What Machines Can't Do

What Machines Can't Do

*Politics and Technology
in the Industrial Enterprise*

Robert J. Thomas

UNIVERSITY OF CALIFORNIA PRESS
Berkeley · Los Angeles · London

University of California Press
Berkeley and Los Angeles, California

University of California Press, Ltd.
London, England

© 1994 by
The Regents of the University of California

Library of Congress Cataloging-in-Publication Data

Thomas, Robert Joseph, 1952–

What machines can't do : politics and technology in the industrial
enterprise / Robert J. Thomas.

p.   cm.

Includes bibliographical references and index.

ISBN 0-520-08131-5

1. Technological innovations—Management. 2. Organizational
change. 3. United States—Manufactures—Technological innovations—Case studies. 4. Manufacturing resource planning—United
States—Case studies. 5. Organizational change—United States—
Case studies. 6. Appropriate technology—United States—Case studies. I. Title.

HD45.T43   1994

658.5'14—dc20   93-15746
                                                                  CIP

Printed in the United States of America

9 8 7 6 5 4 3 2 1

The paper used in this publication meets the minimum requirements
of American National Standard for Information Sciences—Perma-
nence of Paper for Printed Library Materials, ANSI Z39.48-1984.

To Rosanna and Alyssa

Contents

Figures and Table

Preface

"If only it weren't for the people, the goddamned people,"
said Finnerty, "always getting tangled up in the machinery. If
it weren't for them, earth would be an engineer's paradise."

Kurt Vonnegut, *Player Piano*

Virtually every manufacturing company has plans for an automated "factory of the future." The images contained in those plans are stark but powerful: Bright yellow robots pivot and bend in time with silent music. Gleaming blue machines fashion blocks of metal into intricate shapes. Computers trace mechanical heartbeats in amber on flat, black screens. Squat, driverless carriers glide quietly along magnetic pathways, flashing red lights signaling the urgency of their errands. Factory lights are dimmed. People are nowhere to be seen.

Yet just as the factory of the future seems within reach, there is growing concern that industrial survival and economic competitiveness cannot be achieved with machines alone. Japanese manufacturers, for example, have demonstrated that remarkable success can be achieved by investing in what McGregor (1960) has termed the "human side of enterprise" and by improving known technologies more often than inventing new ones. By itself, the Japanese "miracle" has provided a powerful indictment of the technological "fix." Moreover, U.S. companies have found that technological fixes are not only not enough but many times just don't work. Managers in growing numbers point to factory warehouses and aisleways littered with hardware too complex or too unreliable to serve their needs; they openly question whether *more* technology is the key to industrial renaissance.

What is most perplexing and most exciting about the current era is the multiplicity of competing ideas about the "proper" way to organize work. Everyone, it seems, is talking about becoming a "world-class" manufacturer dedicated to "lean production," "total quality," "continuous improvement," and "organizational learning." But the *meanings* people attach to those terms, the routes they plan for achieving them, and the resources they have for seeing them through to fruition are often quite different. For example, it is not unusual to visit a manufacturing company and find hourly employees, supervisors, union representatives, and managers meeting in quality control circles and earnestly devising ways to improve the work environment and the work process while, in a separate set of offices, engineers labor at their workstations designing software and computer controls to reduce worker discretion in the production process. Nor is it unusual to find human resource specialists drawing up programs of training and education for what they envision as the "learning organization" while financial analysts down the hall rank technology proposals on the basis of the number of people they promise to eliminate. One side sees the solution as smarter ways to organize people; the other side sees the solution as smarter machines.[1]

Critical questions are being raised: Is the industrial enterprise being "reinvented," and if so, how? Is new technology driving organizational change? If so, in what direction? Or do organizations decide what they want to *be* and then choose technologies that enable them to create that future? If so, who makes those decisions, and how do they make them?

Unfortunately, there is no consensus among researchers as to the future of the industrial enterprise or to the role that new technology will play in its creation. At one level, dissensus is testimony to the disarray caused by shifts taking place in both economy and society. Like manag-

---

1. For a more tangible sense of the turmoil, sit through a Sunday afternoon football game and you will see General Motors and its products portrayed in remarkably different ways. One ad spotlights computer-driven robots tirelessly and unerringly welding a seemingly endless line of Chevrolets. The people who might, in Finnerty's words, "get tangled up in the machinery" have been eliminated from the process. Another ad showcases a sporty subcompact with all the features and the reliability of a Japanese import. There are no workers in this ad and no machines either: the car *is* a Japanese import. A later ad tells us that upscale GM products are handmade by highly skilled and dedicated union workers. Clearly, we are to conclude that people are an essential ingredient in the making of a fine automobile. Finally, late in the second half of the game, General Motors—in the guise of the Saturn Corporation—emerges as a new kind of car company, a place where "old-fashioned" ideas about quality, ingenuity, and pride in work go into a new generation of automobile. These contrasting images might be passed off as a clever marketing strategy were they not also symptomatic of the turmoil going on *inside* General Motors and thousands of other manufacturing companies.

tive technologies and organizational structures are formulated and selected—as I do the outcomes of change. I strive to portray accurately the
conflict as well as the cooperation that characterize organizational life in
a period of turmoil. Finally, the studies are written in a way that will, I
hope, engage the readers and cause them to take seriously the different
"realities" and experiences of workers, managers, and engineers as they
struggle to give meaning to their work and to redefine the role of people
and machines in the industrial enterprise.

This book is an unusual enterprise in at least two respects. It began as
a fairly conventional academic undertaking: replete with theoretical
propositions and a solid grounding in the relevant social science litera-
tures. However, as I began doing the research, I was immediately confronted by the enormous number and variety of things I did not know
about technology and organizations and for which the literature provided inadequate preparation. Fairly quickly I found myself carrying on
two studies, not one: a deductive analysis, reasonably consistent with
the canons of "normal" social science and dedicated to the testing of my
initial hypotheses; and an inductive analysis that sought to build theory
from the welter of different perspectives I was encountering and the
complex realities I was observing in action.[3] The duality of the process
is reflected in the structure of the book. That is, I consciously and quite
deliberately combine a conventional review of the academic literature
with a set of open-ended questions about the relevance of that literature.
Those questions, explored in some depth in chapter 1, lay the foundation for a "power-process" perspective on technology and organization
and the case studies that follow. The power-process perspective is not
presented as a fully elaborated competitor to existing theories; instead, I
use it as a vehicle to guide the reader through the inductive analysis of
the case studies.

This book is, however, unusual in another respect. To borrow a
phrase, it has one arrow and two targets. One target is the academic
community of social science and engineering scholars. To them I hope to
bring a fresh look at old questions—to fan the fires of old debates about
technological determinism and social choice, but also to suggest ways in
which the heat generated by those debates might be put to newer and
more productive uses. To that target I devote chapter 6. The other
target, however, is the community of practitioners—the executives, managers, engineers, workers, and trade unionists who are struggling to

---

3. See appendix 1 for the approach I took to data collection and analysis.

ers and workers in much of U.S. industry, many researchers are only now beginning to accommodate themselves to the emergence of alternative models of organization—among global competitors and inside their own territorial boundaries.[2] Indeed, the past decade has seen an astounding amount of energy expended in the invention, defense, and rediscovery of both organizational forms and organizational theories.

At another level, however, the same developments have rekindled long-smoldering debates about what technology is and what, if anything, it does. For some analysts, technology is an exogenous force, largely outside the realm of conscious organizational or social control. Technology may not be alive, in other words, but it does "impact" organizations and force them to change. For others, technology is a social construct—it is what people make it be and do—and it is therefore subject to social and organizational choice.

Although it deals with very important issues of theory and practice, the debate itself has thus far generated more heat than light—in large measure because advocates from both sides have tended either to remain distant from the phenomena they seek to explain or to approach them from only one angle (e.g., from the perspective of managers or technologists). In an era when there is general agreement as to the *reality* of large-scale change—if not always agreement as to its details—it seems unwise to study change from a distance or from only one perspective. If, as engineers are wont to say, "The devil's in the details," then we may be better served at this moment in history by understanding the details before launching into the grand generalization.

My goal in this book is to contribute to both the theory and the practice of organizational change by going inside the industrial enterprise to observe, describe, and analyze the struggle to define new processes and structures. I do so by means of a series of detailed case studies of technological and organizational change as they are experienced and given meaning by executives, managers, engineers, supervisors, and workers. The case studies span a wide variety of industries and workplaces—aerospace, computers, metalworking, and automobiles—and a wide variety of technologies. In these studies I contrast symbol and substance, what people say they are doing and what is actually being done. I devote as much attention to the *process* of change—how alterna-

2. In this respect, Benson hit the nail on the head when he argued that the "theoretical constructs of the field are tied to and tend to affirm the present realities in organizations. Radical transformation of organizations would undermine those corresponding theories" (1977, 1).

understand and, in some cases, to expand the array of possible futures for the industrial enterprise. They are an unlikely target for an academic treatise; but precisely because they are the ones who will create the future, I hope to reflect back to them some of what I learned from them. For them I wrote chapter 7.

The perspective I bring is, I believe, unique. As a sociologist I bring a fascination with the way people construct both the relationships through which things are produced *and* the images and metaphors through which those relationships are understood. From my prior research, especially my stint as a lettuce harvester and my detailed interviews with auto workers in Detroit, I bring a profound respect for the capacity of people to care about the work they do even in the face of physically and mentally grueling working conditions. I also bring from my fieldwork a certain skepticism about broad generalizations derived from remote observation. From my position as a faculty member in the Sloan School of Management at MIT and as a participant in the Leaders for Manufacturing program—an innovative effort to integrate engineering and social science research—I bring a deep appreciation for the creative abilities of manufacturing technologists.

In the chapter that follows, I spell out in greater detail the theoretical issues and controversies that motivated me to do the research and to write this book. Chapters 2 through 5 form the empirical core of the book and provide in-depth examinations of the process of technological change in each of four major U.S. manufacturing companies. Chapter 6 draws together findings and broader themes from the case studies. Chapter 7 concludes with a more general set of arguments about politics, technology, and the future of the industrial enterprise.

I am enormously indebted to the nearly three hundred people in the companies and unions who agreed to participate in the study. I cannot name them or the organizations they represent, but I hope that what I have to say will be recognized as a sincere effort to portray the reality they experience and the aspirations they hope to achieve. Fortunately, my academic IOUs are not nearly as great in number. However, special thanks are due to John Van Maanen, Rosanna Hertz, Tom Kochan, Mike Piore, Paul Osterman, and Bob Cole for their unflagging support, sympathy, encouragement, and criticism over the (too) many years of this project. Without the sage advice of Lotte Bailyn, Ed Schein, Tom Magnanti, Kent Bowen, Rebecca Henderson, Jan Odhnoff, Paul Lagace, and Mike Useem, I would still be struggling to make sense of what I'd learned. For their financial and professional support, the National Science Foundation (SES 8822130), the MIT Leaders for Manufacturing program, and the Sloan School of Management receive my enduring gratitude. Neither they nor my colleagues are in any way accountable for the conclusions or arguments presented in this book—unless, of course, they want to share in the credit and the blame.

To Rosanna Hertz and Alyssa Thomas I owe the biggest debt. Rosanna made this book possible when, nearly twelve years ago, she challenged me to do something that was uniquely my own—and then to write it in English. But even more important, her professional dedication, her creative energy, and her perseverance in the face of incredible personal trials gave me the inspiration to keep going. Alyssa provided her own form of inspiration: a persistent banging on my study door in the hopes that I would get finished sooner and come out and play.

ONE

Introduction

Social scientists have struggled for years to develop a theory of organizational structure and change that effectively integrates an organization's social and technical systems. Agreement is virtually unanimous on several general points: that organizations are composed of social and technical systems;[1] that these systems are interdependent; and that changes in one usually occasion adaptation in the other. But agreement breaks down over the relative weight to be given to social and technical systems in explaining why organizations take the shape they do and, more important, why they change. Winner stated the central issue succinctly: "On the one hand, we encounter the idea that technological development goes forward virtually of its own inertia, resists any limitation and has the character of a self-propelling, self-sustaining, ineluctable flow. On the other hand there are arguments that human beings have full and conscious choice in the matter and that they are responsible for choices made at each step in the sequence of change" (1977, 46).

Each idea has its advocates in the field. On the one side are researchers who contend that the technical system of an organization determines its structure (e.g., Woodward 1965; Thompson 1967; Khandwalla 1974;

---

1. Borrowing from sociotechnical systems theory (e.g., Trist 1981), we may define social systems as made up of people—as individuals and groups—joined together by a set of formal and informal relations that regulate their behavior and orient them toward the achievement of particular goals (individual as well as collective). Technical systems consist of the physical equipment and processes through which inputs are converted into outputs.

Adler 1987). From their perspective the social system of an organization is compelled to mold or adapt itself to the contours of the "core technology," that is, the dominant technique for converting inputs into outputs. Changes in the technical system of an organization resulting from external or internal innovation translate directly into changes in organizational structure and functioning. On the other side, however, technology and organizational structure are held to be the product of choice, most broadly of social choice. Organizations choose the markets they compete in, the techniques they employ to produce their goods or services, and the shape or structure they find most appropriate to achieving valued goals (Child 1972; Child 1985; Braverman 1974; Edwards 1979).[2] From this perspective, then, technology is made to conform to the contours of the social system of the organization. Abrupt or unexpected changes in technology may occasion adjustments; but more commonly, the technical system is adjusted within limits imposed by the social system of the organization.

On the surface, it might seem odd that such divergent perspectives could persist in the face of opportunities for an empirical test. Still, as Bedeian (1980), Francis (1986), and others have pointed out, the empirical evidence has yet to yield a clear-cut winner. Only in the broadest sense have organizations been shown to adopt similar structures in response to their core technologies—or to alter themselves in patterned and predictable ways in response to the same exogenous technical stimuli (Woodward 1965; Tushman and Anderson 1986). Even these studies have not demonstrated conclusively that technology has an independent influence on structure (see Hickson, Pugh, and Pheysey 1969; Mohr 1972; Blau et al. 1976).[3] Efforts to show that organizations exercise choice in selecting and matching technology and structure have proven equally inconclusive in part because the data presented—largely in the form of case studies (e.g., Piore and Sabel 1984; Shaiken 1985; Child 1985; Wilkinson 1983; Buchanan and Boddy 1983; Perrow 1983)— do not allow for generalization and in part because the variables that are

2. I include within this "camp" researchers working from Marxist labor process theory because most claim that technologies are chosen on the basis of managerial strategy to control work and workers—a narrow but nonetheless clearly social dimension of the organization. I return to this point later in the chapter.

3. Moreover, they do not easily account for the potential effect of factors outside the set of variables traditionally included in the study of technology and organization. For example, arguments advanced from the "new" institutionalism (see DiMaggio and Powell 1983) could be just as compelling: similarities in structure could be the product of *coercive* pressures (e.g., from regulators), *normative* pressures (e.g., from outside constituencies), or *mimetic* processes (e.g., simple copying of competitor behavior).

hypothesized to intervene in the process of strategic choice are too complex to afford empirical tests of a conventional sort (e.g., Sabel 1982).[4] The stalemate has propelled some researchers into a search for better measures of technology and structure and more refined data sets with which to test their propositions (cf. Stanfield 1976; Comstock and Scott 1977; Kelley 1990). Others have tried to find a middle ground between the extremes (see Clark, McLoughlin, Rose, and King 1988; Hrebiniak and Joyce 1985; Tushman and Romanelli 1985). A few, meanwhile, have proposed wiping the slate clean and starting over.[5]

The unsettled nature of the debate might be of no great interest outside the academic community if not for the fact that social, economic, and technological changes of considerable magnitude are taking place globally. In light of those changes, time-honored notions about hierarchy, bureaucracy, and the structuring of work are coming under increasingly intense and critical scrutiny—by managers, technologists, and workers alike. If, as a growing number of analysts suggest,[6] history can no longer be relied on as a guide to action in the current era—much less to organizational survival in an uncertain future—then the relationship between technology and organization is by no means an idle issue. Once again we are left to answer critical questions: If new technology does indeed drive organizational change, how does it do so? What are the mechanisms through which similarities and differences in structure come about? Alternatively, if organizations can structure themselves through technological choice, who makes those choices and how?

Rather than go back to the drawing board in an effort to answer these questions, I argue in this book that it may be most productive to embrace the divergent (perhaps even contradictory) arguments that underlie the debate and to use them as the foundation for a theory of how social *and* technical systems are jointly responsible for organizational structuring and change. In other words, both the technological determinist and social choice perspectives offer important insights about the properties of the system that they consider to be determinant. These

4. Barley (1986; 1990) provides an important advance in this direction through his systematic observations of the social interactions stimulated by the introduction of new technology in an established social system. Yet his analysis does not account for the process whereby new technology—of a particular sort, with particular objectives already built into it—shows up in the first place.

5. Barley (1986; 78), for example, has suggested, "Rather than continue to scrutinize research for additional methodological and conceptual flaws, a more fruitful ploy may be simply to embrace the contradictory evidence as a replicated finding."

6. See Piore and Sabel (1984), Thurow (1992), Drucker (1988), and Dertouzos, Lester, and Solow (1989).

insights should not be dismissed. But both perspectives share a common flaw: because they focus attention primarily on the structural outcomes or impacts of change, they tend to portray the relationship between technical and social systems as static and unidirectional. By neglecting the process of change—especially the process through which choices of technology are made—they generally fail to capture the dynamic and interactive nature of the relationship between the technical and social systems of an organization.

The core argument of the book can be stated rather simply: to explain what new technology does to organizations—or as it is commonly put, "how technology impacts organizations"—we must also explain what people are trying to do to organizations and, by extension, to themselves by means of new technology. Two points are central to this argument. First, it is not enough to claim that technology "impacts" organizations; it is essential to ask as well how and why particular technologies are chosen. Second, it is not enough to claim that technology is the simple product of social or strategic choice; it is essential to ask as well how technological alternatives were themselves framed, how the objectives or interests of different organizational actors shape the range of possibilities considered, and, most important, how differences in objectives or interests influence the outcomes of change.

The bulk of the research literature has neglected the process of change because it cannot be easily represented as a quantifiable variable; by contrast, structural outcomes or impacts can be enumerated and compared. Unfortunately, this situation has led researchers either to overlook variations in process as an explanation for differences in technology's impacts or to assume that the nature of a process can be inferred from observations of outcomes. However, close examination reveals that at least some of the confusion that has hounded prior research can be attributed to the fact that the process of technological change occurs within a social and historical context encrusted with embedded interests and ideologies about what problems can or should be "solved" by technology. These interests and ideologies *are* influenced by organizational structure, but they are also influenced by factors that cannot be easily deduced from formal structure or inferred from the observation of outcomes. Included among those factors are professional and occupational values and concerns about social status that guide people's thinking about what constitutes meaningful work. A particularly important organizational group whose activities and worldviews have escaped direct attention are the engineers and technicians whose job it is to devise and implement new production technology. The influence of these factors becomes apparent only when we focus explicit attention on the process of change.

In this chapter I lay the foundation for an analytical framework that incorporates insights from both the technological determinist and the social choice perspectives. This framework, which I refer to as the "power-process" perspective, begins by accepting as legitimate two seemingly incompatible assumptions: first, that the physical world does indeed constrain the range of alternative ways human beings can organize the production of social goods; and second, that the social worlds (i.e., the organizations and institutions) that human beings create influence the way they understand and act on the physical world. In other words, neither "world" subsumes or masters the other. Therefore, the core problematic is not which world structures the other, but *how they structure one another*. Of necessity, this framing of the problem forces us to conceive of technology and organization as engaged in an ongoing process of structuring. It also allows for the possibility that differences in objectives and interests among human beings will yield different understandings of the physical world—not only how it does work, but how it *should* work. If no one social group (profession, occupation, organizational stratum, class, race, or gender) can lay claim to the "truest" or the most "real" understanding of the physical world, then we are forced to conceive of the relationship between technology and organization as *mediated by the exercise of power*, that is, by a system of authority and domination that asserts the primacy of one understanding of the physical world, one prescription for social organization, over others.

In subsequent chapters I present the results of a three-year study of the process of technological change in a wide range of industrial organizations. This study focused specific attention on the choices that shaped both the technical and the social systems of work. By contrast to prior works in the field, including those that claim to analyze the change process, I did not limit the investigation to the implementation of new technology. Rather, I extended the definition of "process" to include the activities that preceded, as well as followed, formal decisions to implement new technology.

The case studies offer four significant insights—insights that could not have been derived from the study of technology's "impacts." First, the studies demonstrate that the choice of technology is rarely a straight-

forward and rational affair, despite the many efforts of change proponents to justify their actions in a language and with measures that
proclaim their rationality. A central and previously unexplored feature
of the process of technological change is the opportunity it provides for
different categories of organizational actors to try to put in place their
own unique worldviews about the "proper" way to organize work.
Close examination of these worldviews suggests that neither engineers
nor workers respond passively to change; rather, they actively attempt to
shape the content of technological change to make it accord with their
conceptions of "real engineering" and "real work."

Second, the case studies show that the choice of technology represents
an opportunity to affect not only the performance of work but also the
status, influence, and self-concept of those promoting change. That is,
new technology may be far less attractive for what it does than for what
it says symbolically about its creators and proponents. Critical in this
regard are the efforts of manufacturing or process engineers—who are
considered (and often consider themselves) to be "second-class" corporate citizens—to gain a measure of status and recognition in the eyes of
the product engineering community.

Third, the case studies suggest that, although the structure of power
and authority within an organization often influences the range of
technological alternatives considered, in some cases change may be
initiated in the hopes of altering that structure itself. That is, change may
be undertaken not in adherence to organizational strategies and objectives but in conscious efforts to thwart them. Both situations are possible
because the process of technological choice remains largely invisible to
both top management and shop-floor personnel.

Finally, although the case studies offer evidence that cooperative
approaches to labor-management relations may facilitate more effective
and creative use of new technology than adversarial relations do, real
cooperation requires fundamental change in the process of designing
and implementing new technology. The separation of technology design
and implementation in time and space dramatically reduces the opportunities for meaningful "user" (i.e., worker and lower management)
participation in the change process. Thus, in the absence of a crisis that
forcibly suspends historical practices, technology designers often have
little incentive to solicit input from those who are the object of change.
As a result, new technology frequently confronts the rest of the organization as an exogenous force—one that can be countered only through
overt political action.

Beyond whatever insights the case studies may offer about the process of technological change and its influence on the outcomes of change, the studies are, I think, valuable for what they reveal about the challenges facing managers, engineers, workers, unions, and educators as they contemplate the future of the industrial enterprise. Most important, the research findings suggest that traditional assumptions about the relationships between product and process design and between product and process engineering organizations must be dramatically altered— perhaps even reversed—if manufacturing firms in the United States are to regain a competitive posture in the world economy. Although I am not alone in suggesting the need for structural change,[7] I do contend that structural change by itself will be far from sufficient. A prerequisite for change of that magnitude will be the creation of what I refer to as a "process aesthetic" or a philosophy of manufacturing that values the integration of the technical and the social systems of production, rather than values one at the expense of the other. The obstacles to change are enormous—not simply because existing practices are so deeply entrenched but because changes of the sort I propose will have dramatic implications for the way all the relevant parties (including academic researchers and engineering educators) think about the process of production.

Before presenting the case studies and their implications, I will discuss the body of theory I encountered in preparing to do the research.

BRIDGING DETERMINISM AND CHOICE

For all the brickbats that social scientists have lobbed at technological determinists, valuable insights may be gained from seriously considering technology as an independent entity. Most important among them is the recognition that the physical properties of raw materials do constrain the range of alternative ways that inputs can be made into finished goods. Even in the face of debates as to what might be the most efficient (or safe or environmentally sound) way to manufacture, say, printed circuit boards, our knowledge of physics and chemistry suggests that electronic signals must be provided pathways along which to travel. Thus, physical necessity constrains the range of alternative technologies

7. See, for example, recent works by Hayes, Wheelwright, and Clark (1988), Dertouzos, Lester, and Solow (1989), Cohen and Zysman (1987), and Womack, Jones, and Roos (1990).

for making printed circuit boards.[8] Clark et al. (1988, 12–15), for example, suggest that any given technology has a finite "design space" within which it can be altered or adjusted by organizations. The broadest bounds on design space are the engineering system principles (or known properties of raw materials and transformational processes) and the physical embodiment of those principles in specific combinations of hardware and software.

Moreover, technology may not have a mind of its own, but it is often *experienced* by people and organizations as an exogenous force. Many new technologies are created by one set of actors for use by another set: for example, one firm's product often becomes another firm's process. As Abernathy and Clark (1985) noted with respect to product technology, once a "dominant design" has emerged among a group of competitors, it confronts nonusers and new entrants as an established "fact."[9] Even if a new technical process is the outcome of activities undertaken inside an organization (e.g., an internal research and development [R&D] lab), the origins, limits, and possibilities of a technology are often unfamiliar to the ultimate "end users." Thus, technology tends to be experienced and represented as a "self-propelling, self-sustaining, ineluctable flow."

However, even as we recognize the distinctive constraints imposed by the physical properties of technology, the social context within which technologies are created and used must not be overlooked. Simply put, new technologies do not fall from the sky. Inattention and ignorance may lead technology to be experienced as an independent force, but both inattention and ignorance are themselves the outcomes of social processes. Although many developments and their consequences cannot be anticipated in advance, it does not follow that their production should be excluded from analysis. More important, perhaps, *it does not follow that the social system of an organization is necessarily subordinated to the technical system.*

The contribution of the social choice perspective resides in its emphasis on the "embeddedness"—to borrow a term from Granovetter (1985)— of technology in social processes and relationships. Rather than being

8. This is the case even when we recognize that "laws" of physics and chemistry are themselves social and historical constructs (see Fleck [1935] 1979; Kuhn 1967; Latour 1987). That is, research may result in discontinuous shifts in scientific and technical knowledge, but *at the time in which these laws are being applied*, they represent real and hard constraints on the range of alternative ways to accomplish transformative activities.

9. See also Sahal (1981), Abernathy and Utterback (1978), Marquis (1982), and Tushman and Anderson (1986).

objective, technology is *infused with objectives*. By rejecting the notion that technology does anything by itself, the social choice perspective forces an accounting for the way in which interests and ideologies come to be attached to, and expressed through, physical processes. Although labor process theorists (e.g., Braverman 1974; Edwards 1979; Noble 1984; Marglin 1974) have often oversimplified the issue by asserting that technology is shaped by the interests of a single class (i.e., capitalists),[10] the critical idea is that choices are made even when they are not heralded as formal decisions.

Nonetheless, the social choice perspective falls short in two important respects. First, it subordinates the technical system almost completely to the social system. Technology either appears infinitely mutable in the face of social pressure or receives little direct attention at all.[11] Second, the social choice perspective fails to provide clear guidance or a methodology for examining how interests and ideologies are expressed through the choice of technology, by whom they are expressed, and when in the process of change this expression occurs.[12]

THE POWER-PROCESS PERSPECTIVE

The framework I propose builds on insights offered by both the determinist and the social choice perspectives and addresses their theoretical shortcomings as a prelude to empirical investigation. The power-process perspective responds directly to the pattern of contradictory findings and takes up a challenge posed some years ago by Perrow (1983, 540):

10. To a significant degree this is a product of the failure of Marxist labor process theorists to go inside organizations to study technological change processes. Their hesitance derives in part from the ambiguity of the organization—especially economic organizations—as an analytical construct in Marxist theory. Efforts by Goldman (1983) and Gordon, Edwards, and Reich (1982) clarify the issue somewhat; but on the whole, Marxists have operated from the assumption that class relations are far more significant than organizational structures in explaining the evolution and use of new technology. Ironically, their attribution of single-mindedness of purpose to capitalists and managers far exceeds that which most mainstream analysts would be willing to accept (see, for example, March 1981).

11. Clark et al. (1988, 11) state the issue nicely: "The problem with recent research has been that an obsession with technological determinism has obscured the need to include an analysis of technology as one of the many factors which shape the outcomes of technological change. Put another way, the technology baby has all too often been discarded with the determinist bath water."

12. As I argue later, this failure comes about because both case studies and cross-sectional analyses usually begin in the final stages of change—at the point of implementation or afterward—thus ignoring antecedent activities or presuming that they are largely unimportant.

The early work on technology and structure, including my own, recognized a one-sided and general connection, *but it failed to recognize how structure can affect technology and speculate about the large areas of choice involved in presumably narrow technical decisions,* choices that are taken for granted because they are a part of a largely unquestioned social construction of reality—one that should be questioned.[13]

Most important, to transform the analysis from one that is static and one-sided to one that is dynamic and interactive, it is essential to pay explicit attention to the *process, as well as the outcomes, of technological change.* Inattention to the process of technological change has been even more detrimental than Perrow implies: it has resulted in analyses that are ahistorical, that underestimate differences in the logics that underlie technical and social systems, and that either oversimplify or ignore altogether the mediating influence of organizational choice.

In this section I lay out the major arguments for the power-process perspective. I indicate where we can build from prior research and where we must introduce new concepts and relationships to fill the voids in the literature. From this base I then describe the research design that guided a set of comparative case studies of the process and outcomes of technological change in four manufacturing firms.

HISTORY MATTERS

History ought to play a central role in explaining the relationship between technical and social systems in organizations. Indeed, it seems quite straightforward to suggest that prior investments in social and technical infrastructure (e.g., standard operating procedures, formal and informal production standards, fixed capital equipment, and other technical routines) are likely either to influence future investments or to serve as the historical "legacy" against which visions of the future are juxtaposed. Yet history—especially organizational history—has been neglected in all but a few empirical investigations. Instead, researchers have favored investigations that yield cross-sectional pictures of outcomes for comparative purposes. Decontextualization of this sort may make sense when, as Barley (1986, 79) notes, organizational structure is

13. Emphasis added.

defined in formal and abstract terms and technology is taken as a given. However, when it is not obvious which is the fixed point around which the other pivots, longitudinal study of context and process becomes critical.[14]

History matters for several reasons. Most important, the choice of temporal context has serious implications for how we define "process" and, therefore, for how attentive we are to the variety of activities associated with technological change in organizations. Obviously, cross-sectional studies like the ones that have dominated research on technology and structure (e.g., Khandwalla 1974; Woodward 1965; Tushman and Anderson 1986) stand at one extreme: the temporal context is narrowed to a single moment in time, and process disappears as a potential source of explanation for variations in outcome. The activities associated with the configuration and actual use of new technology, as well as the social system adaptations that may still be evolving at the time of investigation, are pushed into the background in the effort to get a clean "snapshot" of the outcomes of change. At best, proxy measures are substituted for direct investigation of important dimensions of process; for example, R&D expenditures as a fraction of gross revenues serve as an indicator of "ability to change," and the number of days lost to work stoppages substitutes for "worker resistance to change." More commonly, however, process dynamics are ignored altogether.

Although researchers who adopt a case study approach are generally less restrictive in their choice of temporal context, most case studies focus on discrete episodes of change. Their investigations are bounded on one side by a decision to introduce a new technology and on the other side by the incorporation of the new technology into routine operation.[15] As a result, process is equated with "implementation," and analysis of the change process is restricted to efforts to explain variation in the adjustments that occur in the social system—and occasionally in

14. As I argue below, longitudinal and historical approaches pose formidable methodological challenges not normally encountered in cross-sectional, outcome-oriented research. At minimum they require multiple methods of data collection, access to people and records far beyond what is usually required (or usually available to researchers), and interpretive techniques for sorting through what are often very different accounts of the same process. These challenges alone may help explain why studies—as well as theories—of the change process have been few and far between.

15. This limitation is as common in case studies based in a technological determinist perspective (e.g., Adler 1990) as it is in those rooted in the social choice perspective (e.g., Shaiken 1985; Wilkinson 1983) or Marxist labor process theory (e.g., Zimbalist 1979).

the technology itself—as implementation proceeds (see Leonard-Barton 1987; Rice and Rogers 1979; Clark et al. 1988).

Overlooked in both cross-sectional and case study research, however, are aspects of a broader process of change that might provide a more complete picture of the relationship between an organization's technical and social systems. Specifically, I refer to change efforts and options that do not qualify for investigation because they fall outside the temporal bounds normally affixed even to case study research. In fact, there appears to be an implicit hierarchy of attention in studies of technological and organizational change: most likely to be studied are the spectacular successes, followed by the spectacular failures. Least likely to be studied, however, are the change options or alternatives that may have been *considered but were not selected* for implementation (even though they might be resurrected later on), followed by the change options that were *disqualified* from serious consideration because they violated existing assumptions about the "proper" way to structure work. Failures, forgone options, and unorthodox propositions represent no less important a part of the process of change than the "successful" or completed ventures that have received most attention in past research. Indeed, they are likely to provide critical insight as to how and why a new technology comes to be recognized as a candidate for adoption. But to include them, we must consciously extend the temporal context for investigation.

By extending the temporal context beyond a single moment in time or a discrete episode of change, researchers can define process in such a way that it becomes a meaningful venue for investigation. At a minimum, it becomes reasonable to ask how developments in one system (technical or social) influence not only the structure of the other but also perceptions of the range of possible structures. For example, the introduction of automated equipment to a formerly labor-intensive production process is frequently accompanied by growth in staff (even the establishment of entire departments) responsible for overseeing and refining its use (Udy 1959; Hunt 1970; Hickson et al. 1969). This adjustment has been cited as evidence for the "centralizing" effect of complex and sophisticated technology on organizational structure (Woodward 1965; Perrow 1967). Yet this adjustment, viewed as part of a historical process, could also have the "impact" of reducing the range of technical systems that will be considered (or recognized as possible) at any subsequent moment in time; that is, through the accretion of "automation" expertise, the staff is likely to become predisposed to automation of technical systems even when pursuit of further automation is not the optimal response.[16]

More extensively, the power-process perspective forces us to distinguish among the activities that make up the process of technological change. Prior research, as I argued earlier, has usually ignored those activities or treated them as subordinate aspects of implementation. Even when more elaborate multistage models are proposed (e.g., Wilkinson 1983; Buchanan and Boddy 1983; Clark et al. 1988),[17] researchers usually pay greatest attention to the activities that *follow* a formal decision to adopt a new technology.[18] By contrast, I argue that the analysis cannot be limited to the final moments of change, that is, to implementation only. Rather, we must include the full range of activities associated with the introduction of new technology, including the *identification* of problems to be solved and solutions to be attached to problems; the *selection* among alternative technologies and, within a given technology, among alternative configurations; and finally, the *implementation* of a chosen technology. Only by attending directly and explicitly to each of these activities can we uncover variations in process and, by extension, to assess what they add to our ability to understand variations in outcome.

However, as should be apparent from the earlier example of automation's possible "future" effects, the analysis of any individual instance of change—no matter how attentive it may be to the activities that make up the process—cannot be undertaken in isolation from the history of changes in either the social or the technical system of an organization.

16. As Perrow (1983, 521) speculated in an essay on the limited influence of human factors engineering in new equipment design, "It would appear that machines and equipment are designed so that they reinforce existing structures and reproduce those structures in new settings." More recently, Cebon (1990), in a study of energy management in universities, found that institutions that maintained a centralized and highly trained staff of engineers were very good at devising and implementing large-scale and very sophisticated systems for regulating heating, cooling, and electrical usage; they could not, however, easily accomplish relatively small-scale technological solutions (such as substituting energy-saving light bulbs for more conventional ones), and they were even less effective at engaging user involvement in energy conservation. Conversely, institutions that maintained a decentralized system for energy delivery, control, and capital budgeting were quite good at small, money-saving changes and at mobilizing changes in energy usage among faculty, staff, and students; they could not, however, accomplish major system changes.

17. For example, Clark et al. (1988, 31) identify five main stages in the process of introducing new technology: initiation, decision to adopt, system selection, implementation, and routine operation.

18. Unfortunately, it is often difficult to tell whether the added stages have real explanatory significance or whether the concept of implementation has merely been shrunk in scope.

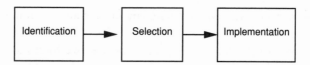

Figure 1. Stages in the process of technological change

Convenience might suggest that investigation be limited to the problems or solutions under consideration at a given moment in time. However, such a restriction would risk the loss of valuable insights about the historical antecedents of what may be defined in the contemporary era as an "important" problem or an "appropriate" solution. Moreover, such a restriction would make it very difficult to gauge the significance of any particular departure from past practice. Likewise, I suggest, to overlook for the sake of convenience the historical roots of the other activities that make up the change process—that is, selection ("choosing within a technology") and implementation—would risk the sacrifice of additional insight.

For these reasons, I contend that it is essential to analyze the process of change from three different directions: first, as an individual instance of change, complete with attention to the sequence of activities that link process with outcome; second, as an instance of change to be compared with other instances of change (both contemporary and historical); and third, as a distinct set of activities each with a history of its own. (See figures 1–3.)

This sort of historical triangulation increases both the breadth and the depth of data available for analyzing the process of change. It allows factors that are specific to the history and circumstances of change in particular organizations to be identified and compared internally and then externally to change processes in other organizations, competitors and noncompetitors alike. It does not limit research only to changes that were completed; instead, it opens the door to learning about the dynamics of change from failed or stillborn efforts. Finally, and perhaps most important, it provides the opportunity to acquire a better understanding of the factors that influence both the real and the perceived range of possible social and technical systems in an organization.

However, the addition of a historical perspective—no matter how sophisticated it may be—cannot by itself resolve the contradictory arguments of the technological determinist and social choice perspectives. Extending the temporal context leads us part of the way to explaining how, in Perrow's terms, "structure can affect technology." But a critical

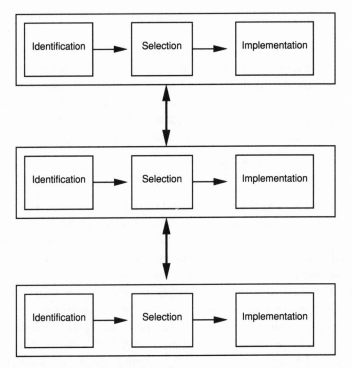

Figure 2. The process of technological change viewed comparatively

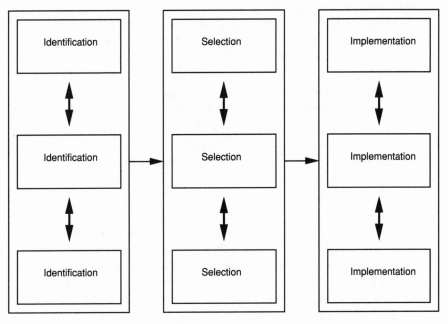

Figure 3. The process of technological change viewed comparatively by stage

feature of the theoretical debate that remains to be addressed is the relative influence of technical and social systems in organizational structuring and change. To that end, we need to extend the organizational context so that we can distinguish the physical properties and limits of technology from the social meanings that may be attached to it, the objectives that may be embedded in it, and the uses to which it may be put.

DISSIMILAR LOGICS IN AN ORGANIZATIONAL CONTEXT

The logics underlying the technical and the social systems of an organization differ in profound ways. Trist put it most succinctly: "The technical system follows the laws of the natural sciences while the social system follows the laws of the human sciences and is a purposeful system" (1981, 37). However independent the social and technical systems may seem, he added, "They are correlative in that one requires the other for the transformation of an input into an output. Their relationship represents a coupling of dissimilars." Virtually all participants in the debate on technology and structure would concur with Trist's characterization. However, as I noted at the outset of the chapter, agreement breaks down when it comes to the relative influence of those systems in organizational structuring and change.

In many respects the simplest and most obvious answer is also the most correct: that is, both are influential. But to be precise, it's essential to add that they are influential in different ways. The key to understanding the influence of each—and the significance of their difference—is to begin with a closer examination of the logics that undergird them. Through such an examination, it will become clear that organizational objectives and the relative capacity of different organizational groups to define them play a vital role in the "coupling of dissimilars." It will also become clear that at least part of the disagreement among researchers can be explained by their tendency to confuse determinism with dominance. That is, those who place their bets on technology as the determinant influence are not completely wrong; however, because they so rarely investigate how technical systems are constructed organizationally, they underestimate the influence of concerns about authority and control in organizations on the choice of technology. Those who argue from a social choice perspective put organizational objectives closer to the heart of the analysis; but because most overlook the constraining influence of technology, they far too often slip into simplistic analyses of the way social systems actually operate. To eliminate this confusion, we must address directly the role of power and conflict in the process of technological change.

The best place to begin is with a closer look at the logics underlying the technical and the social systems of an organization. A technical system is built around fixed and determinate relations among objects. The precise nature of those relations may never be completely known, but what's critical is that neither the objects nor their relations are self-generating. They do not create themselves, and therefore the limits on what they are or can be are real. Absent the ability to self-organize, technical systems can do only what they are commanded to do. The logic of a social system, by contrast, cannot be reduced to fixed and determinate relations precisely because the objects involved—human beings, as individuals and as collectivities—are self-generating and, perhaps more important, self-aware. Rules, procedures, and routines embedded in organizational structure may, as Nelson and Winter (1982) have argued, bind people together and provide a measure of predictability to human and organizational behavior; but it is essential to remember that they are social constructs—and as such, their perpetuation is contingent on their repetition.[19] In other words, social systems, unlike technical systems, are purposive entities that can be amended, dissolved, and reconstructed through the action of their participants.[20]

Three important implications flow from these distinctions. First, the extent to which the logic of one system permeates or structures the other will depend on the organization's objectives or, to be more precise, the objectives as they are negotiated inside an organization and between the organization and its environment. A given technical system may appear to "demand" a particular arrangement of tasks, skills, responsibilities, and authority to achieve the most efficient or productive transformation of inputs into outputs; but the designation of efficiency or productivity (or something else) as an organizational objective is not preordained. It

19. This point echoes the one made by structuration and negotiated order theorists (e.g., Giddens 1976; Barley 1986; Orlikowski 1992), as well as certain institutional theorists (e.g., Zucker 1983), that it is essential to take apart rules and relationships that are "taken for granted."

20. This idea is implied by both sides in the debate on technology and structure, but the lack of explicit attention to history has led to the underdevelopment of the idea and its implications. For example, Trist (1981) raises this point, but largely as a way to distinguish between social and technical systems. As I argue later, this concept does not address the critical issue of their coupling.

is the outcome of a *social* process. Likewise, the translation of an organization's objectives into a division of labor, performance standards, task structures, physical equipment, and so on is also a social process. Thus, the dominance of the technical system can be no more than a reflection of the social processes—and therefore of the relations of power and authority—through which it was created.

This line of reasoning does not mean that organizations have unlimited degrees of freedom in the design of their technical systems. Indeed, as I argued in the last section, history may be (and may be perceived as) a major constraint. Moreover, the technical system should not be viewed simply as a mirror image of an organization's social system.[21] To the contrary, physical objects and their relations are governed by a logic that exists independent of, and prior to, the social system. Technical systems cannot be created that violate the logic that governs physical objects. Thus, the creation of a technical system consists in the discovery and application of rules and conditions that accord with particular organizational objectives.

The second implication is that any study of technological change in organizations will be incomplete if it does not analyze the process through which organizational objectives are defined and translated into the design and operation of the technical system. Just as the technical system of an organization cannot be taken as given but must instead be understood in light of the organization's objectives, so too must the organization's objectives be subjected to scrutiny. At a minimum I suggest that the organizational context for analysis must be extended to include all the parties involved in the different stages of the change process (as described in the preceding section).[22] Only in this way will we be able to make explicit the connection between an organization's objectives and the construction of its technical system—and thus avoid the attribution of agency to technology that is characteristic of the technological determinist perspective.

21. In this regard I concur with Barley's (1986, 104) arguments against a "voluntarist" explanation for technological choice. That is, top organizational decision makers do not completely and directly determine technology's consequences. Many intervening factors can refract or distort top managers' intent. However, recognizing that such distortion can occur should not be reason to ignore top management intent in the selection of new technology.

22. That is, technology developers (even when they are external vendors), line managers, support functions (e.g., maintenance personnel), and financial and accounting staffs are commonly involved in the process of change (cf. Leonard-Barton 1987; Bower 1970). Often their work is also affected by a change.

Particular attention must be paid to the relative capacity of different organizational groups to influence the definition of organizational objectives and the technical means through which they are to be achieved. In situations where access to influence over organizational objectives and technical means is restricted, it is reasonable to expect that the social system of the organization can more easily be structured along the lines of the technical system deemed appropriate by those in positions of dominance. Not only will they possess control over the resources with which to design what they deem to be an appropriate technical system, but their influence in the social system will be enhanced through the representation of the technical system as the "determining" force. Even if lower-level participants have formal representation in negotiation over the rewards for participation (e.g., as in the case of a unionized company), the lack of direct influence in the definition of organizational objectives and technical means is likely to lead to the same result.[23]

When the problem is framed this way, it becomes clearer why theorists and organizational participants alike so often confuse determinism with dominance. The technical system of an organization can be, at one and the same time, *objective*—that is, reflective of a logic, a set of rules and conditions, independent of the social system—and *infused with objectives*—that is, reflective of the interests or goals of particular groups within the social system. Technology can appear to be determinant when its objective features become indistinguishable from the objectives of those who occupy positions of dominance. As critical as I think this point is, it should not be interpreted as implying that those in dominant positions conspire to hide their objectives in or behind technology. This mistake has often been made in labor process theory, including some of the most sophisticated analyses (e.g., Noble 1984). Quite the contrary, those in dominant positions are as likely to believe—if not more likely to believe—in the determinant nature of technology as anyone else, precisely because the attribution of objectivity to technology underscores the idea that their objectives are indistinguishable from collective objectives.[24]

23. I will return to this important point in discussing the obstacles to union and worker involvement in decision making around new technology. See also Thomas (1991) and Thomas and Kochan (1992).

24. This position is reinforced repeatedly in the management literature on technology and innovation. In most cases innovation is considered, almost by definition, to be in accord with a broader set of organizational objectives. For example, Kanter's (1988) life-cycle model of organizational innovation gives considerable emphasis to interest mediation and conflict; but little attention is given either to the innovation itself or to the

The third implication follows directly on the heels of the first two: if the relationship between systems is mediated by the power structure in an organization, then variations in objectives—and the way they are arrived at—ought to yield a range of *possible* couplings of social and technical systems within a given organization or industry. Simply put, we should not expect to discover "one best way" to organize people and machines. In many respects, this point has been made most emphatically in the findings from studies conducted to test the "deskilling" hypothesis. Spenner (1983) and Kelley (1986), for example, have shown that the variety of staffing and control practices compatible with a given technology is far wider than Braverman and other labor process theorists anticipated. These variations in the outcomes of technological change, as I noted earlier, pose an equally significant challenge to theories that treat technology as an independent variable. Similarly, cross-national studies by Sabel (1982), Krafcik (1988), Womack, Jones, and Roos (1990), and Whittaker (1988) have demonstrated that organizations using comparable technologies can divide the necessary work in different ways and that the same goods can be produced competitively using different technologies.

What has been missing in the research literature to date, however, has been detailed examination of the process through which the range of possible couplings between social and technical systems is defined organizationally and then translated into particular couplings. Labor process theorists have largely been content to assume that capitalists/managers have clearly defined objectives and that they hire cadres of willing and compliant engineers who translate those objectives into technical systems (see, e.g., Zimbalist 1979; Gartman 1989). The studies highlighting variation in the use of new technology have based their explanations on conventional measures of structure; insights about process have been limited to what can be gleaned from proxy variables and interviews with small numbers of managers and union leaders. Even the studies that have accorded technology a central role in the emergence of new organizational structures and new approaches to manufacturing reveal little

---

motives that may be driving change proponents. Both are simply *presumed* to be consistent with organizational objectives. Though an insightful sociological analysis, this work shares the same weakness as the studies by Abernathy and Clark (1985) and Utterback (1971): all three implicitly define innovation, a posteriori, as that which has "succeeded." This definition is curious for another reason: most of these writers draw either implicitly or explicitly on notions of "strategic choice" as presented by Child (1972), but they address the issue of domination and control in organizations indirectly at best.

about how technology "facilitated" those developments (cf. Piore and Sabel 1984; Womack, Jones, and Roos 1990; Dertouzous, Lester, and Solow 1989; Sorge and Streeck 1988).

To fill this void, we need to make the definition and translation of organizational objectives an explicit part of the analysis of technological change. In the next section I argue that this end can be achieved most effectively by treating change as a series of choices or decisions.

CHOICE, CHANGE, AND WORLDVIEWS

If the coupling of social and technical systems varies with an organization's objectives and with their translation into specific combinations of machines, people, and rules, then we ought to pay particular attention to how those objectives are interpreted and applied over time and across hierarchical and functional boundaries within organizations. In other words, the coupling of dissimilar logics ought to be an extremely complex activity—one made easier, perhaps, by restrictions that powerful groups can attach to the definition and translation of organizational objectives—but one that by its very nature requires that technical systems be carriers of organizational objectives as well as directors of the behavior of members of the social system.

But achieving a coupling ought to be difficult in another respect: it requires that, across long periods of time and large organizational (e.g., hierarchical) distances, people with very different skills and perspectives will have a hand in translating organizational objectives into hardware, software, task structures, and social relationships. In most cases, forging a coupling and making a change will involve not simultaneous activities but serial ones—not simply because bureaucratic and hierarchical divisions work in this fashion but also because many complex new technologies require the expertise of different technical occupations and functional groups for limited periods of time, much as is the case in the construction of an office building (see Eccles 1981). Thus, as the process of change moves across time, space, and function, the opportunities for translation of organizational objectives increase in number, even though they may decrease in scope as a change becomes more and more fixed. During that transit among stages, many choices will have to be made. For this reason it is appropriate to analyze the change process as a series of choices—choices that are, in many respects, vital to understanding the outcomes of change.

Recent works by Buchanan and Boddy (1983), Wilkinson (1983), Child (1985), and Clark et al. (1988) offer a measure of support for this approach. Though hampered by conceptual limitations that I will address shortly, these studies provide evidence that variations in change processes and objectives or strategies *inside* organizations can help explain differences in the structural outcomes of technological change. Buchanan and Boddy (1983), for example, argue that hierarchy in organizations fosters the creation of "substrategies" among middle and lower-level managers and that these substrategies can filter or, as Child (1985) puts it, "attenuate" top management intent as the change process occurs (see figure 4).[25] Likewise, Wilkinson (1983) has shown that, even if restricted to the final stages of implementation, "shopfloor politics"— that is, the efforts of workers and their unions to affect the skill and employment impacts of new technology—can result in variations in the outcomes of change (see also Jones 1982).

These findings encourage us to view technological change as both a temporal and a hierarchical process involving choices within increasingly narrow portions of the design space.[26] Variations in outcomes can thus be explained as a joint product of differences in strategic intent (between organizations) and differences in the fidelity with which strategic intent is translated into action (within organizations).

As appealing as this approach might appear at first glance, it falls short on two counts. First, Buchanan and Boddy, like other researchers, largely overlook moments in the process of change that precede the formal decision to adopt a given technology.[27] That is, they do not extend the temporal context for their analysis far enough; as a result, they provide little insight as to how and when the options that formed the basis for formal decision were themselves framed. For example, they

25. Specifically, middle managers devise "operational strategies" concerned with technical goals and overall system performance, and lower-level managers devise "control strategies" concerned with operational performance, including human performance in the workplace (Buchanan and Boddy 1983). Their substrategies differ from top management strategy—or what Child (1985) refers to as "corporate steering devices"—not only in their scope but also in their time horizon. As one descends the organizational hierarchy, strategic concerns become narrow and more oriented toward the present tense. Thus, as in the sizable literature on policy implementation (e.g., Wildavsky 1964; Lindblom 1959; Mechanic 1960; Lipsky 1978; Selznick 1949; Stinchcombe 1990, chap. 5), Buchanan and Boddy emphasize the opportunity for lower-level organizational participants to interpret strategy and, through interpretation, to alter, redirect, and even suborn it.

26. Figure 4 is synthesized from text and diagrams in Buchanan and Boddy (1983), Child (1985, 113), and Clark et al. (1988, 12–15).

27. In this respect it is more accurate to say that theirs are studies of *implementation*, not of the totality of the change process.

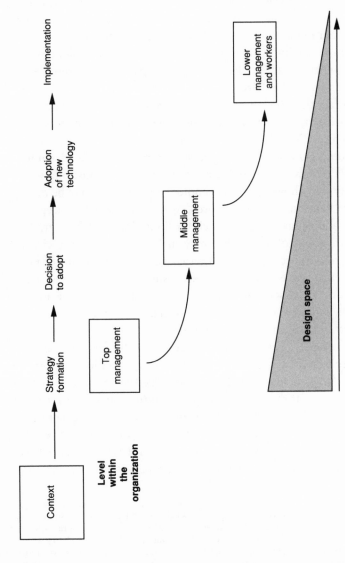

Figure 4. Stages and levels in the process of technological change

lead us to wonder whether top management approval constitutes the formal initiation of a change while the real initiation may occur elsewhere, perhaps lower in the organizational hierarchy or outside the organization altogether.[28] More generally, their model assumes that top management initiates and controls the range of alternatives; it does not allow for the possibility that the range of problems and solutions may be fixed elsewhere, that is, where the design space, as it is represented to top management, has already been narrowed considerably. Thus, despite the fact that Buchanan and Boddy represent technological change as a process open to influence, the model itself is rather static and incomplete.

If a power-process perspective is to emphasize the dynamic and interactive nature of technological change, then it must allow for the possibility that choices about technology and its uses may be made in a nonlinear fashion. In other words, we must not let conceptions of linearity and sequence that fit within limits imposed by a traditional temporal context obscure what may in fact be a far more circuitous, iterative, and indirect process. Alternatively, if conceptions of linearity and sequence prove unavoidable—for example, for purposes of clearly representing or describing a process to readers—then we must also extend the temporal context of the investigation far enough to take into account the complete history of that process.

In this respect, it is essential to recognize the unobtrusive ways in which decision processes can be affected by organizational actors. Three strategies in particular have been emphasized in the broader literature on organizational decision making:[29] (1) *influencing decision premises* in advance of a formal choice by having or acquiring control over definition of the relevant constraints on decision alternatives (Cyert, Simon, and Trow 1956; March and Simon 1958; Carter 1971); (2) *influencing the considered alternatives* through control over the process

---

28. Clark et al. (1988) provide the most extensive coverage of the change process in their case study of the introduction of a new switching technology in British Telecom. Yet the case they analyzed involved a single organization undergoing a dramatic shift in overall corporate strategy (from being a highly regulated public utility to being a commercial enterprise). Absolutely central to the shift in strategy was what they characterize as a radical shift in technology. These factors explain why top management was intimately involved in the formative stages of the change process. In smaller organizations or in ones in which the shifts in strategy or technology are less dramatic, Clark et al.'s arguments may well not hold.

29. For comprehensive overviews of the literature on organizational decision making, see March (1981), Pfeffer (1981), Perrow (1986), and Carroll and Johnson (1990).

of search, for example, using the discovery of a problem as grounds for a claim to control over the search for solutions (see Cyert and March 1963; Pfeffer 1977); and (3) *influencing the evaluation of alternatives* by restricting access to information about the array of possible solutions or the way that information can be interpreted (see Cyert and March 1963; Pettigrew 1972; Pettigrew 1973). Any or all of these strategies may be enacted in the choice of new technology, and their application need not be limited to the choice between technologies: they may be as potent in the process of configuration and implementation.

In elaborating the power-process perspective, therefore, we must amend the analytical framework to take these factors into account (see figure 5). The addition of arrows running "up" the organizational hierarchy allows for the possibility that, at an earlier time, other organizational participants—including middle and lower-level management and engineering staff—or other organizations altogether may actually initiate changes in technology. Their actions—for example, in the form of research, proposals, or other forms of influence—could play a decisive role in setting the premises for decision making at higher levels in the organization. The design space corresponding to technological changes initiated at lower levels of the organization indicates the effect of hierarchical location on the range of possible forms such changes can take. The addition of historical context as an input to the change process—an input that has the potential to affect actions at all levels of the organizational hierarchy—represents, in turn, the limiting effect of structure on choice.

Second, the prior research has failed to undertake a serious effort to explain how or under what conditions substrategies are activated such that they affect the process of technological change. Child, for example, has suggested that "the tightness of coupling between senior management intentions and their actual implementation . . . is regarded as a variable factor. . . . The perspectives or values of middle managers, work organization designers and workers who have the potential to influence the implementation process therefore need to be taken into account, including factors determining their relative influence" (1985, 112). Despite having drawn attention to the issue, however, Child and the others limit their analyses to the reactions of managers, work designers, and workers to hierarchically imposed orders. Their "perspectives and values" may help explain how variations occur in the process of implementation, but we aren't told how they come into being, under what

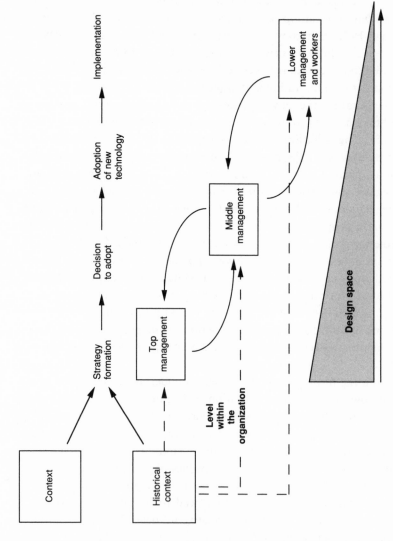

Figure 5. Stages and levels in the power-process model of technological change

conditions they influence the process of implementation, or how they might actively, even creatively, influence the choice of technology in the first place.[30]

The problem is that the concept of substrategy is limited by virtue of its identification with the formal structure of an organization. Formal structure may provide clues as to the responsibilities, activities, and objectives tied to a given position or level, but (1) it cannot by itself tell us a great deal about how potent or influential a given group may be in applying its substrategy to the choice of technology or to the manner of its implementation, and (2) it cannot fully encompass or explain the content of any group's substrategy, especially the values that people in those positions attach to the work they do—that is, values that go beyond formally prescribed duties and responsibilities. Put differently, from a power-process perspective it is not enough simply to recognize the existence of substrategies and to suggest that they can play a mediating role in the process of change; we must also incorporate into the analysis the bases of group power and the content of group substrategy.

Incorporating the bases of group power is not altogether a straightforward undertaking, despite the voluminous literature on the topic in sociology and organizational behavior.[31] Most theories of organizational power suffer from a weakness I earlier attached to the literature on technology and organization: they often take a rather static view on the determination of group power.[32] Notions of resource dependence, control over uncertainty, nonsubstitutability, and centrality may help explain the distribution of power among organizational groups or subunits at a given time and with respect to given events—for example, a specific choice or decision process. They are, however, of limited value when the problem under study—for instance, the relationship between

30. Works by Wilkinson (1983) and Barley (1986), among others, provide valuable insights on the efforts of workers and other "end users" to shape the outcomes of technological change. Yet those efforts are almost always portrayed as *reactions* to initiatives originating elsewhere in the organization. Thus, substrategies or entrenched interests represent filters or lenses through which changes are viewed. Here I am suggesting that substrategies or interests may also *stimulate action* (i.e., efforts to initiate a change), not just responses to some other group's initiative. The shift in perspective requires a concept that allows for both action and reaction.

31. See, for example, Bacharach and Lawler (1980), Crozier (1964), French and Raven (1968), Hickson et al. (1971), Pettigrew (1972), Pfeffer (1977; 1981), Pfeffer and Salancik (1978), Salancik and Pfeffer (1974), and Zald (1962).

32. Pfeffer, one of the most influential and prolific authors in the area, admits as much in his own review of resource dependence and strategic contingencies theories (Pfeffer 1981, 97–135).

technology and organization—is conceived of as dynamic and interactive over time and across events, a quality that is, I propose, a central feature of the power-process perspective.

Reconciling these differences requires that, once again, any individual instance of technological change be analyzed on its own and in its historical context. The ability of a group or a subunit to apply its own substrategy to affect a given change process must be seen as both historically derived (which forces us to ask how it came to acquire the power to intervene) and future oriented (which forces us to ask what the group is trying to achieve by means of its intervention).

Incorporating the content of group substrategy is no less essential for understanding the process and the outcomes of technological change. However, it is one thing to argue, as advocates of resource dependency and strategic contingency theories do, that the formal structure of an organization can give rise to group-specific substrategies and even to argue that power is a critical determinant of a group's ability to apply its substrategy; it is quite another to suggest that the content of that substrategy is reducible to the group's position in that formal structure. Reductionism may not be inappropriate when the goal is simply to assert that technological change affects different groups in different ways. But when the point is to open the door to the idea that different groups may influence the choice of technology and the manner of its use by means of intervention in the decision process, then the content of substrategy cannot be treated so simply.

A more productive alternative to the reductionist approach, I suggest, may be possible if we subsume substrategy under the broader rubric of *worldview*. Worldviews represent the ensemble of norms, beliefs, expectations, and, for lack of a better term, theories that people use to explain the world around them.[33] In an analysis of the political perspectives and values of different strata of workers in industrial organizations, Sabel argued that worldviews "are not just models of the world, they are models *for* the world, as well" (1982, 14). I concur with his characterization, but we can profit from extending the concept over a broader organizational domain—to include the managers and engineers who play a critical role in the process of technological change.

---

33. Worldviews are the product of many influences, as Weber (1978), Geertz (1973), Bourdieu (1977), and Fleck ([1935] 1979) have argued, including one's upbringing, childhood and adolescent experiences, and social class background.

Worldviews are not untethered ideologies. Quite the opposite: organizational leaders seek to shape or guide the worldviews of their participants in ways that will induce certain behaviors and discourage others. They do so by means of rules, rewards, socialization activities, performance measures, job descriptions, and the like.[34] At the same time, however, organizational participants bring with them from their professional, occupational, and social backgrounds norms, values, and beliefs that they seek to express in their personal conduct and, more important, through the work they do.[35] Van Maanen and Barley (1984) stress this point when they describe "occupational communities" as the distinctive languages, symbols, and values among people at the same organizational level and position in the division of labor.

The concept of worldview enables us to think of groups of organizational participants as having the capacity to act as well as react in distinctive ways. Benson (1977, 7) made the point quite effectively when he argued that

> organizational participants . . . are not in any single sense captives of the roles, official purposes, or established procedures of the organization. The participants fill these "forms" with unique "content." Sometimes they may do so in an automatic, unreflective way; in other periods they may become very purposeful in trying to reach beyond the limits of their present situation, to reconstruct the organization in accord with alternative conceptions of its purposes, structures, technologies, and other features.

Labor process theorists have come close to this conception in the effort to explain the organizational behavior of capitalists and managers as the extension of their class consciousness (Burawoy 1979; Wright 1978; Bowles and Gintis 1976). On occasion theorists have also provided evidence to suggest that workers act on the basis of a common consciousness (e.g., Fantasia 1988; Montgomery 1987). But even sympathetic critics (e.g., Wood and Kelly 1982) have noted that class consciousness is a relatively blunt analytical instrument, especially when it fails to take into account differences in consciousness that may arise

34. The literature on control in organizations is, of course, vast. For incisive works on governance arrangements, see Kochan, Katz, and McKersie (1986); on socialization processes, see Van Maanen and Schein (1979); and on performance measurement systems, see Johnson and Kaplan (1987).

35. See also F. Katz (1965), Kunda (1992), Whyte (1961), Gouldner (1954), Roy (1952), and Thomas (1989).

within different strata of working or capitalist classes (Sabel 1982). Absent altogether has been a sensitivity to forms of consciousness resident in other organizational strata. An explicit focus on these other forms of consciousness or worldviews is a central and distinctive feature of the power-process perspective.

Of special interest here are the worldviews of a stratum that has usually been overlooked in prior analyses: engineers and technicians responsible for the design and implementation of new production technology. Though they have been the object of separate study as a professional group (e.g., Zussman 1985; Whalley 1986; Bailyn 1980; Kunda 1992) and as users of new generations of design tools (e.g., Saltzman 1992), their role in the design of new technology has been underplayed. Yet it would seem only appropriate to ask how their perceptions of problems and solutions are formed and how those perceptions influence the process of technological change.[36] If, as I suggested earlier, the coupling of technical and social systems requires the translation of organizational objectives into concrete processes and relations, then we should expect work designers (e.g., manufacturing engineers) to be a major influence in the process of technological change. Moreover, given the fact that their skills and expertise are applied in a domain where neither top management nor most end users are trained (or, in the case of the latter, allowed to move), it could well be argued that engineers and technicians are expected to make critical—yet largely invisible—choices about what constitutes an "important" problem or an "appropriate" solution.

Taken together, these points strongly suggest that a theory of the process of change must incorporate the idea of organizations as a collection of worldviews, not as an entity that may be characterized by a single worldview. As I have sketched it out, the power-process perspective is sensitive to differences in worldviews: how they arise, how they are resolved or accommodated, and most important, how they affect the design and implementation of new technology. Formal structure may provide clues about the prescribed roles and perspectives attached to different participants in the change process, but structure alone cannot predict how participants perceive their roles or how their worldviews will be expressed in the process of change.

36. Analysts such as Perrow (1983; 1984) have commented at length about the way engineers view the world and how those views are reflected in the equipment and systems they design. But the empirical basis for their commentaries is not always clear; indeed, much of what is reported seems largely impressionistic in nature.

UNDERSTANDING TECHNOLOGICAL
CHOICE AND CHANGE

A fruitful way to use these ideas is to think of technological change as a *decision process* along the lines described by Mintzberg, Raisinghani, and Theoret (1976). A decision might be a specific and formal commitment to act, but a decision process consists of a flow of activities culminating in, or punctuated by, formal commitments to act. Mintzberg, Raisinghani, and Theoret put it succinctly: "A decision process [is] a set of actions that begins with the identification of a stimulus for action and ends with the specific commitment to action" (1976, 246).

Making the decision process the unit of analysis for studying technological change has several advantages. It reminds us that change rarely occurs in a smooth, linear fashion. Indeed, the "texture" of the decision process is a critical part of the story: the bumps, the rough spots, and the detours all may contain vital clues for understanding how technology is given meaning and purpose. Equally important, by treating technological change as a decision process we cannot presume that any predetermined stage or moment is more important in understanding the outcomes of a change. If we do not know in advance where and when a new system or technique is given its final shape, we must consider the role of interests and interpretation in the formation of the content of the change, in the allocation of resources to pursue the change, and ultimately in the actual implementation of the change. Focusing on the decision process also forces us to be sensitive to the category of acts Bachrach and Baratz (1962) referred to as "non-decisions": decisions to refrain from acting that can be made directly or indirectly but that are likely to have consequences for a change process.

CASE STUDIES IN CONTEXT

To capture process dynamics, we must extend the temporal context to include the full range of activities—from identification through implementation. Concretely, any specific change effort should be (1) analyzed within the ongoing flow of action within the organization; (2) compared with other efforts that preceded it; and (3) linked, where appropriate, to developments beyond the organization that may either accelerate or retard change. For purposes of consistency and comparability, I distinguish between three "moments" in the change process:[37]

37. These activities may overlap in time, or a decision process may involve iterations

1. *Choosing between technologies*, that is, the activities involved in selecting among alternative approaches to a given task. For example, this moment would include choices between a manual and an automated production process.

2. *Choosing within technologies*, that is, the activities involved in selecting among alternative approaches within a given technology. For example, this moment would include choices about the degree of automation to be employed in a production process.

3. *Implementing the chosen technology*, that is, the activities involved in selecting among alternative approaches to operating the chosen technology. For example, this moment would involve choices about the manner in which skills and operational control will be distributed.

We must also extend the organizational context to include the groups or levels responsible for initiating a change, those who must authorize the change, and ultimately those who are the object of the change. The investigation must cut across hierarchical levels and functional lines, paralleling where possible both the formal and the informal pathways of power and influence. In case studies undertaken from the power-process perspective—in contrast to the bulk of prior research—data collection cannot be limited to a single individual (e.g., who fills out a questionnaire designed to capture the attitudes and behaviors of an entire organization) or to a small subset designated to speak on behalf of the organization.

RESEARCH METHODS

The research methodology most appropriate to the questions I have posed is principally qualitative.[38] Direct observation is the best way to capture process dynamics, especially where multiple interpretations of events and explanations are anticipated. However, given the long time frames involved in most technological change efforts (several years in most cases), direct observation is extremely difficult. For this reason I chose to study changes that, for the most part, were already completed

---

between them, but each will be important in providing clues to the outcomes of the change.

38. The appendixes provide greater detail about the interview questions, the interview sample, and the techniques used for data analysis.

but that were sufficiently recent to allow participants to be interviewed in depth about the process of change and their perceptions of it.

The trade-offs between "real-time" observation and observation via historical recollection are not insignificant, but the loss of information and the potential for reconstructive bias can be compensated for by systematic efforts to collect data from multiple sources (see, e.g., Schwenk 1985; Denzin 1978; Jick 1983; Pettigrew 1983). Many organizations routinely generate paper trails that include project proposals and comments, memoranda and letters circulated internally, purchase specifications, bids from equipment vendors, and capital equipment requests. As I describe in appendix 1, these documents can be used to construct detailed chronologies of events that can then be employed to corroborate or challenge dates, events, and interpretations provided by interview subjects. In addition, information on the organizations and technologies can be gathered from public sources (e.g., annual reports, business and technical presses, and the written accounts of external observers).

Of course, the most important sources of data about change processes are the participants themselves. Because the meanings and the objectives participants attach to change are central issues in the research, interviews must provide detailed information of two different sorts: (1) *description of the change*, that is, what changed, how the change process occurred, and what role individuals played in the process; and (2) *explanation of the change*, that is, why it occurred, why it took the form it did, and why it had the consequences it did. By asking a common and structured set of questions that probe for descriptive detail, the researcher can obtain a more complete picture of change as a process and can also compare processes across cases and organizations. By asking questions that probe for meaning or intent, the researcher can bring to the surface aspects of the change process that might not be immediately evident in the outcomes of a change or that might be overlooked in an effort to make the change process appear, in retrospect, to have been simple and straightforward. By combining both types of questions in interviews with people from different levels and functions, the researcher can track how both the technology and the participants' perception of it evolved over time.

Unlike cross-sectional research designs, especially those that employ survey methods, interview-based qualitative research requires that data be analyzed (and reanalyzed) as it is collected. Every piece of information and every interview transcript must be considered on its own and then in relation to all other pieces. This is inherent in both the method and the phenomena it seeks to explain. If it were possible to infer process from simple observation of outcomes, then data collection could be organized in a very different way: one could simply speak to the "right" people or get the right outcome measures and proceed to tell the story. However, if outcomes are not capable of explaining processes, the story itself must be treated as an emergent phenomenon.

The importance of continuous analysis—or what Glaser and Strauss (1967) refer to as "constant comparative analysis"—is underscored by my concern with keeping the study of process in context. As I suggested earlier, context must be understood two ways: as the ongoing flow of events that organizations and individuals initiate and respond to and as their perceptions of the meaning and purpose of those events. To do an adequate job of analysis, it is essential to evaluate continuously what people say in light of the context to which they are referring and the context in which they are saying it.[39] The point is not that "truth" will somehow emerge from continuous analysis and evaluation; this notion is no more valid than the contrary notion that truth is uniquely associated with quantification. Rather, the point is that a richer and much more credible account of a multifaceted process can be achieved.

SITE AND CASE SELECTION

The selection of cases and research sites was influenced by two principal criteria. First, I required broad and relatively unrestricted access to people and documentation in order to do a thorough study of the decision processes surrounding technological change. Second, the cases themselves had to be sufficiently similar to allow for both comparison and generalizability.

As it turned out, the first criterion raised enormous practical problems. My request for breadth and depth of access was unprecedented in many of the organizations I approached. Most were familiar with case study research, but their prior experiences involved one- or two-day "visits" by academics (or their research assistants) who spoke mainly to

---

39. For example, if someone—say, a manager in charge of a factory—reports that she "chose" a particular process because "it made sense," her remark has to be understood two ways: first, in reference to what she perceived to be the limiting factors operating at the time a choice was made (e.g., capital constraints, product life cycles, or the state of labor-management relations); and second, in reference to the position she occupies (or occupied) in the setting (e.g., as a plant manager, a spokesperson for the organization, or a person whose actions are constantly being monitored and evaluated).

top managers and other credentialed spokespersons. In some instances, my initial contacts found merit in my proposal but could not persuade others in positions of authority to open the doors to me. In other instances, companies would allow me to study only a part of the decision process. Several companies, including some that are included in this study, offered to provide access on the condition that I *not* include competitor firms in the sample.

Difficulties in negotiating access carried over to the selection of the cases themselves. Although I had originally intended to limit my sample to specific types of change in process or production technology (e.g., flexible machining systems), only two of the companies that agreed to give me access employed comparable production technologies. I was thus forced to choose between very limited access to data in companies employing roughly equivalent new technologies and much broader access and data from companies employing very different technologies. Given my overriding concern with analyzing the full process of change, I chose to pursue the latter course.

I was, however, able to structure the sample of cases and sites in three important ways. First, all the cases represent instances of technological change that were considered to be substantial departures from prior processes employed by these organizations. Second, all the cases were instances of change in process technology, that is, in the physical and social organization of the production process. Although several cases include significant changes in less visible elements of production technology—most notably in software and control systems—all are principally concerned with alterations in manufacturing techniques. Third, all the cases involve large, U.S.-based companies whose principal lines of business are the design and manufacture of industrial goods.

The sites are differentiated by the manner in which they organize research and development around manufacturing technology. Although this differentiation was not an explicit criterion in the selection of sites, the companies fall into two groups: those in which manufacturing research and development is centralized (that is, carried out as a corporate function), versus those in which it is decentralized to the level of operating units or divisions. As indicated in table 1, the structural location of manufacturing R&D coincides roughly with the broad characterization of core production technologies.

The empirical core of the study consists of six cases drawn from four different companies. The cases drawn from the aircraft, aluminum, and

TABLE 1. CHARACTERISTICS OF RESEARCH SITES AND INTERVIEW SAMPLE

Site	Case Study	Core Technology of Organization	Location of Process R&D	Total Number of Interviews
Aircraft and aerospace	Flexible machining system	Large batch	Division	26
	Robotized assembly cell	Large batch	Division	31
	Computer numerical control machine tools	Small batch	Division	24
Computer and electronics	Surface mount circuit board assembly	Large batch	Division	118
Aluminum products	Continuous casting	Continuous process	Corporate	51
Automotive	Flexible machining system	Mass production	Corporate	46
			Total	296

auto companies involve changes in manufacturing technology specific to a single division. The sixth case involves a change in process technology that spanned several divisions in the computer and electronics company.

I conducted a total of 296 interviews in the four companies over the course of three years. In each case, interviews included all levels of the organizational hierarchy and representatives from all the functional groups involved in the change. Initial interviews were usually conducted with R&D managers. I then interviewed people whom this group recommended as knowledgeable about some aspect of the design or implementation of the final system; in most cases the second round of interviews included representatives from product and process engineering, facilities maintenance, purchasing, industrial engineering, training, human resources and industrial relations, marketing, and finance. Finally, I interviewed production supervisors, hourly workers, and, where appropriate, union representatives closest to the change. The interviews averaged an hour and a half in length. The interviews were tape-recorded and fully transcribed for later analysis.

In addition, I did library research on the companies in which the research was to be conducted and on the technologies that would be the object of analysis. All available documentation associated with each case was requested to augment the interviews. My immersion in company records and library research on the specific technologies helped make me a credible interviewer. My prior knowledge of esoteric project acronyms and technical terms impressed many of the managers and engineers; one went so far as to suggest that I apply for a job since one of his secrets of success was "knowing the jargon better than anyone else."[40] In most instances, company representatives were very forthcoming in providing me with available records. However, a significant portion of that documentation was labeled proprietary, and reporting of some of its contents therefore had to be approved before publication.

Finally, I kept detailed field notes on the time I spent at each site observing the equipment at work and questioning the operators, supervisors, and technicians in attendance about the technology, particularly in terms of how it departed from past practices and how it affected adjacent processes. These notes provided a measure of continuity to the

40. I did, however, query interviewees as to what the jargon meant to them, rather than feigning understanding of the jargon and risking the loss of valuable meanings in the process.

analysis in progress and were especially useful in generating new questions and lines of investigation.

REPORTING FINDINGS

The use of a qualitative approach has some obvious and some not-so-obvious implications for how research findings are reported. Most evident is the fact that findings cannot be reported in the same manner as experimental results (Van Maanen 1988; Glaser and Strauss 1967; Strauss 1987; Becker 1986). Although, as I have suggested, the research is designed to include all relevant actors, stages, and perspectives on the change process, the inductive nature of the research precludes use of either the procedures or the rhetoric of deductive hypothesis formation and testing. Conclusions can and will be drawn from the case studies, but they cannot and will not be presented as constituting "proofs" or "critical tests" of specific propositions.

To many readers, the preceding points may seem obvious—both as a strength and as a weakness of this style of research—but I emphasize the obvious for two basic reasons. First, at least a portion of the audience to whom this book is addressed does not routinely read case studies in the manner in which I intend these to be read. Case studies that appear in management texts and in the business press commonly present a set of "facts" that describe a particular situation or problem and either challenge readers to figure out the "right" answer or encourage them to accept a heavily massaged summary of events as evidence for or against a particular proposition. My case studies, by contrast, are intended to be "open" to interpretation. I will, of course, suggest what I feel to be appropriate or plausible interpretations—directly in words and indirectly in the way I have edited the story I tell. However, I will also emphasize the fact that the story I am telling is the product of multiple informants, each with his or her own interpretation. Thus, rather than obscure the existence of contending views or interpretations by presenting a single authoritative voice, I will attempt to reproduce with fidelity the "multiple and competing rationalities" that characterize organizations.

Second, throughout the book I will emphasize the emergent nature of both the change processes I studied and of my analysis of those processes. Concretely, this approach means that each case will be presented in such a way that the reader can be aware of how I developed my interpretation over the course of the research. Not only does this style of writing add an element of action to what might otherwise be turgid academic prose, but it also makes the reader aware of the way in which social realities (and sociological analyses) are constructed. Thus, unlike much social science writing in which the researcher is absent or invisible, I will be present in the writing.

ORGANIZATION OF THE BOOK

The next four chapters constitute the empirical "heart" of the book. Each chapter is organized around a case study—the exception being chapter 2, which incorporates three cases from different parts of the same company. I begin each chapter with a brief overview of organizational and technological context and then proceed to lay out the cases in the broad phases I described earlier: choices between technologies, choices within a technology, and then implementation of the chosen technology. I accumulate insights from the cases to provide the reader with a clearer sense of how the analysis developed over time.

Each chapter focuses on the core questions I outlined earlier: If new technology does indeed drive organizational change, *how* does it do so? What are the mechanisms through which similarities and differences in structure come about? Alternatively, if organizations can structure themselves through technological choice, who makes those choices and how?

Chapter 2 analyzes the process of change involved in the adoption of three different technologies in a large and successful manufacturer of commercial aircraft. Two of the three were large-scale undertakings: budgets in each instance were in the millions of dollars. The third was much less costly, though no less important for what it says about the organizational dynamics of choice and change. Of particular interest is what each case study reveals about the screens or criteria that different groups used in deciding what was an important organizational problem. Chapter 3 shifts to a single case of change in production technology that cross-cut the boundaries of what were otherwise very independent product-based divisions in a large computer and electronics company. In this case, by contrast to the aircraft company, the absence of a heavily bureaucratic system of administration seemed to provide greater opportunities for experimentation with new technology. Yet as the detailed description will show, getting a technological alternative on the agenda for choice may require far more than convincing experimental evidence. Chapter 4 concerns what is, in many ways, a far older and more traditional manufacturing environment: a major aluminum products company. Ironically, this traditional environment was the site of a surprisingly unconventional approach to the process of technological choice and change—one that by its emphasis on collaboration across functional and hierarchical boundaries stands in dramatic contrast to the first two firms, which pride themselves on being progressive and inventive organizations. Finally, chapter 5 focuses on a parts-producing plant in the automobile industry. The auto industry, as we know from the extraordinary attention it has received in both the academic and the business press, has been a hotbed of experimentation—some of which has been carefully controlled. In this case we encounter what has been described inside the company as a successful instance of new technology implementation—only to find that much of the success is owed to highly sophisticated political maneuvering and powerful political alliances between traditional adversaries.

In the final two chapters, I assess what the case studies offer as insights for both theory and practice. In chapter 6 I review the perspectives presented in this chapter in light of the research findings. There I elaborate the power-process perspective in greater detail, indicating how it diverges from and yet bridges the technological determinist and social choice arguments. However, I also push the analysis a step further by suggesting that what the case studies have to tell us about the politics of technological change may also apply more generally to the process of organizational innovation and change. In chapter 7 I depart from the tradition of social science writing and direct my attention to the practical implications of the research. I offer two modest contributions to the discussion on technology and the future of the industrial enterprise: (1) that the future industrial enterprise may be better served by embracing organizational politics rather than trying to eliminate them; and (2) that durable organizational change will require not only restructuring but an imaginative reconceptualization of the *process* of manufacturing as an art form in itself.

TWO

Technology as a Power Tool

*Technological Choice
in an Aircraft Company*

Under normal circumstances, people who fly in airplanes don't spend a lot of time thinking about how airplanes are made. They assume that somewhere—if not in the cockpit—somebody or some organization has the problem of flight and flying machines all figured out. In other words, airplanes fly and stay together in the air because they are the product of a rational, logical, and, indeed, scientific process of design and manufacturing. The same descriptors, we assume, apply to the organizations that make airplanes.

For the most part those assumptions are quite valid. Yet in this chapter I will suggest that the people in those organizations are making more than just airplanes. They are engaged in a complex and occasionally contentious process of giving meaning and purpose to the work they do, to the environment in which they do it, and to the relationships that bind their work to the work of others. In short, they are designing and manufacturing organizations as well as airplanes. Physical technology, in the form of machines, computers, and the like, plays a critical role in the building of airplanes; but it plays a critical role in the way people interact in building organizations, too. Thus, choices among alternative physical technologies are also choices among alternative ways to organize people.

In this chapter I examine three recent cases of change in manufacturing technology in a large commercial aircraft company. I give specific attention to the physical and the social "impacts" of technological change. But real insight about what new technology "does" to work and organizations requires equal, if not greater, attention to what people are trying to do to organizations and to each other *by means of* new technology. Thus, in each case the focus shifts with the evolution of each technology: from an analysis of the problems or solutions that initiated the choice between technologies, to the choices that are made within alternative forms of a given technology, and, finally, to the manner of implementation itself.

The three cases examined in this chapter vary in useful ways. The first case centers on the development and introduction of a flexible machining system or cell (referred to as an FMS). FMS technology combines computer-controlled machine tools and sensing devices to automate the cutting, grinding, and shaping of metal parts. The second case involves an effort to apply robotics technology to an assembly process. The third case focuses on the introduction of a new generation of machine tools, computer numerically controlled (CNC) machines. Although these cases do not stand in opposition,[1] they do offer a useful contrast in both the magnitude of departure from the technologies that preceded them and in the manner in which they were chosen and then incorporated. Specifically, the FMS represents a large and expensive undertaking that made extensive use of in-house research and development. The robotized assembly cell (or RAC) was an even more expensive undertaking, but it also involved far greater reliance on external expertise. The CNC case involved a relatively incremental and less expensive shift in technology undertaken as part of an equipment replacement process.

THE INDUSTRIAL
AND ORGANIZATIONAL CONTEXT

The companies that design and manufacture commercial aircraft are a study in contrasts. They are at once risk-seeking and risk-averse, flexible and organic but also rigid and mechanical, rewarding of innovation yet jealously protective of tradition. These contrasting qualities—how they arise and how they are reconciled—constitute a vital part of the story of technological change in aircraft manufacturing.

A useful place to begin is with the images people in this business use to describe their product and the organizations that produce them. Top aircraft company managers, for example, speak with pride of their

---

1. That is, they are not commonly used for the same tasks and therefore are not usually seen as alternative approaches to machining activities.

organizations' ability to create a product that can safely and reliably perform an extraordinary variety of tasks under hostile and unpredictable conditions. They delight in describing the miles of wire and tubing, the tons of aluminum and graphite, and the dozens of electronic systems that go into the average airliner. They point to thick planning documents and detailed flow charts as evidence of the precision with which they orchestrate the thousands of separate fabrication and assembly tasks carried out all over the world.

Yet working engineers and middle managers describe their product as "a million spare parts flying in formation." This comment, though perhaps disquieting to the airline passenger, is a common one. Like most insiders' jokes, especially in industry, it is an exaggeration, a form of self-deprecation intended to poke fun at an otherwise extremely serious and safety-minded business. However, it also contains several essential elements of truth about the business of designing and building a product as complex and as precarious as, in the words of one engineer I interviewed, "an aluminum tube stuffed with grandmothers flying near the speed of sound."

A "million parts flying in formation" connotes several things about the design and manufacture of a jet airliner. It says a great deal about the complexity of both the product and the organization: there are, quite literally, a million parts in a jumbo jet (counting rivets and fasteners), and virtually every part has a corresponding organizational grouping that exercises responsibility for it. Both the parts and the organization "fly in formation" because they share a common focus—the airplane as a totality—but the glue that holds the organizational parts together often appears as tenuous and as fragile as the thousands of individual rivets, fasteners, and spot welds that give shape to the airplane itself. The pieces fly together, but left unchecked, they would fly apart; in describing "airplane principles" to me, a structural engineer offered an apt characterization of both the product and the organization that produces it: "Engines provide the thrust and wings provide the lift. They work together. However, if we didn't design things right, if we didn't exercise the proper control, the engines would tear the wings off the body." Similarly, to build an airplane, control must be exercised over the thousand separate groupings that must simultaneously fly together; otherwise, both the plane and the organization would fly apart.

Perhaps most revealing in the "million parts" comment, however, is the underlying recognition that both systems—aeronautical and organizational—are so complex that no one individual really understands how they all work, much less how they all come together. Both are human creations, but both are beyond human scale. Thus, despite the extraordinary assemblage of scientific, engineering, and production expertise that enables a jumbo jet to be designed and built, there remains an essential mystery to the endeavor . . . and to the social relationships through which it is undertaken.

A closer look reveals that the mystery is accommodated, though not resolved, in the creation of two distinctly different organizations *inside* each company. One organization, the design organization, confronts the complexities of the system directly and leverages from that confrontation substantial organizational power and influence. The other organization, the manufacturing organization, addresses it indirectly, through the designs and plans—the formal objectifications of the unknown—provided to it by the design organization. Manufacturing follows design's lead; it is expected to translate the theory into practice, to execute but not to conceive.

The differences between these organizations are demonstrated most graphically in the launch of a new airplane program. The launch of a new airplane program is a momentous event in the life of a company.[2] It doesn't happen very often—perhaps once in a decade—and when it does a great deal hangs in the balance: hundreds of millions of dollars, thousands of jobs, and in some cases the economic health of an entire region are at stake.[3] Thousands of people are assembled—many are pulled away from the more mundane task of updating and customizing existing models—distributed into teams, outfitted with plans and offices, exhorted from on high, and unleashed on a campaign of creation that can last seven to ten years from concept approval to testing and certification. Schedules and flow charts provide the exoskeleton (and the discipline) for an extraordinary array of functional and cross-functional groups. Time, above all, is critical: a slipped schedule in so complex and interdependent an undertaking can have disastrous consequences, especially where anxious creditors and customers are concerned. During these campaigns, careers as well as fortunes can be made or lost. "Battlefield" promotions are common, and both successes and failures become the stuff of corporate legend, at least until the next campaign.

2. See *Seattle Times* (1985) and Dertouzos, Lester, and Solow (1989).
3. Given the large role that exports of U.S.-made commercial aircraft play in the nation's balance of trade, the fate of a new airplane can have even more dramatic consequences. See, for example, Dertouzos, Lester, and Solow (1989).

At the heart of the campaign is what Burns and Stalker (1961) termed an "organic" organization made up of engineers who design the parts and integrate them into a coherent system. They accomplish this task through an iterative movement from part to whole to part again. To give a simplified example, hydraulic lines, electrical cables, fuel lines, and physical structures are designed independently, overlaid to check for intersections and blockages, and then redesigned to accommodate one another. Design is extremely information- and communication-intensive; computer-aided design tools augment (and accelerate) the process, but a workable design demands close, even continuous, contact. In the harried effort to keep to schedule, the design organization relies most heavily on mutual adjustment as its central coordinating mechanism (Mintzberg 1979), especially on trust in the competence of the associated engineering professions.

Indeed, it is the intensity of interaction and trust that enables this part of the organization to surmount the mysteries of so complex a product and so seemingly incomprehensible a process. It is, however, also the means by which the design organization comes to exercise hegemony in the power structure of these companies. That is, having accomplished what appears to most outsiders (and many insiders) as a miracle—a dissolution of the mystery—the design organization cloaks itself in that very mystery as a symbol of its unique, even virtuous, skills. The act need not be interpreted as crass or conspiratorial, any more than the power of doctors in a hospital need be attributed to simple egotism. Rather, it is, as Hickson et al. (1971) argued, symbolic of designers' ability to claim that they manage a (if not *the*) critical uncertainty facing the organization and then to translate that claim into organizational power.

Yet even this explanation does not account for the subtle moral overtones that accompany the design activity. Airplane designers, like medical doctors, simultaneously embrace the mystery in what they do (holding one or three hundred lives in their hands) and reject the mystery by representing themselves as practitioners of science and purveyors of rationality. This duality both establishes their claim to power and legitimizes it as well. The effectiveness of the claim is manifested in myriad ways, as the case studies will indicate. But the most telling in the organization I studied was the informal rule that no matter where someone earned his or her college degree or in what field he or she concentrated, *only* designers are referred to as "engineers." In other words, designers are the "real" engineers, and by definition, only they do "real engineering" work.

If the organization that designs the new airplane appears organic, the one that builds the plane tends to be remarkably mechanical in nature. Once a plane has been certified and the attendant mysteries accommodated, teams are replaced by far more traditional functional departments. Back-of-the-envelope plans give way to standardized forms and procedures. Informal agreements and understandings are subjected to mind-numbing documentation. And the sense of mission that encouraged improvisation and experimentation across intellectual and hierarchical lines yields to more mundane concerns about departmental boundaries, chains of command, budgets, balance sheets, time studies, and head counts—all the trappings of a bureaucratic organization. Though manufacturing or, as it is referred to in the case study company, "operations" is by no means considered an irrelevant activity, it is neither considered nor expected to be a creative one.

Certainly the managers, operations staff,[4] supervisors, and workers do build the airplanes, but a very strong distinction is made between building and creating. Creation involves imagination, innovation, and risk taking; these qualities are, however, actively discouraged in the operations organization except under the explicit oversight and approval of the design hierarchy. Various means are invoked to justify the distinction, not the least being the external controls imposed by regulatory agencies such as the Federal Aviation Administration, which insist that every part and every part change be recorded and retrievable should later problems arise. Thus, building an airplane may require a special sort of knowledge, and building it to engineers' designs may demand high levels of ingenuity, but by virtue of the engineers' successful claim to coping with the mysteries of the airplane, the manufacturing organization is limited to routinizing the creative acts of others and claiming control over the process of production.

This contrast forms an important part of the context for the case studies of change in the process of aircraft manufacturing. It makes clear, for example, that this company comprises not one but *two* engineering organizations and that each has a decidedly different style and mission. Moreover, it strongly suggests that the incentives and resources for undertaking change are differentially distributed: to wit, the product is expected to lead the process and, perhaps more important, the process (i.e., manufacturing) must not inhibit or render uncertain the creation of the product.

---

4. *Operations staff* is the term used inside the company to refer to the industrial, mechanical, and electrical engineers who focus on the process of manufacturing.

THE AIRCRAFT COMPANY

The organization from which the case studies are drawn is a large and financially successful manufacturer of commercial aircraft and aerospace products. It is based in North America and employs more than one hundred thousand people worldwide. Like its major competitors, the company maintains an extensive infrastructure of design, fabrication, and assembly processes, although it subcontracts a substantial share of parts fabrication to an army of firms around the world. In-house manufacturing is dedicated to the molding and machining of precision parts and to the final assembly of the aircraft itself.

The company employs a divisional structure, with commercial jet aircraft forming one of the principal divisions. The aircraft division controls its own design, manufacturing, marketing, and sales functions. Engineering staff consist of the two distinct groups I described earlier: design (i.e., the "real" engineers) and manufacturing. The manufacturing engineering group is an admixture of industrial, mechanical, and electrical engineers responsible for the development, implementation, and maintenance of manufacturing technology. The manufacturing engineers devoted to developing new production technology are dwarfed in size by the design engineering group. They report to operations management and are physically housed at some distance from their counterparts in design.

The majority of production workers are unionized, but as has been common in the United States, neither workers nor their union have been actively engaged in the development or implementation of new manufacturing technology. Several years prior to the initiation of my research, however, the company and the union did negotiate clauses in the collective bargaining agreement pledging both sides to cooperate in enhancing quality and productivity. A central part of that agreement involved the creation of a joint committee to serve as a vehicle for information sharing between the parties concerning the company's plans for introducing new technology and for overseeing the development of programs of worker retraining and reallocation.[5] The existence of the agreement thus provided a valuable opportunity to assess the effects of more cooperative

5. At the time of my study, however, the joint committee had reached an impasse in their efforts: both manufacturing R&D engineers and labor relations representatives were ill equipped to discuss the human and organizational implications of new technology, and the union officials were overwhelmed with the mass of technical information presented by the company. The joint committee, and the company more generally, agreed to sponsor the case studies in an effort to break the impasse. Neither I nor the committee could anticipate where the research might lead. For a more detailed discussion, see Thomas (1991).

labor-management relations—on the order of what Kochan, Katz, and McKersie (1986) characterize as a "transformed" industrial relations system—on the process of technological choice and change.

I turn now to reporting the findings from the research—and I explain why, in this setting at least, technology is a power tool.

CASE 1: THE FLEXIBLE MACHINING SYSTEM

Automation has been of great interest to engineers, managers, and academics for well over three decades (Bright 1958; Piore and Sabel 1984). For most of that time, "fixed" automation, dedicated to the production of enormous volumes of identical parts, was the dominant approach. However, over the past decade new approaches have greatly reduced the limits of fixed automation; these more "flexible" machining systems (FMS) allow a wider variety of small volume parts to be made at a much lower cost (Noble 1984; Jaikumar 1986; Shaiken 1985). In 1980, when this case begins, FMS technology was in its infancy; it represented a major departure from this company's prior experience and, arguably, put it at or near the leading edge of its industry.

This change took nearly four years to complete. When put into operation in 1984, the FMS cell departed in significant ways from the process that preceded it (the cell is sketched in figure 6). Formerly, each of the three machines at the heart of the cell was operated independently by a skilled machinist. Now the three machines form a system controlled by a computer and linked by a conveyor. The computer not only directs the operation of each machine but also orchestrates the movement of parts from one machine to the next.

CHOOSING BETWEEN TECHNOLOGIES

My introduction to the FMS came in the form of a stack of documents pulled from company archives. The centerpiece was a lengthy proposal asking for several million dollars to be allocated for research and development of what was characterized as a "dramatic new approach to precision machining." Along with the proposal, however, I also received a sheaf of memoranda, letters, and notes (some of which were hand-written) from the manufacturing R&D group that had drafted the formal request for funds. My review of the proposal and documents surrounding the FMS left me puzzled. On the one hand, it was not clear

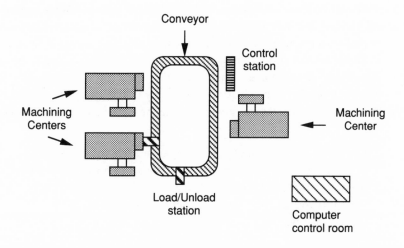

Figure 6. Flexible machining system

that the authors of the FMS proposal had much confidence in either the technology or their ability to develop it. Internal memos from the R&D group expressed concern about the failure of more experienced companies with similar efforts. Other reports suggested that the level of R&D's expertise was not sufficient to the task: engineers would have to be sent to special seminars, and other skills would have to be acquired through "additional hires." On the other hand, the proposal submitted to corporate executives showcased very explicit and attractive return-on-investment (ROI) calculations. Great confidence was expressed in the ability of the R&D organization to develop the FMS—to the extent that all the major work should be done in-house instead of going to a more experienced equipment manufacturer. Moreover, no reference was made in the calculations to the expense of acquiring new skills and new people or the potential costs of delay. Thus, even before I had a chance to ask why this technology was chosen, I was puzzled by the difference between R&D's confident portrayal of the FMS to upper management and its private tentativeness, uncertainty, and possible underestimation of the system's true costs.

Although these contradictory impressions were irksome, I held them aside to focus my first interviews on contextual factors, especially on the role that organizational objectives played in the choice of problems to be solved by means of new technology. If the company had chosen to pursue an expensive example of advanced manufacturing technology, I expected it to reflect some broader strategic goals. In a lengthy interview with the divisional operations manager in charge of manufacturing and manufacturing technology, I asked whether corporate management specified the direction of production technology development. He responded by suggesting that corporate management's guidance was indirect at best:

> Corporate doesn't exactly dictate which direction we ought to go. They're more influential when it comes to how much money we have to spend. If you're given a budget of so many dollars, it's up to you to come up with a scheme for making the best use of that money.

Less expensive changes in manufacturing technology are made at the discretion of the divisions, but large expenditures or "big ticket items" like the FMS have to undergo scrutiny by corporate executives and financial staff to make sure they are in line with corporate strategic objectives. Even then, he said, corporate objectives were not particularly explicit; they consisted in three simple rules: "curb costs, increase productivity, and lose heads" (i.e., reduce the number of production workers).

If corporate executives did not give guidance but still retained their right to review divisional spending, perhaps divisional management played that steering role. When asked about the budget cycle in which the FMS was initiated, the operations manager said he'd offered "hints" to his line managers and to the R&D department about what he felt were some major production problems. But, he added, his hints were largely "echoes of the message we got from corporate." In passing on the message to his subordinates, he said: "I sort of threw down the gauntlet to my people to see who would respond."

Symptoms Versus Causes   In this case, the gauntlet took the form of a memo in June 1980 requesting proposals for investments in new technology. By October a dozen proposals had been submitted. The majority requested replacement of worn-out machines or extension of ongoing development projects. However, two stood out—in terms of both their projected expense and their focus on technologies that were unprecedented in the division and the company. One, expressed in a two-page memo from a pair of production superintendents, called for a computer-controlled system with robot carriers to automate the storage and retrieval of parts in several shops. According to the proposal, the system would enable the shops to track their inventory more closely and to reduce the time it took individual parts to get through the machining process. It offered little in the way of expectations for the cost of the system or the savings it might generate.

The second proposal came in from manufacturing research and development, neatly bound and complete with transparencies and preliminary cost justifications. It urged consideration of a flexible machining system. According to the proposal, the division's largest machine shop was in serious trouble: "Of the total time a part spends in the shop, only 5% is spent on a machine. For the remainder of the time, the part is either waiting for processing or is in transit from one station to the next." The proposal identified two major causes for the shop's problem. First, it argued, the current process for scheduling the movement of parts through the maze of machines and machining steps was "archaic" and "out of control." It could be saved only by a "*modern material handling system*" (emphasis in original). Second, the proposal went on, the existing process was overly labor intensive. The lack of adequate control over scheduling and parts movement allowed "outdated staffing practices to persist, especially compared to modern (Japanese) methods." In other words, there were not only too many workers, but too many workers standing idle for long periods of time. The proposal went on to point out that several major Japanese companies were already running their FMS systems unmanned in "lights-out" factories.

A side-by-side comparison of the two proposals revealed several significant similarities and differences. For example, both proposals targeted the movement of parts through the shop as a major cause of idle machines and workers. The shop superintendents' proposal implied that the system for routing, tracking, and storing parts was the culprit. The R&D proposal essentially concurred, but in its use of phrases such as "out of control" it hinted that human systems were as much to blame as paper systems. The point was underscored by reference to "outdated staffing practices" that, by contrast to "modern (Japanese)" methods, were "archaic." The evocative phrasing and the polished form of the R&D proposal highlighted another important difference: new technology was their business; they were prepared to launch it; they were, by comparison to the shop, purveyors of modern production practices.

This textual analysis was corroborated in interviews with the authors of the FMS proposal. An R&D manager who had supervised the writing recalled his explicit efforts to use "the same words and even the same phrases" he'd heard the operations manager use to describe an "antiquated factory" run by a competitor company. He told me proudly:

> I really think he bought the idea because of the way we presented it. We pushed the right buttons . . . cost reduction, losing heads. I think we succeeded because I understood him. I understood how to sell this guy something.

Familiar imagery would enhance the proposal's chances, but equally important was the distinction to be drawn between R&D and the shop: R&D was in touch with new technology; the shop was not.

However, those interviews also revealed that R&D's advocacy of the FMS system was hardly coincidental. The proposal came close on the heels of a major machine tool show in Chicago that had featured the first FMS created by a major equipment manufacturer. Several engineers had attended the exhibition; at least one had gone with the explicit intent of viewing the FMS. Moreover, their wording of the FMS proposal borrowed liberally from brochures that extolled the virtues of the system on display. Inspired by the sales brochures and videotapes of Japanese factories, the FMS advocates had found a solution. Hints from the operations manager provided them with a problem. Thus, a proposal was conceived.

When it came to judging the relative merits of the proposals he had received, the operations manager gave credence to the R&D group's assessment of the importance of imagery in decision making. He preferred the FMS because "harder-working machines" and fewer people were something he thought his superiors could understand. The automated storage system might have been worthwhile, but the proposal was not nearly as compelling as the FMS and it did not promise to eliminate any workers. According to the operations manager, the automated storage system was a "band-aid":

> It didn't get to the heart of the action: getting control over the process by getting the parts in and out of the machines. You don't get that unless you have a way to keep bottlenecks like people and paper from getting in the way.

A closer look at the "heart of the action" brings to the surface an objective familiar to labor process theory—control—but it also reveals that the problem to which the operations manager referred was not limited to workers. On the one hand, the FMS would significantly alter the allocation of workers to different jobs in the machine shop. In theory, at least, the use of conveyors, sensors, and computer controls would eliminate the existing practice of allocating one operator per machine. It could also do away with many of the stock handlers who moved parts between machines and the set-up workers who changed the tools and fixtures between machining operations. In other words, by substituting machines for workers, control over the process would be hard-wired. Moreover, by exercising its contractual right to introduce new production technology, management could avoid a direct confrontation with the union over work pace and production standards.

On the other hand, when I pressed the operations manager about the issue, he admitted that idle workers were as much a symptom as they were a cause of what he perceived to be the shop's inefficiencies. He pointed to shop management as contributors to the situation:

> It's hard for them to see the real problems sometimes. They don't
> always see that they're part of the problem. . . . So, they set their
> own rates about how much work should get done. They allow
> things to slack off. There's no shortage of excuses, of course.
> And maybe some are valid. A shop like that can be a tough
> place, especially with the kind of union we have. And a lot of
> foremen came out of the hourly ranks, so they have commit-
> ments to this guy or that way of doing things. But my job is to
> get the work out. To keep things under control.

He then tempered that remark by arguing that he could understand the reasons behind shop management's "myopia":

> Shop supervision had the same concern about job security that
> the guys operating the machines did. In other words, if you don't
> need as many machine operators, you don't need as many super-
> visors to supervise them.

In other words, a real attraction of the FMS was its promise to alter dramatically the social organization of the shop and its historical accumulation of customs and informal norms—seemingly independent of whatever tangible economic benefits the technology might provide. The operations manager confirmed this assessment when he added that it would "let us clean house and start all over again. Wipe the slate clean."

These comments, as well as the slippery distinction between symptoms and underlying causes, led me to search out the superintendents who had authored the competing proposal. One had retired, but the other provided several important points of contrast with what I had been told by the operations manager and the R&D engineers. When I queried him as to the justification for an automated storage and tracking system, he smiled, held up three fingers, and launched into a monologue:

> First, you have to understand that we are not in charge of our own world here. We don't schedule what comes in here; a logistics department does. They get orders from engineering [design] about what they want and when they want it, and then they tell us what to do. So we don't have the chance, really, to control the flow of work in the shop. Second, the parts tracking system is old and a mess. Every part has a number, but we still use paper to track everything. So if paper is lost or a part gets sidetracked, we probably don't know where it is. We thought that a new system could solve that. Maybe we could use bar codes and light wands. We couldn't convince the guys in logistics that they should do it, so we thought we'd try to do it ourselves. And, third . . . we wanted to build something that would help us cope with engineering. You see, engineering is the boss in this company. . . . They need a part today, and so they tell you to drop everything else and to make their part. Problem is, there are all kinds of "theys." There's the they who's got this big order in and he's expecting you'll do it on schedule. Then there's the they who's got these parts he needs made today and he didn't think about sending it in until yesterday. And then there's the they who sent in his order two days ago and wanted it done today but now he's decided he wants to make a change and still have it today. That's what we were up against. Still are, to be honest with you.

The shop, it seemed, wanted control over itself. The automated system would bring discipline to the logistics department responsible for scheduling and provide a means for the shop to cope with the unpredictable and largely uncontrollable demands from engineering.

New technology in the form of an automated system was not, however, intended to replace workers with machines. From the superintendent's perspective, there was "always room for improvement in productivity" by finding ways to increase the attentiveness of machine operators; but, he added:

> If the machines are idle 95 percent of the time like you said, you can't blame the guys on the floor. Sure, they could work harder. But if they're waiting because our logistics and scheduling are all fouled up, who's to blame?

This comment explained the absence of calculations for the number of heads that would be lost in the superintendent's proposal. It was not at all clear that heads would be lost or, for that matter, whether any needed to be.

Bringing Interests to the Surface   At this point in the research, I found it hard to see this decision-making process as an example of strategic choice (Child 1972). Although all participants in the contest struggled to justify their choices in the language of corporate objectives, the actual decisions seemed to be influenced as much by the availability of solutions as they were by the importance of problems. Indeed, the FMS appeared to be a clear instance of a solution searching for a problem (see Cohen, March, and Olsen 1972).

There were, however, two further dimensions to the story that argued for the incorporation of a political perspective on the choice of technology. First, as I questioned the operations manager about his reasons for choosing the expensive FMS and forgoing other requests (including the automated storage system), I found that the FMS also coincided with a distinctly personal objective: "I wanted to be the guy who did it first." Being the first operations manager in the company with the technology could have significant career implications, suggesting that the fact of innovation may be as important as its usefulness. It would also be very much in character with this particular manager: his aggressive pursuit of resources to support modernization of manufacturing processes had won him fierce loyalty among manufacturing engineers.

In order to do it first, he argued, he had to be sure that it was "done right, done cheaply, and done quietly." Thus, after reviewing the initial proposal, he authorized R&D to begin by investigating how other companies had set up an FMS; learning from others' mistakes could help it be done right and cheaply. He also cautioned R&D to proceed without fanfare. As he told me:

Those guys [from a larger division] were looking over my shoulder all the time. If they had caught on to what I was thinking about, you can be sure they would have said they deserve to be the first ones with an FMS.

Second, the FMS held a major attraction for R&D engineers. It gave them the opportunity to distinguish themselves—to do what their department's formal mandate espoused but what many said they rarely had a chance to do. For example, one engineer was inspired by what he had seen at the machine show and learned from peers in other companies. He listed the opportunities submerged in the proposal:

This gives us the chance to be real engineers. To do what we do best, to do what we're trained to do, and to do what this company needs. We need to be at the front end of technological change.

When I asked what he meant by "real engineering," he thought for a moment and then replied:

It's hard to say exactly. In my mind it has to do with creating something, . . . seeing a problem and using all your skills to solve it. Something that's real, important, and creative. Something you can see through to the end. I'll tell you what it's not: it's not the firefighting we usually do: the fixes to somebody else's mistakes, the leaky hose, the faulty programming, the band-aid that squeezes two more months out of a machine that should have been scrapped ages ago.

In a more personal vein, a colleague in the project added:

Projects like this don't come around that often. You have more of a chance to bring some positive attention to yourself when you're onto something new. It's not exactly a career maker, but it sure doesn't hurt either.

The opportunity to be "real" engineers was important in both relative and absolute terms. In relative terms, engineers in the manufacturing R&D organization felt themselves to be, at best, subordinate in status to product designers. Many with whom I spoke chafed at the fact that they were not even referred to as engineers. One younger machine-control specialist expressed an anger shared by many of his colleagues:

You know, I have a good mechanical engineering degree from a very good school. I just happen to like this end of things . . . the manufacturing end of the company. I like it better than design. I graduated from a better place with a higher GPA than at least a dozen guys I know over there [pointing to an adjacent building housing a design group].

Differences in pay scales and promotional opportunities exacerbated the manufacturing engineers' resentment.[6] In absolute terms, the FMS held out the possibility that the manufacturing R&D engineers could accomplish by themselves a smaller version of the much larger and more expensive FMS they had seen on display. In other words, on top of introducing an innovation to the company, they could engage in something much closer to invention.

Thus, early in the history of this change process—before any money was spent—important choices had been made and significant parameters for later choices had already been set. Of the alternatives generated by the request for proposals, the FMS was deemed the more appealing because it aligned corporate objectives with the personal and professional interests of the divisional manager and R&D engineers. By defining the problem as one of control, however, managers and engineers made choices that virtually guaranteed that neither workers nor shop-level supervisors would have a direct role to play in the choice process. Indeed, the change proposal initiated by shop management was dismissed as myopic and the FMS proposal was supported because it promised to forcibly alter the web of obligations and traditions that characterized social relations in production.

At this stage, the contradictory impressions I had received from my earlier review of the documents became more pronounced. Return-on-investment calculations had initially appeared to serve as a filter for screening out unprofitable investments. However, nothing I heard in the early interviews suggested that profitability really mattered in the choice among alternatives. Moreover, the lack of in-house expertise neither deterred development of the proposal nor created excessive concern about the ultimate cost of the undertaking. Instead, what seemed most important was the identification of an attractive concept: one that

6. At the time of the study, the company was working to equalize titles, pay scales, and promotional tracks.

evoked powerful images (heads lost, a shop under control) and opportunities (career advancement, "real engineering" work).

However, because of its anticipated cost, the FMS required corporate review. If strategic objectives had practical force over the politics of divisional decision making, then profitability might take back center stage.

CHOOSING WITHIN THE TECHNOLOGY

Corporate approval depended heavily on the ability of R&D and divisional management to justify the FMS financially. Direct labor costs figure prominently in ROI calculations, and, as I was told, they are critical in a proposal's funding chances in competition with other investment alternatives. A cross-country tour of FMS vendors and users showed the R&D project group that labor savings were not guaranteed. One engineer suggested that "even when you held constant the size of the cell and what they were making, the staffing solutions were all over the map," that is, from less than one machine operator for every three machines to one person per machine.

Finessing the ROI   The high level of uncertainty about the true cost of the FMS combined with the lack of experience among R&D engineers to create a great deal of tension. According to the previous engineer:

> I had to come up with a payback . . . and the best I could come up with was four years. Around here, the corporate rule, the ground rule, is if the thing can't be paid back in less than two years, preferably one year, your request has a chance of a snowball in hell of flying. Well now, that either makes you damned smart or a good liar.

The manager of R&D sent this engineer off to work with staff from the industrial engineering department to come up with more acceptable figures. Industrial engineering staff apparently helped; however, when I sought to find out how those figures were arrived at, I was told: "I'm not going to tell you how we generated that ROI because it was really silly. We had a number to hit and we hit it."

The R&D engineers, with new calculations in hand, went back to divisional management. However, the numbers were still not acceptable, particularly to those wary of the discerning eyes of corporate "bean counters." The operations manager resolved the staffing problem by making a supervisor the system operator. In the words of one participant, this arbitrary change enabled the assembled group to "finesse the ROI."

Given the amount of work by the operations manager and the R&D project team, it might seem reasonable to conclude that the story would end at this point. However, many elements of the *content* of the FMS still remained to be determined, and these elements could not be fixed outside the context of its use. The proposal reflected the perceptions and the encapsulated interests of only a subset of the organization. For example, one of the principal engineers came back from the cross-country tour enthusiastic about the technical possibilities and challenges but worried about organizational and procedural consequences of the new technology. As he explained to me later:

> A user contemplating the system has a lot of homework to do.
> You have got to consider combining project requirements. In
> that very statement there—about combining project require-
> ments—you run into organization restructuring. Because we had
> [listing of current programs] and each one of these programs has
> a program manager, and under that program manager is a manu-
> facturing manager, and so on. . . . What that means is that when
> you start saying all your parts are going to go through a com-
> mon machining cell, politics start entering.

In other words, he feared that a single program or contract alone would not be enough to support the project.

Pitching the Technology   As a result, the idea and its proponents would have to move from a center in R&D in three different organizational directions: outward to embrace the functional groups it would affect; downward to the shop where it would be housed; and upward to corporate executives and staff on whose approval the proposal ultimately rested. The different tactics employed to organize support—or placate resistance—not only varied among these three groups but demonstrated the importance of adroit political strategy for accomplishing technological change.

Outward. Project team members were dispatched as emissaries to allied functions (e.g., quality control, scheduling, maintenance). Each of these departments had its own set of interests and its own chain of command. A close examination of their prepared scripts made it clear that, despite higher-level backing, the project representatives were willing to bargain with allied groups over the ultimate configuration of the FMS. For example, a dispute arose over the method for linking the machines: one group wanted robot carriers to shuttle parts between the machines, but the group that would have ultimate responsibility for maintaining the system detested the idea and held out for a conveyor line. Because the conveyor would reduce the overall cost of the project and stifle resistance, the conveyor was chosen.

As important as the bargaining and trading, however, the presentations were designed to provide allied groups with a way to pitch the projects to their own bosses. A software engineer described the process:

> It wasn't anything new, really. You always wind up briefing a guy who doesn't really know what the hell he's talking about to send him up to another guy who doesn't know what the hell he's talking about, but may have heard enough pitches that he can ask some good questions and have some kind of expectations of an answer.

Thus, a coalition was formed to back the proposal.

Downward. Because shop-level supervisors and workers had already been identified as part of the problem to be "solved" by the FMS, they were given little opportunity to affect the content of the proposal. This did not mean, however, that they could be ignored entirely. The operations manager, it will be recalled, did not want to telegraph his plans to other divisions. Thus, the project team set out to co-opt lower-level management. Specifically, the operations manager instructed the project team to assemble a "user group" with a shop-level supervisor as its nominal leader. Engineers acknowledged the appropriateness of the tactic but still complained that the exercise was futile since, as one put it bluntly, "Most of those guys have to be dragged kicking and screaming into the twentieth century."

The general supervisor put in charge of the user group admitted to being opposed to the FMS project when he first heard about it. He anticipated a repetition of past experiences, with R&D developing a new system or machine in a curtained-off area, unveiling it to supervisors, and "leaving the shop to pick up the pieces." Over time his opposition turned to cautious acceptance: "They may not have listened to me, but at least they heard me out."

Neither the union nor workers in the area were included as part of the user group. In fact, the union learned of the FMS long after the machinery was bolted into the ground and on its way to operation—three and a half years after the project was initiated.

Upward. The operations manager's presentation to his boss and then to corporate management drew heavily on his earlier work with R&D managers to find the right numbers and the right language with which to pitch the project. When asked how he described the FMS to his bosses, he was very clear: "I'd be kidding you if I didn't say we leave out some of the negative things when we're trying to sell this stuff upstairs. So we forget about some of those things." And when I asked how technical he gets in making the pitch, he responded:

> Oh, I don't try to get technical. I go on emotion as much as anything. It's got to be something that turns them on. They can visualize in their own mind that this is going to be a good idea, it's going to solve the problem—at least in the way we've set up the problem—and it'll get good savings.

The process was not complete without supportive economic figures. However, financial considerations had been well covered with the "finessed" ROI calculations—so well covered, in fact, that the final proposal promised to eliminate direct labor entirely. This meant that there would be no direct cost associated with the operation of the FMS. In the end, funding was approved, and the FMS project was launched into its final stages.

Thus, profitability took back center stage in the closing moments of the second act. But it played a curious role. On the one hand, corporate review required ROI figures in support of the proposal; this requirement, in a sense, encouraged FMS proponents to play games with the numbers. On the other hand, divisional management and R&D took the corporate review seriously enough to make bold claims despite their fragile numbers. The net result was that technological choices were made largely on the basis of personal and professional interests and what was perceived to be an archaic social context in the shop that could not be altered without the external pressure of technological change. In other words, two years before the FMS went into operation, R&D had committed itself to a course of action that dramatically reduced the degrees of freedom available for modification of the system once it was in place.

IMPLEMENTING THE TECHNOLOGY

The installation and construction of the FMS occurred under guarded conditions. The machines were taken over by engineers, and the project team draped a large canvas curtain around the area. They spent the next twenty months in relative seclusion. Supervisors and workers were discouraged from eavesdropping on the work in progress.

As the work of implementation proceeded, the system began to prove far more complex and sensitive to bottlenecks than anticipated. For example, debris from certain metals jammed up the conveyor, slowing the overall process and rendering it far less "flexible." Software engineers experienced great difficulty integrating the system; eventually, an outside company was hired to write an entirely new program. A full-time technician had to be added to oversee the computer, and a programmer was assigned part-time to respond to intermittent glitches.

Symbolic Sensors   Problems with the sensors proved most intractable, but they also demonstrated the significance of the entrenched interests that had guided technological choices made early on in the process. Sensors, like those that open and close supermarket doors, use light beams and electronic eyes to identify the position of a metal part and to signal the beginning and ending of machining activities. They are intended to replace the eyes and ears of the individual machinist. When sensors malfunction, damage can be done to the metal parts or, more commonly, to the machines doing the cutting and grinding. Despite continuous setbacks the engineers doggedly continued in their efforts. In separate interviews two engineers provided virtually identical explanations for their persistence: (1) the sensors were one of the "real" engineering challenges associated with the FMS, and in the words of one, "We had a lot of pride invested in solving that one"; (2) without the sensors, someone would have to monitor the individual machines, meaning that some heads would not be lost; and (3) the sensors were a central part of the tracking system that had promised to "get the shop under control." Thus, failure to fully integrate the sensors would not only shoot down the expected return on investment and undermine the effort to reorganize the shop but also threaten the interests and careers of the "real" engineers.

The symbolic importance of the sensors was so great that when a production superintendent suggested that workers be brought back into the system, the engineers nearly revolted. As evidence of his claims, the superintendent circulated a memo written by an R&D engineer when the initial FMS proposal was drafted. The memo warned that the sensors would be a "linchpin" in the whole undertaking. He argued that replacing the eyes and ears of the skilled machinist would be difficult and cautioned against excessive reliance on the electronic alternative. The engineer's warnings had been ignored, he told me in a later interview, because they "were just the ravings of a guy from the old school." Under pressure from the operations manager, who was becoming increasingly nervous about excessive delays, the project team reluctantly scaled back the use of sensors and a former machinist was assigned to monitor the machines.

At the end of the nearly two years set aside for construction and implementation, the FMS was officially turned over to production management. According to the formal "close-out" report in the files, the project was completed on time and only slightly over budget. A comparison between the proposal and the actual system revealed, however, that the FMS was not exactly complete. The scaled-back use of sensors had curtailed many of the more sophisticated feedback and control functions originally intended for the machine. The system required not one but three full-time hourly employees to operate it. Additional software programming support was necessary, and even more was anticipated. And problems with cooling and debris removal persisted, restricting the kinds of parts that could be run through the system. The project team's success in meeting formal schedule and budget criteria were thus artifacts of these relatively invisible amendments to the original design.

After a year of operation, the FMS demonstrated modest improvements in the flow time for parts in the shop, but it did not come close to the time and cost savings predicted in the proposal. Technical problems continued to plague the system, and the higher level of staffing (direct and indirect) rendered the FMS much more costly to run than had been anticipated.

Despite the vigorous attention that ROI figures had received early on, the company never did review the economic performance of the machine. According to my interviews, the absence of an audit was not unusual, even for an expenditure of this magnitude. What mattered, I was told, was that the close-out report did not draw attention to any economic and performance shortcomings. But those shortcomings did not prevent the FMS from garnering "managed" attention. As one participant recalled, shortly before the system was turned over to the shop, the operations manager ordered a crew to "paint and polish" the machines and set up a demonstration run that would allow him to "put on a show for corporate brass." A symbol had been sold and a symbolic demonstration was in order. Shortly after the start-up of the system, the operations manager was promoted to a higher-level post in the company.

CONCLUSION

New technology in the form of a flexible machining system "impacted" this organization. The number of hourly workers used in the area was reduced from seven to four.[7] Machine operating time increased by about 20 percent. Control over the shop appeared to have been centralized; at least the installation of a central computer allowed the work of the three machines to be more closely monitored by a supervisor.

However, it would be extremely difficult to understand why those impacts occurred—or, more specifically, why that technology appeared—without attending directly to the process through which it was given meaning and purpose. This case study has shown that the choice of the FMS was not a simple matter of rational economic calculation and that the evolution of the system was not simply a technical affair. Both choice and development were directly affected by the perceptions and interests of managers and engineers and by their efforts to shape the context within which it would be used. Those perceptions and interests were largely opaque to the corporate decision makers who sat in judgment on the FMS proposal.

Organizational objectives were influential in the choice of both the problem and the solution. However, the *interpretation* of organizational objectives seemed most paradoxical. As I suggested in the first chapter, it should not be particularly surprising to find that the distribution of expertise and resources influences the range of problems and solutions an organization identifies and from which it selects. But it is surprising that organizational objectives should be deemed so important and then be so clearly ignored. The admonition to "get rid of heads" told operations management and R&D what they would have to promise in order to get the resources—and the opportunity to gain attention and to do "real engineering" work—but in practice the ROI calculations and all the preliminaries appeared to be little more than a charade. The rules of

7. The other three "heads" were transferred to jobs in an adjacent area of the shop. No one was laid off as a result of transfer.

the game required that all participants present themselves as rational, calculating utility maximizers, but beneath the official rules an entirely different game was being played.

The workings of this game emerge more clearly in the second instance of technological change.

CASE 2: THE ROBOTIZED ASSEMBLY CELL

In a uniquely American display of enthusiasm for technology, *Time* magazine proclaimed the robot "Man of the Year" in 1981. A year later the company under discussion here launched its first large-scale venture into robotics technology. At least one person I interviewed would suggest that the timing of the second event was not coincidental.

The effort to create a fully integrated robotized assembly cell (RAC) offers two important points of comparison with the preceding case. First, and most significant, this decision process can be best characterized as a solution in search of a problem. By contrast to the FMS, where it could be argued that long-standing problems were finally mated to a solution, the RAC case indicates that the early stages were dominated by the interest of upper-level (divisional and corporate) management in high technology as a solution that would eventually find a problem. Second, even though a relatively simple example of robotics technology had been successfully introduced into the assembly activity several years earlier, the notion of an integrated cell multiplied the number and complexity of operations to be performed. Most important, it introduced a feedback dimension of much greater sophistication (and therefore of greater potential difficulty) than was the case in the FMS. This led the R&D engineers to be far more dependent on other departments inside the company and on external equipment vendors. Thus, departments largely restricted to the sidelines in the FMS case emerged to play a critical role in shaping both the meaning and the purpose of the new technology.

The robotized assembly cell (shown schematically in figure 7) is located in one of the assembly facilities of the aircraft division. It is dedicated to the assembly of interior panels for commercial aircraft. Interior panels (such as those for ceilings and sides of airplanes) are among the few high-volume subassemblies made in the company.[8] The

8. The overwhelming majority of final assembly is undertaken in conditions not well suited to the use of robotics equipment: either the parts are too delicate, complicated, or unwieldy, or they are located in portions of the airplane inaccessible to robot arms.

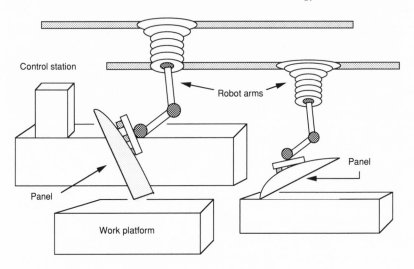

Figure 7.   Schematic drawing of robotized assembly cell

cell is designed to attach pieces of hardware to the backs of the panels that face inward to the interior of the airplane. Among other things, small metal studs must be glued on the backs of the panels to allow them to be attached to the fuselage. In addition, mounting brackets for windows (and the sliding shades that allow passengers to "close" the window) and housings for lights are attached in this process. These pieces are attached to the panels by means of two robotic arms (gantry robots) that hang from an overhead structure in the work area. The overhead structure allows the arms to be moved forward and backward and from side to side within the work area. Each robot arm uses a coupling system to pick up various tools (called "end effectors") to perform different tasks: for example, one uses vacuum suction cups to lift a panel onto a work fixture; another holds a supply of studs that can be placed on the panel, heated, and bonded in place; and yet another can grasp the aluminum alloy bracket for the window in place.

The RAC requires four integrated computers to operate the arms and the auxiliary equipment. These computers must synchronize the movements of the arms (e.g., so they don't crash into one another), sequence the tasks, control the flow of materials, and keep track of the various back-up and emergency systems needed to avoid the work being done improperly (e.g., not allowing the robot arm to continue a task when it encounters an obstacle). A control station for the work cell, located directly alongside it, allows the system operator to track the robot arms through their various stages; also, in the control station problems are registered and inquiries are placed for future action.

The system was designed to completely replace a crew of eight workers. The present assembly process is mirrored in the general actions and sequence of robotic tasks, but the number of people required to do the work is substantially reduced. Given that the robotics work cell was not in full operation at the time I did my research, it was unclear how many people would actually be required to staff the system. Estimates varied from one person replacing eight to four people replacing eight.

CHOOSING BETWEEN TECHNOLOGIES

Even though the project was not complete at the time I initiated my study, I quickly sensed that it had a murky past. The executive who championed the undertaking had since retired and was not available for interview. The present divisional manager hesitated to take responsibility for the project, though he admitted that it may have looked worthwhile at the time it was initiated. In the initial interviews personnel in R&D were vague about the project's opening stages. An air of uneasiness surrounded the undertaking.

Further investigation revealed that this case could best be described as a solution in search of a problem. As in the case of the FMS, the process again involved R&D (this time in a different division), but now the process of framing took on a decidedly different cast from the outset. My early interviews indicated that a solution had been specified well in advance of the development efforts; only the problem was left up for grabs. Manufacturing R&D was the only contestant in the process.

Despite the fact that my early research had unearthed a formal proposal from the assembly division's manufacturing R&D group to develop a robotized assembly cell for the interior panels, the division-level operations manager revealed that the development effort was stimulated by an announcement from high-level corporate executives that "robotics technology was the wave of the future and that the company ought to be on the crest of that wave." An R&D manager put it succinctly: "We were given a kind of mandate from our bosses. Robotics was something that was hot and it ought to be applied in our operation." In other words, money would be made available to automate or robotize labor-intensive activities. A vice president argued that this was part of a broader corporate pressure to force the division to gear up for more cost competition by "getting the labor out" and "losing heads" and to dampen the fluctuation in the demand for labor.

The Dangers of "Real Engineering"   Advance knowledge about the availability of money to pursue the robotics "solution" and active top management interest in the undertaking generated a mixture of excitement and apprehension in the manufacturing R&D group. On the one hand, they were being handed the opportunity to do "real engineering" work: that is, within fairly broad constraints, they could create a self-contained, visible, working symbol of their technical talents. They were being told to invent something. The project manager spread his arms widely as he recalled his feelings at the time:

> We had this incredibly wide range to work in. There were con-
> straints, of course. We couldn't spend a billion dollars. It had to
> work, eventually. But at that time we were really revved up
> about the whole thing. Some of us were in shock, too. Nobody
> could remember getting this kind of freedom before.

However, after the initial shock wore off, R&D engineers became aware of what they *didn't* know about robotics technology. The project manager continued:

> If there's one thing we didn't do right as a group from the begin-
> ning, it was to look very soberly at what skills we had and what
> we didn't have. We . . . or at least I didn't think we had all the
> skills we needed. But I figured that what we didn't know, we'd
> find someplace else. If not here, then outside.

Concerns also began to surface about other, decidedly organizational constraints. For example, a senior engineer who was several years older than the project manager recalled his own impressions of the early project team:

> It was fascinating to watch. The older guys on the team started
> out real cautious. They'd seen things like this start up and then
> evaporate when the big bosses lost interest. I'm not going to say
> they dragged their feet, but they were trying to tell the young
> cats to go slow. Take it easy. Be careful. And, especially, don't
> forget that people are going to be looking over your shoulder.

Four kinds of people, he explained, would be looking over their shoulders: other R&D engineers, perhaps jealous of the group's opportunity to do "real engineering" work; other departments, many of which suspected R&D of being a "black hole" for scarce resources; production management, especially plant supervisors, who resisted the introduction of anything they considered exotic; and, finally, design engineers. Despite the distance—organizational as well as temporal—between the developmental work on a robotics cell and the process of aircraft design, the engineers who designed the parts to be assembled robotically would eventually have to pass judgment before any equipment could be integrated into the production process.

Within this context, the R&D project team began a search for portions of the assembly process that might yield themselves to robotics. After several months of investigation, panel assembly was identified as "ripe for robotics." Panels were relatively high-volume parts, and the production process was labor intensive. A relatively simple pick-and-place robot arm had already been rigged up to perform one highly repetitive chore in panel assembly; thus, some knowledge was available about the process and the characteristics of the materials being assembled. The area also had a reputation for erratic quality levels: misaligned parts were common, and human error, according to several engineers, was the principal culprit. The downstream consequences of quality problems in the panel area were fairly serious since misaligned parts did not become apparent until final assembly. Once in assembly, defective panels would interfere with a highly interdependent sequence of tasks. All these factors made panel assembly a very appealing problem for the robotics solution. According to the project manager, there was an additional appeal:

> If we could integrate all those separate steps, the whole process
> could be run by a single person. All of it would be under control.
> We could just turn it on and it would go. We'd be heroes to the
> guys in assembly.

Whether motivated by the vision of a ticker-tape parade or a desire to avoid the watchful eyes of others, the R&D team quietly proceeded to define their project. Tentative and very informal "what if" discussions were held with design engineers to see how they might react to a change in assembly technology. A team member told me that he was "told explicitly to be vague about what we were up to. If we let on that things were going to change, the design guys might step in. Luckily, nobody raised any objections at that point." Similarly, panel parts and assemblies were pulled from inventory and set up in a distant corner of the factory so that experiments could be conducted without drawing attention. Project meetings were held in the offices of the R&D group with no one but team members invited to attend.

Going Outside, Not Inside, for Help   The first major milestone the project manager set for the group was a broad definition of what the robotized assembly cell would need to do. It was in this activity that the group began to discover just how little they knew about the task they were seeking to accomplish. To "scope out" the RAC adequately, the group would need either to ask much more explicit questions of others who might have the information and the skills they lacked (e.g., plant-level software engineers, facilities specialists, and design engineers) or to go outside the organization to other companies with roughly equivalent systems or to companies that sold robotics equipment. The first route would have prematurely unveiled their plans; the second would be less risky in that regard but probably was more expensive and time consuming.

A decision was made to contact a pair of robotic equipment manufacturers. Phone calls to contacts in other companies led team members to conclude that there were no comparable assembly cells to learn from. Going outside had the added advantage of enabling R&D to retain control over the definition of the technology. Two companies were given contracts to determine whether the entire panel assembly could be done with robots.

Not surprisingly, both vendors answered the team's question with a resounding yes. By far the most important outcome of the subcontracting was a videotape from one of the vendors. The tape demonstrated that most of the things R&D wanted done could be done. But more important than simple confirmation for R&D, the videotape provided a very graphic frame for convincing divisional and corporate managers of the feasibility of the solution and therefore of the need for additional funding.

Armed with a solution, a problem, and the funds to mate them, the team prepared to give shape to what they saw on the videotape. The choice between technologies had proven from the outset a much more complex affair than had been anticipated. Yet the opportunity to do real engineering work had encouraged the team to overlook, if temporarily, their trepidations about their ability to make good on their promises. They had succeeded thus far in part because they had kept their plans out of public view. Now, however, as they moved toward actual development of the RAC, they would have to present the contents of their plans to at least some of the others who would have to make it work: that is, they would have to expose what they had learned outside to inside review.

CHOOSING WITHIN THE TECHNOLOGY

Despite the positive reception their plans and videotape had received from higher-level management, R&D management recognized that the RAC would still have to be justified economically and organizationally. The vendors' reports had indicated that substantial direct labor could be eliminated. Though enticing, their calculations were suspect; these vendors would likely be interested in bidding on the project. The issue became acute when the vendors' feasibility studies and the videotape were presented to the industrial engineering department.

Part of industrial engineering's responsibility, as described by a staff member close to the project, includes their role in a system of organizational "checks and balances." As he told me:

> They [referring to R&D], they'll say, "We'll save this much
> money," and go on and on about the great savings. Some of
> them are legitimate and some of them we just have to pro-
> test. . . . Our main concern is to look at rates, capabilities, qual-
> ity and productivity. So when they come to us, we do a little
> simulated study . . . to see if this machine or whatever has the
> capability.

On the initial pass, industrial engineering raised a list of questions about the vendors' promises. R&D was forced back to the vendor, and after several lengthy interchanges, the project team returned with a new video-tape and new calculations. The new data provided by the vendor suggested that the RAC would pay for itself in less than two years.

Industrial engineering reexamined the data and the videotape. In the process, according to one staff member, they discovered that an important part of the assembly operation had been, in his words, "artfully edited." Close scrutiny revealed that a piece that was supposed to be snapped into place by the robot arm had actually fallen through the panel and off the screen. Industrial engineering also raised the objection that the present labor-intensive system was more flexible than the robotics application: labor hours could be expanded and contracted fairly easily; robot hours, by contrast, were going to be heavily influenced by the interdependent character of the system and the fixability of the various parts. Industrial engineering concluded that a more realistic payback period for the system was nearly four years. And as the staffer told me, "We made sure it was documented so that there would be irrefutable evidence if there was a possibility of a flaw."

Preventing a Range War   Much to the dismay of the R&D team, industrial engineering's disagreements with the early vendor calculations opened the door to expressions of concern from other quarters, several of whom complained that the money would be better spent on less exotic projects. For example, representatives of shop management expressed strong objections: first about the inflexibility of what they saw as complex equipment dedicated to one task, and then about the sensitivity of the robotics equipment to the panels made from light and relatively flimsy materials. They also raised questions about the reliability of the system—recognizing its newness—and about its employment consequences. The manager of the maintenance department registered complaints that far more critical equipment and systems were "failing all over the place" for lack of resources to do preventive maintenance.

In an effort to avoid what he called a "range war between the cattle ranchers and the sheep herders," the manager of R&D decided to expand the project team to include representatives from all the major functional support areas and shop management. It was a move similar in intent to the outward framing undertaken in the FMS case, but this time it was not intended so much to sell the technology as to rescue it. Team members from outside R&D differed in their opinions as to the viability of the RAC, but they did not feel they could kill the project either. One member told me that "the big bosses wanted this thing, and that meant the best thing we could do was prevent it from becoming a white elephant."

When I questioned the R&D manager about the expansion of the project team—especially as to why such a move was necessary, given higher-level management support—he shrugged his shoulders and replied: "Look, I can't tell you what was going on up there in the clouds. First they gave us a big go-ahead and then they were nowhere to be seen." Another manager speculated that conflicting opinions among higher-level managers had led some to tell their subordinates to "kill the RAC or at least wound it without letting on where they got the okay."

However the behind-the-scenes maneuvering occurred, the expanded project team took charge of the endeavor. Their first move was to scale down the assembly cell plans, reduce its complexity by narrowing the variety of panel lines it would cover, and instruct the R&D engineers to go back to the drawing board with product designers to see if some steps in the assembly process could be eliminated by reengineering the parts. For the next eighteen months, the original core of R&D engineers worked to design the more modest assembly cell.

Though the expansion of the team opened doors for data collection, the engineers labored under what several described as the "suspicious eyes" of the allied departments. For some, the project retained its earlier excitement, if only because they were learning a great deal in the process and remained convinced that they would see their plans through to fruition. The "fun part" was yet to come, I was told; real engineering was not complete without the opportunity to actually build the system. For others, especially the more senior engineers, the limits imposed by the contending departments eroded their enthusiasm. The "bureaucracy," in the words of one member, "had snapped down on us like it always did." The opportunities to do real engineering were rapidly slipping away.

The senior engineers' fears were confirmed when the expanded team reassembled to review the R&D engineers' redesign. The changes they had requested were complete, and although the industrial engineering department estimated that the new cell would pay for itself in three years or less, the representatives from the allied departments remained skeptical, even hostile. The extent of their hostility was not fully revealed until the end of deliberations when it came time to decide on next steps. The R&D engineers assumed that, having been the principal architects of the RAC, they would be its builders as well. They had made that case to the expanded team, citing the lower anticipated cost of such an approach. However, their detractors disagreed vehemently and, after demanding a vote on the proposition, forced the construction of the RAC out of R&D's hands. The proposal would be supported only if the entire RAC were subcontracted to a vendor.

Sensing he'd been trumped by his opponents, the R&D manager had little option but to concede. He told me: "Oh yeah, I could have gone upstairs and bitched and moaned. But it was pretty clear I'd lose. At one level, we got what we wanted. We just didn't get what we really wanted." Accepting the situation, he received a letter of support from the expanded team. In relatively short order, the proposal was approved by higher-level management.

Least Common Denominator   Bid specifications were drawn up and distributed. Six months later, three proposals came in to be reviewed. Two of the bids were from the vendors who had done the feasibility studies; the third came in from a small robotics manufacturer whose equipment had been included in the bid from one of the original vendors. Given the level of conflict that had already occurred, the R&D project leader was careful not to endorse one proposal over the others. Instead, he presented the proposals to the project team without identifying the vendors by name. Despite the careful preparation, team members disagreed as to the relative merits of the proposals. An R&D engineer recalled his anger at the time: "That's an example of what can happen when people who don't know the technical issues get a chance to stick their two cents in!" When the dust settled, the team could agree only on a least common denominator: cost. The contract was let to the low-cost bidder, the small robotics manufacturer.

The system was promised for delivery in twenty-six weeks, roughly equivalent to the projections made by the other two vendors. However, the actual (and incomplete) delivery occurred sixty-six weeks later. According to R&D personnel, "Everything that could have gone wrong went wrong." Most devastating was the organizational and financial failure of the vendor: turnover in the vendor's engineering ranks left it unable to fulfill its obligations to new and existing contracts; then, faced with bankruptcy, the firm was acquired by another company and forced to reorder its priorities. At several points along the line, R&D and company personnel discussed the possibility of simply buying the vendor in order to assure that the work would be completed. After much wrangling, pieces of equipment, boxes of designs and documents, and dozens of diskettes were delivered by truck to the R&D team.

The irony, of course, was that R&D was now presented with an even more challenging opportunity to do real engineering work. If the RAC were to be salvaged, R&D would have to complete the hardware development, finish off the programming chores, and link the pieces together to make an integrated cell. However, in the intervening period most of the engineers originally assigned to the project had been given other duties, and many of their supervisors were reluctant to release them. Moreover, the project had been tainted—"a jinxed affair" according to the R&D manager—and no longer held its earlier allure.

IMPLEMENTING THE TECHNOLOGY

At the end of this study, the robotics work cell had been bolted into the ground, but R&D personnel were still struggling to make the overall system work. Problems with pieces of the system continued to foul up the whole. The adhesive delivery system, for example, still did not work adequately. Without the proper delivery of adhesives and quick drying times, subsequent assembly steps were orphaned. In order to get the system to do *something*, even at a low level of integration, the stud-bonding portion of the process was activated. However, the single-armed (and, in relative terms, very inexpensive) robot that had been installed several years earlier continued to operate faster and more efficiently than its muscular two-armed "big brother" a few feet away.

Epilogue   Six months after completing this case study, I met with a group of product engineers who were redesigning the interior panels. They had successfully designed a panel that *eliminated* the hardware attachments for which the RAC was intended. They were not, however, aware of the manufacturing R&D team's work. As I later discovered, the R&D team was equally unaware of the designers' achievement.

CONCLUSION

New technology in the form of a robotized assembly cell did not "impact" this organization. Still, the preceding analysis reveals a great deal about the process of change and the organization in which it emerged. Top-level management was enraptured by the *idea* of robotics technology, seemingly independent of whether the organization needed it or could productively employ it. R&D engineers were enraptured by the idea of doing real engineering work, of being inventors, even though they were aware that they lacked the skills necessary to go it alone. Allied departments, in turn, were threatened by an idea not of their own creation. To protect their interests, they adopted adroit political maneuvers to thwart the idea without appearing to contradict top management. The failure of the robotics equipment vendor could not have been predicted by any of the parties. But in a sense, enough traps had been laid that the technology seemed bound to fail anyway.

I turn now to the final case from the aircraft company.

CASE 3: SHOP-PROGRAMMABLE MACHINE TOOLS

After burrowing through the mounds of paperwork produced by the FMS and the RAC, I was somewhat relieved to find only a small, neat stack of documents attached to the third case. Differences in the scale, cost, and complexity of the technology led me to anticipate that the story behind the introduction of a new generation of machine tools would be relatively simple and straightforward. Yet the process of change was no less influenced by the social context and political maneuvering than in the previous case. Important once again are the perceptions and interests of change proponents and the political tactics they employed to advance a vision of what new technology should do to their organization.

Shop-programmable (or computer numerically controlled [CNC]) machine tools are used to cut, grind, and shape metal parts. CNC machines differ from other types of machining equipment largely in the way they are controlled. For example, in contrast to the older generation of hand-cranked machines, each CNC machine tool is equipped with its own small computer, which can be programmed to guide its actions;[9] but in contrast to other systems, such as the FMS described earlier, each machine is run independently and does not require programmed instructions from a central computer. CNC equipment varies enormously in expense and in the range of tasks it can perform, from simple rough grinding to intricate and detailed cutting and shaping.

In mid 1986, four new shop-programmable machine tools purchased from an equipment manufacturer were introduced into one of the largest machine shops in the company's parts fabrication division. At an average cost of roughly $100,000 each, they replaced six aging machines judged too costly to repair. The shop into which they were placed was referred to as the "conventional side of the house" because it contained traditional operator-controlled machine tools and was used largely to produce parts in small batches.[10]

---

9. Data are input on the type of work to be done, the type of material to be machined, and the tolerances required in cutting, and the computer generates a program that can be stored on a floppy disk.

10. The other side of the shop contained a variety of large numerically controlled machines that were individually controlled by a central computer. Those "NC" machines were used largely in the manner of past generations of fixed automation: for long runs of identical parts.

CHOOSING BETWEEN TECHNOLOGIES

When I began exploring this case, I was aware that the implications of changes in machine-tool controls had been the object of debate in the academic literature. Noble (1984) and Shaiken (1985), for example, argued that earlier generations of equipment controls had been designed to embed traditional machinist's skills in the software that "drive" the machines and thus to deskill craft work. However, CNC machines represented a potential departure from that hypothesized trend: they could be programmed locally, allowing a skilled machinist to continue to run the machine (even to override the computer); or they could be programmed in such a way that the operator could simply follow directions prompted by the internal computer and displayed on the machine's built-in video screen (in much the same way most people "operate" their microwave ovens and VCRs). Given that these alternatives were available as options from the equipment manufacturer, I was especially interested in understanding which route this company had taken and why.[11]

In my initial interviews I asked representatives of shop management why they bought the CNC equipment as opposed to some other equivalent technology. Before I could understand their choice, I was told, I had to understand the context. A significant chunk of the work performed in the conventional side of the shop consisted of emergency orders for customers in need of out-of-stock replacement parts and new parts being produced in relatively small numbers for testing or use elsewhere. The unpredictable arrival of emergency orders, as well as competing demands from various sources for small production runs, led to a great deal of negotiation, juggling, and occasionally overt conflict between shop management and the internal and external customers making claims on the shop's machining capacity.

A major contributor to the tension experienced by shop management—who described the situation as "chaotic," "ulcer producing," and "impossible"—was the shop's dependence on external departments

---

11. See Whittaker (1988) for a fascinating discussion of the alternative approaches taken by British and Japanese machining firms to the use of CNC equipment. Kelley's (1986; 1990) findings from a cross-sectional survey of machining companies in the United States suggests that the distribution of responsibility for programming is influenced by the markets in which firms operate and the character of labor-management relations. Uncovering the causal relations behind her findings, however, is made problematic by the fact that her survey provides few clues to the process through which programming duties were distributed.

for the plans and programs necessary to meet the orders they received. In particular, the Resource Planning and the numerical control (NC) programming groups, located in a separate set of offices, exercised a claim to "configuration control" that directly affected shop management's ability to accommodate the demands of its various customers.[12] When parts were cut on numerically controlled equipment, Resource Planning directed the NC programming group to write or retrieve a program for making the part and distributed the tape to the appropriate portion of the shop. Thus, Resource Planning played traffic cop in directing the flow of parts and programming as well as librarian in revising, storing, and retrieving blueprints, programs, and documents.

From the viewpoint of shop management, dependence on Resource Planning and NC programming was the problem and new technology was the solution. If the shop acquired the CNC machines, it would be able to short-circuit the otherwise highly centralized system by writing its own programs, storing them locally, and scheduling its work load. Implicit in this definition of the problem and the solution was a strategy for acquiring the new technology strikingly similar to that heard in the FMS case: it would have to be done "right, cheaply, and quietly."

The process began in earnest in 1985. Each year the shop submits to divisional management a five-year plan that ranks needs for equipment replacement or repair. This process routinely takes place outside the purview of R&D, and in this division at least, it is an activity orchestrated by the facilities maintenance department. Prior to 1985 each five-year plan had included a request for replacement of a number of badly worn machine tools with newer but largely similar versions. Starting with the 1985 plan, however, the request specified CNC equipment. Shop managers told me that they had known of the technology for at least a year before they made their request. One shop superintendent had visited several other companies that used the CNC equipment and had discussed the tools with salespeople at an equipment exhibition in late 1984. However, when the request was made in 1985, CNC was largely undefined, and it was therefore not clear that "shop programmability" was the underlying desire. The shop request went forward with an unexceptionable problem statement: "Existing equipment is over 20 years old. [It is] experiencing 10% downtime. Worn beyond repair." The solution statement accompanying a technician's review of the equip-

---

12. Configuration control, briefly put, involves control over plans, programs, and specifications for the large variety of parts machined in the fabrication division.

ment recommended: "Purchase [CNC] machining centers that allow operators to input data. This will eliminate layout time and increase productivity. . . . [W]ill allow 4 machines to replace 6."

In the normal course of its duties, the facilities and maintenance department helped devise the formal proposal, including calculating the payback periods for the investment. The payback figures appeared respectable, but again there was some question regarding the accuracy of the calculations. When asked how those figures were arrived at, shop managers admitted that they were "based as much on guess as on fact." To that was added the admission that there were never more than four people operating the six machines being replaced (because of frequent breakdowns in the older machines). Still, the facilities staff followed the standard procedure of producing transparencies to form the basis of the proposal to divisional management.[13]

CHOOSING WITHIN THE TECHNOLOGY

Gaining independence from other departments may have been a major part of shop management's private goal in seeking the new machines, but the choices they made among alternatives within CNC technology were profoundly affected by social organization at the level of the shop floor. In the words of one manager close to the process, the CNC equipment was attractive because it would "preserve and extend" the skills of machinists already in the shop. In this instance, shop management's perspective could be viewed as simple rhetoric, but it was, in fact, accompanied by efforts to involve the machinists in the area: acknowledging, in effect, workers' positional interests. Two of the workers who ultimately came to staff the machines were consulted in advance about the feasibility of this kind of equipment, and the four workers who were assigned the machines were sent out for special training several weeks before it arrived. The significance of this move is greater because, as I noted earlier, the machines do not presuppose a lengthy apprenticeship in the range of machining skills in order to be run adequately.

Interviews with the CNC equipment operators revealed that shop management's action was appreciated, but it was also expected. Conventional machinists are traditionally very protective of their skills and resist the incursion of new control systems, especially when they dimin-

13. They recommended a specific number of transparencies for each $100,000 in capital requested.

ish operator discretion (Shaiken 1985). In this instance, however, the impact on skills was discounted as a source of contention. For example, when asked his opinion about the CNC equipment, one of the operators described them as an extension of past technology:

> It's really something the way it reduces the time we used to spend doing set-ups. But it doesn't require any less skill because you can override the controls. You can also make a part faster for a customer because you don't have to sit and wait for NC programming to do their thing. We spend a lot of time trying to figure out how to program them to do trickier cuts.

Another machinist readily admitted that simple operation of the machines could be possible by someone who had no experience with conventional machine tools, but, he added, shop management's closeness to the work being done in the area made them "aware of what it takes to get the most out of this equipment." That awareness, he suggested, derived in large part from the fact that several of the higher-level supervisors in the shop had begun work as hourly machinists. Another operator added, however, that any attempt to force a new piece of equipment into the shop without "smoothing it out with the guys" would likely have set off at least a mild confrontation.

With a pitch and transparencies prepared by the facilities maintenance department, shop management presented its proposal for the acquisition of four CNC machines. The presentation was concise and carefully timed to fit into an agenda of more than two dozen similar presentations from other shops. According to several observers, the large number of presentations reduced the evaluation process to a review of problem statements, estimates of productivity increase, and cost projections. The CNC proposal urgently requested replacement of worn-out equipment and showed acceptable payback periods (and labor force reductions). Divisional management approved the request without discussion.

IMPLEMENTING THE TECHNOLOGY

Whether motivated by regard for machinists' skills, commonality of experience, or desire to avoid confrontation, shop management made local conditions a significant factor in the selection and deployment of the new technology. That approach—corroborated by both managers and workers—had a substantial payoff in the response of the area machinists. Moreover, machinists interviewed in the course of the study suggested that the new equipment represented a welcome challenge: they enthusiastically took to the machines and reported spending many lunch and break periods discussing ways to maximize the capabilities of the new technology.[14]

Outside the shop, however, the process quickly degenerated into a decidedly political conflict. Although the Resource Planning group was unaware of the events that led up to the acquisition of the CNC equipment, it found out soon after the equipment arrived. For many of those involved, what transpired was further evidence that "the shop ought not be left to its own devices." In the words of one well-placed observer:

> What you see there is a demonstration of how oriented shop management is to their own small world and to their personnel. And, obviously, they grew up in the shop. They came up through there. So when you analyze what they tell you, you have to re-member where they came from.

Within six months after the equipment arrived, the aggrieved stake-holders (which by that time included Resource Planning, NC programming, manufacturing R&D, and manufacturing engineering) began meeting to formulate a response. According to one engineer involved in the process:

> Just recently, manufacturing engineering recognized that they should be in the loop of acquisition of new technology. What we're doing now is getting the procedure changed so . . . we have a say because we're closer associated to the prime divisions as to what we expect in the future. I think in that regard we know a lit-tle bit more than the shop. So at least we'll have a say in the equipment they purchase as to what it should be.

After a period of intense organizing, the group presented a protest to divisional management. Although divisional leaders claimed to see noth-ing wrong with the acquisition of the new equipment, they did send out a directive to production managers "encouraging"—but not requiring—

14. The union, which had not been informed of the impending arrival of the CNC equipment by either management or the designated machine operators, filed an inquiry soon after the machines were bolted down. The union contended that the new technology warranted an increase in pay and a change in job classification. After negotiations the job classification was changed, and seniority rules were applied; however, pay rates were kept at their original level. See Thomas (1991) and Thomas and Kochan (1992) for a further discussion of union strategies for dealing with new technology.

them to circulate their five-year equipment purchase plans to other department heads.

CONCLUSION

Shop management used new technology to sever external dependencies and to regain a measure of control over their piece of the organization. This technology came off the shelf, and because it was used extensively in industry, shop managers could reasonably anticipate it to do what they wanted it to do. They carefully prepared for the economic review—including defining the problem and solution in the language of organizational objectives (e.g., "heads lost") in order to minimize questions about the technology itself and thus to avoid the appearance of overt conflict with other groups. Although their choice of technology and the tactics they used to acquire it demonstrated what R&D labeled "myopia," shop management actively engaged interests ignored in the FMS case—most particularly those of shop-floor employees. Thus, they made clear that from their perspective the shop was not "out of control"; rather, peer and superior organizations were.

CONCLUSIONS AND IMPLICATIONS

At the outset of this chapter, I suggested that people in the aircraft company make more than just airplanes. The case studies offer ample evidence to that effect. People do make airplanes, but at the same time they make jobs and careers, allies and enemies, monuments and epitaphs. They invest tremendous energy in the attempt to give meaning to the work they do and to express things they value as individuals and as members of a group in a large and complex organization. What distinguishes people's ability to achieve these ends is their relative access to power and influence in the organization.

Concretely, the case studies show that choices between technologies are rarely simple or unfettered by human interests. They suggest that the attractiveness of a technology is not a function simply of its technical attributes or its expected contributions to economic performance but also of its political and symbolic value. If these cases are any guide, a technology must satisfy technical and economic criteria in order to be recognized as a candidate for adoption; but among equally qualified candidates, greater likelihood of adoption goes to those that can express—or can be made to express—the interests of powerful individuals or groups. Indeed, the choice between technological possibilities involves three screens: (1) a *technical* screen (e.g., does it physically do what we need it to do?); (2) an *economic* screen (e.g., will it achieve a recognizable or organizationally acceptable payoff?); and (3) a *political* or interest-based screen (e.g., does it express my/our vision of the proper way to accomplish the task? what will it do to my/our role in the organization? and, what does it say about me/us?).

The questions that make up the political screen are, in many ways, the ones most frequently overlooked in analyses of technological change in organizations. There are three basic reasons why this is the case. First, the questions and answers are the least likely to be expressed openly. Arguments for and against a candidate technology are almost invariably expressed in a language of *organizational* interests (i.e., the interests of all) through the use of evaluative criteria that are superficially objective (i.e., devoid of interests)—even (or especially) when the motivation to put forth a candidate technology is inherently personal or factional. In those instances where a candidate technology has been "proven" feasible by another organization, the use of such evaluative criteria is relatively nonproblematic and not subject to dispute. However, in cases where the anticipated performance of the candidate technology is uncertain or existing evaluative measures cannot be adequately applied—as often occurs with an unprecedented technology—the reliance on symbolic representation increases and political interests come dangerously close to the surface. This was most evident in the FMS case, where everyone with whom I spoke privately agreed that the return-on-investment calculations verged on fiction and that the operations manager sold the technology on the basis of its symbolic, indeed its emotional, appeal. Still, despite their private ridicule of ROI as an accurate measure of the appeal of the technology, all sides clung to it tenaciously: without such a measure, the choice would all but publicly be a political one.

Second, the questions behind the political screen are, in their own way, far more complex than the technical ones. Virtually every candidate technology means something different to those who view it, and what each group sees in the technology is likely to be tinted by their own individual and positional or professional interests and worldviews. The analogy to an art exhibition comes to mind: viewers of, say, a sculpture form opinions that are based, at one and the same time, on the object itself, the associations it evokes (e.g., like objects, images, and/or emotions), and the purposes that can be attached to it (i.e., what it could be used for). Comments about the sculpture—or the technology—mix elements of description (what it *is*) and analysis (what it is *to the viewer*). To extend the analogy to the case studies: both the FMS and the RAC appealed to line managers as examples of "modern" technology, above and beyond any immediate use either might have had in the production of airplane parts. Modernity was invoked repeatedly by the R&D engineers when they pitched the FMS to the operations manager and by the operations manager when he pitched the project to his superiors. In both cases, modern meant automated, purged of people and paper, shorn of custom and informal accommodation, instilled with a discipline that did not allow for interpretation, and yet flexible enough to be easily adjusted to a wider variety of tasks than might have been possible with "traditional" automated equipment. FMS proponents sought to add authority to these images by associating them with highly successful Japanese firms, who were even then pointed to as exemplars of modern, "world-class" manufacturing.[15] Robots, as *Time* magazine asserted, were the wave of the future. Moreover, to be associated with these new technologies, let alone to be identified as a champion, was to *be* modern and therefore to draw positive attention to oneself—a point not lost on the operations manager in the FMS case.

R&D engineers were also attracted by the idea of being modern, but the opportunity to do "real engineering" had even greater appeal. Both the FMS and the RAC represented the opportunity to create artifacts that embodied many of the attributes of what the real engineers (i.e., designers) created. The automated storage and tracking system might have served the same purposes, but it was not R&D's invention—indeed, it was suggested by "premodern" shop managers whose very shop was "out of control"—and it would be neither as visible nor as independent an invention as the FMS. That is, the storage and tracking system was more infrastructural than structural, more like the wiring behind the walls than the object to which the wires deliver power. The FMS, by contrast, would be visible and independent.[16] The significance of this distinction was evidenced in the importance that engineers attached to the sensors: if sensors could be successfully adapted, the FMS could run without people. Like an enduring sculpture or painting, the skill and creativity of the artist(s) would be evident in the beauty of the object.

15. The term *world-class* had not achieved currency at that time. However, the Japanese had already gained considerable attention among U.S. manufacturing firms through their use of new technologies—among other things—to outcompete giant U.S. companies in the steel and auto industries.

16. Indeed, at the suggestion of the R&D manager, all the pieces of the system were painted bright yellow to set them off from the surrounding dull green equipment.

The CNC case offers an instructive contrast. The new technology represented a tool that would enable the shop to cope with conflicting demands that the Resource Planning group did not adequately manage or buffer. Being modern was far less important than being able to achieve greater autonomy in determining the flow of work. CNC machine tools were attractive for their promise to aid shop management in quietly accomplishing organizational change and, in particular, changing the distribution of power over the affairs of the shop.

Third, answers to the political questions are likely to build from worldviews that are themselves quite often unspoken and even unexamined. These worldviews, as I suggested in chapter 1, involve basic beliefs about core features of human beings and social organization. As in Schein's (1985) theory of the foundations of organizational culture, worldviews about technology and the social organization of work must be analyzed not only in terms of artifacts and espoused values but also at the level of assumptions. Their influence is best demonstrated in a comparison of the FMS and RAC cases on one side with the CNC case on the other.

Apart from differences in the magnitude and the expense of the technologies, one clear distinction between these cases was the role accorded to the lowest levels of the organization in conceptualizing and carrying out change. In the FMS and RAC cases, production supervisors and workers were excluded entirely from involvement in the change process. Their exclusion was explained in various ways, but most important were the unspoken assessments: that neither workers nor lower-level managers (many of whom were former machinists) were capable of contributing to either problem identification or solution. To claim, as managers and engineers did, that they *were* the problem was obviously a value statement—a debatable one, given the operations manager's admissions in the FMS case—but beneath that resided a pair of assumptions: first, that workers and their supervisors were incapable of contributing because they lacked knowledge and willingness; and second, that only managers and engineers were capable of acting in a knowledgeable and committed fashion. Only managers and engineers were modern. A very different set of assumptions was at work in the CNC case and in the proposed automated storage and retrieval system. In those cases lower-level managers assumed first that workers were quite capable of contributing to the change process *precisely because* they were knowledgeable and committed and second that engineers and managers neither trusted nor understood shop-floor people and the conditions under which they worked. Inclusion of workers may have been part of a political strategy for surreptitiously bringing in the new technology, but even then shop managers had to believe that workers possessed the knowledge and the willingness necessary to secure the shop's autonomy. The unspoken and contradictory assumptions in these cases led to an ironic result: the same kind of people who were considered suspect and who were to be driven out by the FMS and the RAC technologies were the ones who masterminded the introduction of the CNC technology.[17] Moreover, each validated the others' assumptions through their actions: the actions of managers and engineers in the FMS and RAC cases "proved" shop-floor assumptions; likewise, the actions of shop managers and workers "proved" their inability to see the world the way managers and supervisors did.

In sum, the political questions and criteria represent an important though complex screen that influences the choice of technology. They are not immediately evident in public discussions of technological possibilities, and they are virtually impossible to infer from the outcomes of change alone. Nor can they be extrapolated from histories of change efforts provided by articulate organizational spokespersons. Rather, what is required is careful examination of the process of technological change.

However, it is important to reiterate that worldviews are not untethered variables in the analysis. That is, they are not formed in a vacuum, and the assumptions that have currency in an organization (and that influence the process of technological choice) are not simply a product of the aggregation of people with similar backgrounds. They are, by contrast, as much a product of action as they are a precondition of it. Thus, worldviews—and the power to enact them—must be understood in their historical and organizational context.

The summary points I made about industrial and organizational context at the beginning of this chapter—the "million parts flying in formation"—can now be directly connected to the discussion of technology politics. The hegemony of design engineering in this organization is itself a product of core assumptions about the nature of the product and the organization necessary to produce it. The "mystery" of an airplane has been captured by those who design it, and the routine of executing design has been accorded to the manufacturing organization. In other words, manufacturing is the last in the chain of activities that

---

17. Even more ironic, perhaps, was the association of "modern" and "Japanese" among managers and engineers in the FMS case since Japanese firms tend to have a much higher regard for (and reliance on) lower-level employees. See, for example, Cole (1979).

commences with the conception of a design, the last in its ability to alter or amend a design once it is chosen, and the least able to claim mastery over the mysteries of the product. Manufacturing is, therefore, actively discouraged from conceiving of its task—or its technological alternatives—in terms other than an ability to respond to the commands of the design organization. This relationship puts a clear priority, indeed a premium, on manufacturing management's ability to *control its own environment* in order to respond adequately to hierarchically imposed demands. And it suggests that if manufacturing engineers (such as those found in the R&D organization) are ever to approach the status, or earn the respect, of their counterparts in design, they must bring to fruition technologies that are "airplane-like" in nature.

In this sense, we see that manufacturing managers and engineers are subject to the same suspicion and disdain that they hold for those who work "beneath" them. Therefore, the range of technological and organizational possibilities they construct is not simply an outgrowth of personal prejudice: it is intimately tied to the structure of status and power in the organization. To change the way technology is used—or technological possibilities are conceived—would require a change in the distribution of status and power in the organization itself.

For all the theoretical mileage I have tried to squeeze from these cases, they are only three instances of change in one organization. It makes sense now to see what can be learned from a similar set of questions and a similar approach in a very different setting.

THREE

Between Invention and Convention

Technological Choice in a Computer Company

Companies in the computer and electronics industry are generally thought of as innovative and unconventional—in organizational form and behavior as much as in the products they produce. Textbooks and business journals delight in describing the things that set them apart from more traditional manufacturing enterprises, such as the aircraft company depicted in the last chapter. Even oblique references to geography (e.g., Silicon Valley, Route 128, the Research Triangle) are enough to evoke images of laid-back organizations where jeans and running shoes replace pinstripes and wingtips and "flat" organizational structures take the place of bureaucratic hierarchies. The creativity as well as the quirkiness of these enterprises has been popularized in best-selling treatments such as Kidder's *Soul of a New Machine* (1981).

Yet what *The Soul of a New Machine* does not tell us is how the unconventional organization does conventional things, such as manufacturing. The "skunkworks" tales may capture our attention, especially when told in the manner of a suspense story, but what of the organization whose responsibility it is to realize the invention in practice—to crank out fifty thousand replicas of the "new machine"? If product developers and software engineers are the test pilots, the elite units, and the pioneers of the computer business, are those in manufacturing the ground mechanics, the foot soldiers, and the settlers? How are technological choices made and implemented in the unconventional organization?

To answer these questions and to extend my analysis of the process of technological choice, I collaborated with my colleague Rebecca Henderson, an applied economist, in studying a large and successful U.S.-based computer and electronics firm. Our common goal was to explore how the company made and evaluated investments in new manufacturing technology.[1] My interest, in particular, was to study technological change in an industry where, by reputation at least, organizational forms were less rigid and hierarchical than those of the aircraft industry. Whether "political questions" would be any less influential in the process of technological choice was unclear; however, I did expect that the absence of a bureaucratic structure would render the decision-making process more open and therefore less contentious. This industry—and this company—held an added appeal: both had a reputation for a decidedly nontraditional approach to employment practices. By contrast to the aircraft company, with its long history of adversarial relations with trade unions and its thicket of bureaucratic rules regarding job descriptions and work organization, this company had been nonunion since its founding, maintained a policy of employment security, and offered an extensive menu of employee benefits, including training and tuition rebates for all its employees. In such a setting it would be hard to imagine technological choices being predicated on, or justified by, "heads lost."

The focus of this chapter is the choice and implementation of a major change in the process of printed circuit board assembly. In contrast to the preceding chapter, here I will analyze the process and the "impacts" of a single change in two product-based divisions of the same company. The findings I report are derived from interviews with more than a hundred managers, engineers, supervisors, and operators spread across three divisions and corporate headquarters. As in the preceding chapter, however, this study pushes the boundaries of the analysis in two important ways: back in time, to include the prehistory of the technological change, and outward from the specific settings in which change took place to factor in the competitive and organizational contexts that surrounded the choice process.

There are two plot lines to the story. The first involves the use of technology as a vehicle for making organizational as well as technical change. Whereas an "official story" (prepared by the company) portrays the choice

1. Henderson is preparing an empirical analysis of the methods used to evaluate investments in new technology. For a description of her approach—and the departure it represents from traditional thinking—see Henderson (1988) and Henderson and Clark (1990).

of the new technology as linear and purposive, the story as told by the participants is one in which the choice—its origins and its subsequent history—is best encapsulated as a "movement" to change the dominant status system among engineering professionals and the relationship between manufacturing and design in a product-driven company. Borrowing from Zald and Berger's (1978) application of social movement theory to the analysis of organizational conflict, I will suggest that this case represents an example of "unconventional politics"—an insurgency intended to alter the established order, the extant "rules of the game." This chapter, however, extends Zald and Berger's analysis by providing detailed data on the history of the change and careful examination of the perspectives of both those who supported and those who opposed it.[2]

The second plot line, however, has to do with differences in the impacts of the same technological change for the organization of work and workers in two divisions of the same organization. The relative success of movement advocates in realizing their goals had serious and direct implications for the manner in which new technology came to be used in practice. In this latter domain unconventional politics have had very serious consequences for an unconventional organization.

THE INDUSTRIAL AND ORGANIZATIONAL CONTEXT

The company is a large but decentralized designer and manufacturer of a wide array of electronics products for consumer, medical, and industrial markets. Its products include small- to medium-range computers and workstations, electronic measurement devices, and communications equipment. Founded by a small group of engineers over fifty years ago, it grew largely through invention. Top engineering talent was recruited from competitors and nearby universities and provided with resources and opportunities with which to invent state-of-the-art products for the growing post–World War II electronics market. Over the next four decades, the company grew division by division until in 1990 it encompassed several dozen product-based divisions.

---

2. In building their theoretical arguments, Zald and Berger (1978) rely on secondary sources and newspaper accounts of organizational politics and conflict. As I note in chapter 1, the virtue of the case studies I have done is that they are built on primary sources and seek to incorporate divergent views.

Insiders describe the company as an "engineering sandbox," a "lot of small businesses that happen to share the same name," and as one young woman engineer put it, "a place where adolescent propeller-heads get to play out their techno-macho fantasies." The company *is* an engineer's dream inasmuch as it has built its reputation on the quality and sophistication of its products; in virtually every market in which it competes, the company is considered a technical leader. Its history of ardent devotion to the autonomy of the product-based divisions gives it the appearance of being a confederation of small businesses rather than a multibillion dollar corporation. Autonomy and invention have been supported through the practice of spinning off new divisions with the invention of a new product line—making inventors entrepreneurs of sorts when their creations succeed in the market. Though the depiction of engineer/inventors as "adolescent propeller-heads" may seem derogatory—the comment contained elements of pride and embarrassment—the ethos of "techno-macho" is strong in the company.[3] There is tremendous pride in the sophistication of the company's products, and at all the levels I interviewed, people repeatedly referred to the ability of the company's products to "out-perform" the competition—even when high performance did not translate into market dominance. Propeller-heads, gear-heads, nerds, and techno-weenies, as product engineers are referred to, may be derided for their purported lack of social skills, but their creative talents are held out as the principal explanation for the company's longevity in the often turbulent computer and electronics marketplace.

Autonomy and invention are important products of the decentralized structure of the company. There are, for example, few centralized resources. Each division has its own product development organization—referred to as a "lab"—as well as its own marketing, finance, and manufacturing departments. Divisions are loosely organized into groups of similar products, but even within those groups products may differ substantially in the type and level of competition they face. Life cycles of some products may be quite long (e.g., five or more years) whereas others may be quite short (on the order of six to eight months), and the factors deemed critical to success vary accordingly. For long-lived products, cost containment and reliability may be deemed paramount; for short-lived products, cost may be secondary to the ability to rapidly enhance or

---

3. It is not clear whether these terms are applied as frequently to female engineers as to male engineers.

revise product features. Variability in markets and products encourages the divisions to attend to their own situations and to pay far less attention to developments across divisional or group boundaries. The history, as well as the historical success, of decentralized divisions has led managers and engineers to take fierce pride in their independence from direct corporate control. As one divisional manager put it, "I don't trust any building that doesn't have a loading dock." Another manager claimed that one of the secrets to his business's success resided in the fact that "we're out of range of the corporate jet."

Autonomy and invention are also important for understanding the distribution of power and resources between the labs and their respective manufacturing organizations. Three aspects of the relationship stand out. First, according to the cross-section of people I interviewed, process or manufacturing technology has historically been driven by product needs. That is, given a product by the labs, the manufacturing organization is expected to find a way to build it. This hierarchy of influence is reflected in the funding for changes in manufacturing technology: equipment acquisition depends on the willingness of the labs to pay for it, and "rate of return" calculations on manufacturing technology are rudimentary. Although manufacturing engineers may be less constrained by ROI benchmarks (by comparison, for example, to their counterparts in the aircraft company), they do experience real limits on their ability to acquire and use new technology. A divisional manager explained:

> One of the real impediments to bringing any major new process
> in is the Catch-22 syndrome. . . . What you need is a major prod-
> uct that will . . . pay for the process or justify someone else's pay-
> ing for the process. On the other hand, most people developing
> new products do not trust new processes to be in place when
> they need them and are under constraints to develop their prod-
> ucts as quickly as possible.

This restrictiveness has led to what many described as an "underfunding" of manufacturing research and development and a strong orientation on the part of manufacturing engineers to purchase new technology "off the shelf." In the words of one manager, manufacturing operations are "never very close to the forefront of new processes. We've always been back there paddling like crazy to try and keep from getting swamped by the next wave."

Second, the historical influence of the labs is also embedded in their preference for stable and well-understood manufacturing methods. Indeed, although product designers conceded that their conservatism contributed to an "over the wall" syndrome,[4] many also argued that stable production technologies actually helped coordinate design and manufacturing processes. Although designs and products might evolve rapidly—pushing the state of the art in terms of product performance and functionality—stable manufacturing processes did not challenge the accumulated knowledge of design rules and restrictions.

Third, manufacturing achieves a measure of visibility only when product introduction schedules are tight. Then, manufacturing personnel told me proudly, they "jump through hoops to cut a day or two off the delivery date." This state of affairs led a manufacturing engineer to conclude, "The sad thing is that all of our manufacturing innovation has gone into making their products manufacturable." A former divisional manager explained:

We don't invent or improve processes in a sustainable way. We use our creativity to figure out how on God's green earth we can make this funny thing that just came out of the lab. And that's not a repeatable sort of thing. Once we tweak the process to do that, then the next funny product comes out with another few characteristics that are different. So all the stuff we've done before that was useful is not transportable.

The positive "spin" put on this relationship is that manufacturing works best when it is geared to respond rapidly to the needs of the labs; the not-so-positive spin is that manufacturing should never jeopardize the ability of the labs to get a product designed, developed, and off to market.

Employment and human resource practices are guided by corporate policies that stress the organization's commitment to both individuals and the communities in which they reside. For example, the company maintains a well-developed internal labor market with training, promotion, and relocation opportunities designed to support employment security and skill development. Employment security, according to the hourly workers I interviewed, was a key attraction of the com-

4. Rigid distinctions among functional groups and serial development processes lead groups (e.g., product designers) who have completed their task to "throw it over the wall" to the next group in the sequence (e.g., manufacturing).

pany.[5] Jobs are ranked by a standard evaluative tool used across the company, and wage levels are competitive with prevailing levels in the labor markets from which the company draws. In addition to employment security and competitive wages and benefits, the company offers a smorgasbord of amenities that set it apart from most conventional manufacturing organizations: for example, exercise facilities, common parking and eating areas, and, most recently, on-site childcare.

Since its inception, the company has been nonunion. Without adopting an openly antiunion stance, it has nonetheless sought to provide an economic and an organizational environment that, in the words of one manager, "makes unions unnecessary." Apart from its employment and human resource policies, the company's decentralized organization has made it a difficult organizing target: divisions are spread out geographically, and as is the case with many of its competitors, manufacturing facilities tend to be located outside major urban centers. This decentralization allows the company to draw from labor markets less experienced with unions. In place of a contractually mandated grievance system, an extensive employee representation program allows complaints and conflicts to be managed.

THE TECHNOLOGY

Technological change in the assembly of printed circuit boards is the focal point of this case study. Printed circuit boards are among the electronic "guts" inside computers, television sets, VCRs, answering machines, calculators, and so on. The boards are flat, usually rectangular, and studded with computer chips or microprocessors, resistors, heat dissipators, and so on. The process of circuit board assembly, simply put, consists of the attachment of these components to the board. In the "old" process, known as through-hole assembly, components were inserted or "loaded" with small metal leads through holes drilled in the circuit board. Components could be loaded onto boards mechanically or manually; however, once loaded, the boards would be passed over a bath of liquid metal (solder) that would secure them to the board and make the necessary physical connections among the components so that electricity (or, more precisely, electronic signals) could be transmitted along

5. Employment security is not normally guaranteed. Moreover, it is not the same as job security. Employees are told that the company will make every effort to find them a job in the event of a downturn or a change in technology; however, it makes no pledges that the job will be equivalent to the one held previously.

predetermined paths. Thus, components would reside on one side of a board, and soldered connections would be made on the other side of the board.

The "new" process, referred to as surface mount assembly or surface mount technology (SMT), introduces significant changes.[6] First, components are literally mounted on the surface of the circuit board. The elimination of holes increases the amount of "real estate" or board space available for components to be mounted: components can be loaded together more closely, and with advanced soldering techniques, they can even be loaded on both sides of a board. Thus, the functions of a given size of board can be increased more than twofold; alternatively, the same board design can be maintained, but the board size can be reduced by more than half. One immediate attraction of surface mount technology is its contribution to the miniaturization of electronic products.

Second, surface mounting renders the assembly process more complex. Most important, the mounting process is far more sensitive to error or to misplacement of components than is the through-hole method that it replaces. Components are mounted closer together, and the contact points are more difficult to see; moreover, the physical means for attaching the components changes from one of metal leads holding the component in place to one of an adhesive solder securing the components to the board. Thus, the possibility for errors in placement (by either a machine or a human being) are greater and harder to detect.

Third, surface mount technology changes the way printed circuit boards are designed and the way component layout is conducted. In what one engineer described as "the ancient and honorable through-hole approach," board designers could literally handcraft mock-ups or prototypes of the boards they would later send to the manufacturing process. Engineers would design the boards (with the electrical pathways charted and the holes for the components designed on a computer) and then plug the appropriate components into the board to see if it did what was desired. With surface mount technology, however, design and prototyping became far more intricate; prototyping with a "breadboard" (a standard, multi-purpose board that allows various configurations to be tested at a workbench) became impossible. Moreover, the new process required engineers to incorporate new rules about component layout (e.g., greater component density can lead to higher temperatures on the board itself), to learn a

---

6. For a more detailed description of the technical changes occasioned by the development of surface mount technology, see Mangin (1990).

new inventory (or parts list) of components, and to understand the new set of physical, as well as chemical, parameters that would condition the board assembly process. As a product engineering manager explained:

> Traditionally, the way engineers had done a lot of their designs was that they would go and breadboard their designs. They had nice little parts with color codes on them, and if they wanted to change from part A to part B they could rummage through their drawer and find a different one and solder it on the board. Here [with surface mount technology], they couldn't even tell what the parts were. Some of them claimed they couldn't even see them!

Even the language for describing boards and defects had to change: new terms such as "tombstones," "drawbridges," and "micro-drawbridges" were introduced to the engineering lexicon.[7]

In short, SMT could contribute to product miniaturization, to increases in board (and product) functions, and, conceivably, to reductions in board cost. However, achieving those advantages made certain skills obsolete and enhanced others, a change in the traditional relationship between product design and manufacturing, and it increased the complexity of the manufacturing process itself.

CHOOSING BETWEEN TECHNOLOGIES

The foregoing leads to an interesting question: given this history, structure, and culture, how would the organization respond to a major change in manufacturing technology change "out there" (i.e., beyond the boundaries of the organization)? The question is especially interesting in that the change at issue here appears to make obsolete an extant knowledge base of design rules and procedures, to render it difficult to sustain a traditional division of labor between product development and manufacturing, and to call into question the ability of manufacturing to maintain a routine process.

In this case, my research began with a series of interviews with corporate staff, who provided an overview of the technology and the change process. Documents provided at that time included a staff report

---

7. "Tombstones" are components that come loose from the board during the soldering process: they literally stand on end. "Drawbridges" are components that are partially detached from the board. "Micro-drawbridges" are components that separate from the board but can be detected only with a magnifying glass.

prepared for public consumption. That report provides a convenient point of departure for this analysis. I refer to it as the "official story."

THE OFFICIAL STORY

The script of the official story begins in the late 1970s, when the company is reported as becoming aware of the growing trend toward miniaturization and an increased market demand for improved product performance. In the words of the report:

> We are often asked to explain our decision to go with SMT when it appeared to be less economical than existing through-hole technology. The answer is simple: our product specifications—driven by customers' needs—required it.

Thus, market demand required the company to invest in SMT.

However, according to the report, in responding to customer needs, the company chose to break with tradition and to pursue this process development in a centralized fashion. Three major reasons were cited for this shift. First, the historically decentralized approach to manufacturing had resulted in the proliferation of several dozen through-hole shops with incompatible equipment and processes. Centralized development and control over a burgeoning technology promised to standardize equipment and processes and to increase the effectiveness of technology transfer. Second, the potential cost of equipment and engineering time would be enormous if the divisions pursued SMT on their own. Centralized development would improve use of engineering talent, lower equipment costs through volume purchases, and reduce the cost of process improvement. Third, centralized "roll-out" of the new technology would enable the company to construct "greenfield factories"—that is, to question old methods and processes and to restructure the relationship between the labs and the manufacturing organizations. The report concluded that "through centralization and, more importantly, standardization, we expect to realize gains that will provide us with lasting competitive advantage in the electronics marketplace."

The key elements of the official story can be restated simply: Recognition of a "problem"—changing market demands—was relatively straightforward. Recognition of a "solution," though not so straightforward, was nonetheless obvious once the problem was well understood. Slower to emerge were the problems associated with the solution; however, once they were diagnosed, the implementation of the solution was straightforward. Thus, a linear recounting is possible: problem seeks solution; solution raises internal problems; internal problems seek internal solution; new technology is selected and implemented.

In this sense the official story seems to be quite consistent with a strategic choice perspective. That is, driven by an increasingly competitive marketplace, top organizational leaders identified a new technology that would enable them to achieve competitive advantage. The technology, however, required changes in organizational structure if it was to be employed effectively: to wit, a more centralized approach to development and implementation and a more centralized structure seemed to be called for. In other words, the existing structure would not support such a strategy.

THE UNOFFICIAL STORY

The "unofficial story" is quite different. It is, I will contend, the story of SMT as the banner for a social movement. Corporate analysts may have claimed a strategy for SMT, but interviews in the divisions offer substantial evidence that the strategy was forced on the corporation. It is a story of covertly subversive behavior in which innovation is accomplished by means of a fascinating combination of legitimate and nonlegitimate behaviors, of appeals to a "higher moral order"—that of the company as a whole—coupled with efforts to realize distinctly "local" interests.

Although it may be a bit extreme as a comparative frame, the difference between the official version of the SMT story and the local story told by SMT advocates in the divisions is similar in several ways to the disagreements among social movement theorists over the history of the civil rights movement in the United States. One side stresses the importance of support from urban liberals, the Democratic party—especially its liberal wing in Congress—and the presidencies of John F. Kennedy and Lyndon Johnson. Their combined influence "explains" the success of the civil rights movement after decades of discrimination against African Americans (Turner and Killian 1972).[8] The competing explanation, told from the perspective of Southern black activists, is a story of the mobilization of indigenous resources and organizations—churches, the clergy, kin networks—that enabled movement leaders not only to gain the attention of national political elites but to build a platform with

8. For a similar explanation for the success of the farmworker movement, see Jenkins (1984) and Jenkins and Perrow (1977).

which to put forth claims against national and local polities (Morris 1986).

The story as told "in the trenches" of this company portrays a fascinating process of local network-building and resource mobilization for the purposes of restructuring the role of manufacturing. It is a process through which independent development and advocacy efforts across the divisions forced a corporate response. But, as in the resource mobilization analysis of the civil rights movement, the movement behind SMT was not the simple product of a single event or grievance. The grievance level did not change dramatically prior to the appearance of SMT, and historical grievances had not stimulated prior movement efforts. The movement was not simply the product of technological determinism: at the time the movement emerged, SMT was not the only technology option, and there was no corporate thrust into SMT prior to the appearance of divisional efforts. Finally, the movement did not represent a simple power play on the part of a few disgruntled manufacturing engineers: the method by which change took place was very much influenced by engineers' perceptions that the commonwealth, the company, had to change in a particular way if it were to remain competitive.

To understand how SMT became the banner for a social movement, it is important to focus attention on the early history of development efforts. Here I will concentrate on the process in one division—"East Coast"—for purposes of brevity. Later I will blend in the process as it unfolded in the other divisions.

BETWEEN CONVENTION AND INVENTION

East Coast is a division focused on a line of products for the medical care industry. Its product line consists largely in diagnostic equipment for use in medical laboratories and hospitals. East Coast was and remains a dominant force in the markets it serves, especially in the high-end and sophisticated segments of the market. Product design labs, marketing, and manufacturing are all located in the same metropolitan area; in close proximity are a number of computer and instrument manufacturers, equipment vendors, high-tech and aerospace design companies, and research universities.

Despite its reputation for state-of-the-art products, East Coast, like many of its competitors, was until the mid 1980s quite dedicated to the use of through-hole technology for the assembly of the printed circuit boards that went into its products. Interviews with managers and engineers in product development, manufacturing, and marketing strongly suggested that divisional management did not deem the process of circuit board assembly (and manufacturing in general) to be a particularly crucial part of the business. Assembly costs, for example, were not considered to be a significant part of competitive strategy. A product development manager explained:

> Usually the priorities we use to evaluate an investment go this way: significant technical contribution, minimum feature set, and then somewhere further down it's time-to-market. Cost sometimes doesn't even make the list.

Moreover, the division's emphasis on product advancement resulted in little resource allocation to improving, altering, or researching changes in the assembly process. Finally, as one lab engineer argued, product designers were more willing to take risks themselves than to allow others to take risks that might affect them: "It's very difficult to accept a new process as a boundary condition unless you really trust the organization that's putting it in place."

Indeed, when I began doing the research, I was told repeatedly how traditional the product orientation was. For example, manufacturing engineers contended that it was virtually impossible to replace aging equipment or to buy new equipment without the explicit sponsorship, approval, and funding of the product development organization. The lead engineer in the SMT effort put it this way:

> Oh, sure, little things you can get in. You're not entirely constrained. What I mean, though, is that if it ain't broke, we don't fix it. In general, if you wanted to buy something new or different, you had to convince somebody with a project that they're going to die if you don't get it. Makes you a little less than aggressive, I guess you'd say.

This attitude led East Coast, like other divisions, always to be someplace behind the process technology leaders in the computer and electronics industry.

However, to suggest that manufacturing was a subordinate activity and that divisional managers acted conservatively is not to suggest that everyone was satisfied with the situation. Many times I was told that manufacturing as a function and manufacturing engineers as a group chafed at the status they were accorded. Product engineers were referred to as "guys who play frisbee during lunch while we sweat our asses off." Perceived disparities in pay and promotional opportunities were characterized by statements such as "you'll never see a manufacturing guy become a divisional honcho" and "we all get our profit sharing, but when it comes to passing out the 'attaboys' they always start with the labs first." Manufacturing engineers believed themselves to be second-class citizens:

> They [product designers] think of us as the guy with a second-rate education and a greasy rag in his back pocket.

Though stopping short of overt hostility, these comments nonetheless voiced a sense of long-standing grievance—of perceived inequality as built into both the structure and the culture of the organization. As one manufacturing engineer put it:

> What gets you recognized around here is the whiz-bang product, not the process improvement. The [company] culture still values individual contribution. And your highest-ranked engineer is doing leading-edge technology.

In the eyes of many on the process side of the fence, what manufacturing lacked was a means to address the imbalance, to demonstrate, if only in symbolic terms, the significance of its contributions to organizational performance. Most emphatic in this sense were the manufacturing engineers—those whose responsibility it was to fix and improve the equipment and systems that made up the production process. Manufacturing engineers in this organization, not unlike their counterparts in the aircraft company, occupied a position between the product designers—the "real engineers" in the aircraft company—and line manufacturing management. Though they formally reported to manufacturing management, almost all were college educated and identified themselves as professional engineers. Yet, given the relatively small size of the division, they were close enough to the manufacturing process to be aware of, and sensitive to, the social system of production and the pressures faced by manufacturing management to resist dramatic process change.

Thus, their position at the intersection of the unconventional, change-oriented design labs and the far more conventional, stability-oriented manufacturing organization created seriously divided loyalties. On the one hand, to be real engineers and to gain currency or value in the status system dominated by products and invention, they needed their own invention. Process improvement was not by itself enough, certainly not in the form that engineers described it as being approached at the time, that is, "tweaking" or fine-tuning the existing through-hole process with resources grudgingly provided by the labs and out of the time left over after supporting manufacturing management. On the other hand, to improve the status of manufacturing and, in particular, to enable it to demonstrate its value to the organization, manufacturing engineers could not veer too far from convention or jeopardize manufacturing's ability to "do the impossible routinely," as one engineer put it.

If any real change in the status of manufacturing and of manufacturing engineering was to come about, it seemed that it would have to be "driven" by the needs of a new *product*. Yet it was precisely in this setting that a new process was to emerge.

Key to understanding that development was—as the literature on innovation would lead us to expect (see, for example, Maidique 1980; Burgelman 1984; Dean 1987; Van de Ven 1986; Kanter 1988)—the emergence of a champion for change. But, as critics of the "great leader" theory of social movements and social change would argue (see, e.g., Tilly 1978), it was not a leader alone who made the movement. More important was the recognition on the part of the manufacturing engineers that an exogenous development—SMT—could serve as a vehicle for organizational change. At the heart of the innovation process was the use of SMT to mobilize a social movement.

BUILDING A MOVEMENT

In addition to its core responsibility for supporting the existing through-hole process, the East Coast manufacturing engineering department was responsible for monitoring the environment for developments in manufacturing technology. Still, only two of the ten people in the department were given the assignment. The lead manufacturing engineer had few resources at his disposal, and he and his assistant spent most of their time trying to improve the existing through-hole technology.

However, in the course of visiting other printed circuit board assembly facilities in 1983, they discovered a military contractor soldering components directly onto printed circuit boards. In a subsequent trip to an equipment vendor, they encountered engineers from one of their competitors experimenting with robots that placed chips onto their boards. Astounded and excited by what they saw, the two searched technical journals for background information and conducted rudimentary tests with materials they bought and borrowed from vendors. Still not sure whether SMT was applicable or even economical for their division's product line, the pair reported their findings enthusiastically to higher-level management. The response was not what they hoped for, as the lead engineer explained:

> I remember one day my boss came by after we'd told him a bit
> about what we'd seen. He looked at it and he said, "I don't like
> this. We used to do this in [a military contractor company]."
> And he ordered us, he gave us a direct order to stop this develop-
> ment of surface mount.

Despite their boss's warning, the engineers decided to take a risk and experiment with the new technology. The lead engineer explained:

> We ignored him, essentially, and we did it when he wasn't there
> or when he wasn't around. He wasn't a very progressive guy and
> we figured we could take a chance.

After hours and in out-of-the-way places, they put together what they referred to as their "pocket lab"—a lab beaker and a dime-store hot-plate—and tested the new soldering technique. They arranged impromptu demonstrations of the new technique for anyone who would stand still long enough to watch. As one of the engineers told us:

> That's the only way anything gets done [in this company]. You
> can go to R&D with the greatest analysis in the world and it's
> not going to be near as good as taking hardware to them and say-
> ing, "Look what we built."

As they got more deeply into the process—beyond simply a new soldering technique and into actually mounting components on their boards—the need for equipment became much greater. As one of the engineers recalled:

> That's how we did our initial prototypes. We'd call up [the ven-
> dor] and say, "Can we get some time in your lab?" and then
> we'd zip down in the car, careful not to take any sharp corners.

Even though the pocket lab was a "great hook" and the manufacturing engineers had received positive feedback from some product designers, their experiments were largely perceived as "cute, even clever" but not convincing. By and large, the lab's objections held sway: until the process in its entirety could be proven, no resources would be forthcoming; of course, lacking "legitimate" resources, the process could not be proven.

Yet the pair remained convinced that what they held in their hands had tremendous potential. Two aspects were enticing. First, the lead engineer was convinced that an SMT process would make it possible to dramatically reduce defects and other quality problems attributable to the hand-loading of components. In what he characterized as a "thorough review of the through-hole process," he had concluded that nine out of ten defects were caused by human error. To get the system under control, he argued, it was essential to do away with the reliance on hand labor. Earlier efforts to alter the through-hole process convinced him that only some form of automation could solve the problem. Second, and more expansively, SMT offered a lever for making organizational change. The lead engineer explained:

> We knew it was going to be very difficult in [the company] for manufacturing to lead this kind of a process technology improvement. It just never was that way before. We were always driven by R&D. But we also saw it as an opportunity, in fact, to get ahead of R&D in terms of their [board] density requirements. We could basically change the whole ball field so that the game changed and that we would have a chance to start to lead the technology for a change—rather than be dragged along.

Development might have remained restricted to "clever tricks" had it not been for three loosely connected but simultaneous events: (1) the creation of a network among independent, division-level development efforts; (2) the growth of concern within the company about the encroachment of Japanese competitors into American markets; and (3) the appearance of an "opening" in the East Coast product line that could be served by SMT. Because each of these events is important to the emergence and the growth of the SMT movement, I will discuss them in turn.

NETWORKING

As related in the official story of SMT adoption, at the time that experiments were being conducted in East Coast, the company contained a large number of through-hole shops. Many of these employed incompatible machines and processes; in other cases, what had originally been similar machines and processes had been modified over time so that they were largely incompatible.[9] For the divisions this situation was acceptable, even if it was occasionally bothersome. It was acceptable because each division preferred to remain in control of its own operations, especially when times were good. It was bothersome when times were bad because it was difficult to transfer work across divisions to sustain employment. A corporate executive responsible for manufacturing development explained:

> Sure, people did get together. We occasionally had symposiums of sorts on things like printed circuit loading. And everybody would come together and we'd talk about having standard processes. And then it would just kind of break down because processes were so different and because everybody wanted to do their own. We'd say, "Okay, which process should we use?" And the answer would be "Well, it will have to be mine. If it's not mine, I'm going home." Then they'd go home.

Comfort outweighed discomfort since equipment costs were relatively low or, as was the case in most divisions, the equipment had already been paid for. Thus, there was no reason to standardize, and the incompatibility of equipment sets meant there was little call for information sharing across divisions.

Frustrating as it may have been to be consistently rebuffed in their efforts to eliminate duplication of efforts, corporate staff continued to push for information sharing across divisional boundaries. One such effort, in 1984, finally bore fruit—but, as I will show, it was a decidedly different outcome than the one that the corporate staff had anticipated. Specifically, a meeting was called by the corporate manufacturing development group to create a "technology management team" composed of manufacturing engineers from across the divisions. The team was assigned to do what they could to improve the performance of the various through-hole shops. A participant on the team from the East Coast division recalled his confusion as to why they were even meeting: "So we got together, a brand-new team, and kind of went 'What are we supposed

9. Such incompatibility occurred even *within* divisions. For example, East Coast had problems of compatibility between manufacturing facilities in the United States and Western Europe. A manufacturing manager noted, "We have run into that problem where we transfer products back and forth with our plant in Europe. They have a different brand of machine than we do, so that even on the products that we build in common with them, we've had problems."

to do?' Nobody knew, but we met three or four times." The team initially focused on common technical problems, and as two participants argued, they did achieve some marginal improvements in operating efficiencies. Yet few came away convinced that they could or even should consolidate (i.e., give up) their own through-hole shops.

What did emerge from the teaming effort was a network among manufacturing engineers that would provide a critical foundation for the spread of surface mount technology. The engineer from East Coast who had begun experimenting with SMT turned the group's focus toward the new technology:

> As we met, we began to appreciate that there was this thing, surface mount, out there and so, through the management, we sent a note to [the CEO] that said, "Do you want us to save $10 million by squeezing the old [through-hole] process or do you want us to work on something new and better?"

The team received no response to its query—a development one member described as resulting from the "fact that nobody understands rhetoric in this company"—and the issue was dropped from their formal agenda. Soon after, the team was disbanded.

However, the topic did not die with the dissolution of the team. In fact, the team served as the nucleus of a network for spreading the word about this new thing called SMT. The network began to work overtime when it was discovered that a newly formed small computer division was undertaking a concerted effort to develop SMT on a larger scale.

Response to word of development activity in the small computer division was significant in two regards. First, it provoked anger and resentment because that division was operating at a loss. In the value system of the company, the lowest place on the totem pole was reserved for the least profitable divisions. A Midwest division manufacturing manager put it bluntly:

> The psychology of [the company] is you make a profit. Otherwise you're whale dung. Stuff on the bottom of the ocean. That's right. People joke and make really awful comments about any division or business entity that does not make a profit in this corporation.

Second, it provoked tremendous interest. In the new division, manufacturing engineers were doing "real" engineering. Interest came to outweigh anger when word passed through the network that the engineers in the small computer division were proposing to develop a fully automated process. According to one observer, they proposed to develop a self-contained manufacturing facility designed by experts to be run by experts:

> They were working very hard on a fully automated line. And the value added from the production organization would be to monitor the monitors. In fact, their optimum would be just technical staff to monitor. A "lights-out" factory was what they were trying to achieve.

In the eyes of those who had been experimenting on their own, in isolation, here was a process that was itself an invention. Thus, despite the antipathy toward a division that was losing money, a bond of solidarity caused manufacturing engineers to applaud peers who were doing something worthy.

This network and feelings of solidarity might not have resulted in the formation of a movement at this time any more than in the past were it not for the fact that it now provided the means to support "local" actions in a coordinated fashion. The network enabled resources—real and symbolic—to be mobilized. Most important at the outset was the mobilization of a new definition of process. At the time, SMT was not the only form of new manufacturing technology being considered in the company or being promoted by equipment vendors and consultants. As in many American manufacturers, there was in this company a great deal of talk and piecemeal experimentation with computer integrated manufacturing (CIM), flexible manufacturing cells, and information technologies of various sorts. But to the division-level manufacturing engineers, SMT held several unique attractions: (1) it was contained, not diffuse: that is, it offered a discernible, even if dramatic, set of changes; (2) it rearranged known activities: that is, it did not completely eliminate or make obsolete existing manufacturing skills or competencies; and (3) it maintained assembly as a largely mechanical process. Thus, the critical contribution of the development activity in the small computer division was its demonstration that a significant process change could itself be conceived of as a product—a tool as precise as the products the divisions made.

The network not only provided a means for diffusing this definition of the "process as product" but also provided a conduit for channeling information that could bolster the previously isolated division-level efforts. For example, the engineers at East Coast tapped into the network to gather information and then reproduced it as a paper at an outside professional conference. One of the authors explained:

> To put that paper together, we made use of our good contacts in the printed circuit shops. We built off the experience of people in the Midwest divisions and all over. We discovered that in this company we have really learned incredible details by tapping into the school of hard knocks. The folks in the fab shops gave us really detailed data. So that all became part of the paper, and we felt at last that we had some kind of grasp on what was going on . . . what it's going to take to make a real surface mount process.

Their paper extolled the potential virtues of SMT. Presenting a paper at a professional conference was a valued and legitimate thing to do; it also enabled them to apply gentle pressure from "below."

The network even provided the East Coast engineers with the raw materials to engage in an inventive effort of their own. With printed circuit boards provided by colleagues from another division, they hand-crafted surface mount boards equivalent to through-hole boards from an existing product and then secretly swapped the boards on instruments going out to a customer. The lead engineer described their efforts:

> We were saying, "How can we finally convince these people that it's the right thing to do?" What we did was we took one of our current products which was an all through-hole product and we took one of the printed circuit boards—it's used twice in the product, side by side—and we stuck in one of the surface mount boards we'd done by hand. We did this after hours. . . . We said, "What we're going to do when my boss isn't around is we're going to re-lay this board out in surface mount and we're going to ship it in our product in a twin experiment."

He added quickly:

> I don't want to say we did it in a clandestine way. Low profile might be a better way to describe it. . . . We tried to keep as low a profile as we could. 'Cause it's the kind of thing that the more publicity it gets, the more people worry about it and it's not the

right thing to do. We figured, "Hell, fifteen systems at the worst can fail. What kind of risk is that compared to the potential benefit?"

When I asked whether he perceived his "experiment" to involve personal risk, he replied:

I didn't worry about it much. I mean, I think the worst that could have happened to me is I would have been called into somebody's office and gotten hollered at for those fifteen failures in the field. Now that I think about it, I was more concerned about whether I . . . wanted to invest my whole future in surface mount. The payoffs could be real big, but it could also turn out to be a dead-end, too.

His assistant was less concerned about personal risks:

Actually, personally I didn't think a whole lot about that. I was just having a ball with this stuff. It was just a lot of fun, you know, working on the new technology and bringing it in. So, honestly, I have to say that it really didn't cross my mind much.

Once convinced that the boards had been out in the field long enough to prove their durability (with no complaints coming from the customer about product failure), they "revealed" their secret to the design lab as further evidence of the viability of surface mount technology.

At the same time that East Coast engineers were shipping out instruments with secretly implanted surface mount boards, their counterparts in other divisions were working to build their own surface mount capabilities. Three Midwest divisions were undertaking independent experiments with boards from their own product lines. The independence of their efforts was justified, according to those we interviewed, by the widely varying needs of the respective product lines. In one division the product line was large, but product designs changed rather slowly (e.g., every three to five years); thus, experiments were aimed at introducing SMT as a way to increase the flexibility of the production process. In the second division a race was on with competitors to pack as much computing power into as small a workstation as possible; SMT was sold on the basis of its promise to miniaturize circuit boards. A manufacturing engineering manager explained:

We made the biggest inroads in those areas where they [product designers] almost absolutely had to have it in order to build the product in the box they wanted to build. You couldn't convince them that the cost was going to be less. Quality was questionable. But they could see that the density they would achieve would be significant.

In a third Midwest division the product line was relatively narrow, but the life cycle of a given design was very short; experiments were aimed at using SMT to reduce the time it took to bring a revised board into production.

In all three cases the engineers' network provided critical support to early efforts. As one participant argued:

We leveraged very heavily. We took advantage of the fact that others in [the company] were further ahead of us. . . . People were very open. They would provide us parts we couldn't get from vendors and insights on how the machines were run.

This situation promoted a kind of group risk taking, he added: "All the way up through the first year or so I had very little support as far as product willing to commit to it. We went out on a limb."

Thus, while each division insisted on pursuing product-specific applications, manufacturing engineers searched hungrily for information that others in their emergent network might be able to provide. The network supplied not only news but, as I will suggest, images, metaphors, and visions of a future state in which the company would be better off as a result of the inventive efforts of those who had been considered second-class citizens.

AN EXTERNAL THREAT

At the same time that the movement network was solidifying, managers across the company were beginning to take seriously the potential entrance of Japanese and other Asian competitors into their markets. Division-level SMT proponents quickly tapped into the perceived threat by emphasizing their belief that Japanese electronics firms were "years ahead" in the application of surface mount technology. At the East Coast division the engineer in charge of manufacturing technology bent the ear of people he knew in marketing, arguing that

we ought to worry more about a low-cost product and this was specifically to start to protect our flank against the Japanese. . . .

What was happening, in typical Japanese fashion, the Japanese
were coming out with imaging equipment—very low end, very
low feature, very low cost—but they're getting their foot in the
door with the same strategy that they followed with automobiles.

A manufacturing engineer in the Midwest division dismantled a Japanese competitor's product and saw surface mount boards inside:

I began to see this as a strategic investment for the nineties . . .
one that would enable us not only to compete against the Japanese but so we could get more features into our product.

The competitor's product became his hook to attract the attention of
the design lab. This engineer and colleagues in other divisions pointed,
for example, to the fact that the most advanced SMT equipment was
manufactured by Japanese firms.

By combining the market threat with a warning that Japanese firms
had already leapfrogged through-hole technology, local proponents
painted SMT as the answer, even in the absence of evidence that they
could reliably develop and use the technology. Here, too, the manufacturing engineers' network proved significant: metaphors, stories, and
successful arguments were swapped through the network to such a
great extent that managers on separate coasts recalled their surprise
at hearing their subordinates use the same language to describe SMT.
One explained:

We had to laugh, really. Here they were using the same
buzzwords: "SMT is like atomic energy in the fifties. SMT will
make the factory of the future. SMT will be so efficient that all
you have to be concerned with is the cost of the parts themselves."

PRODUCT OPENINGS

Movement proponents also scouted out points of advantage for employing SMT. In most cases this scouting meant finding a product in need of
the advantages promised by the new process. In East Coast, for example,
a critical opportunity appeared with the initiation of an effort to develop
a line of low-end equipment for a market niche considered vulnerable to
Japanese competitors. The idea was to develop a product sufficiently
different from what had been produced in the past that, according to the
project manager in charge of development, the team was "forced to start

with a blank slate." Released from historical constraints and precedents, the manager in charge of the development effort recalled the "rantings of our friends over in manufacturing engineering" and decided to give them a chance to put their ideas about SMT to a test. He explained:

> The worst we could do is fail in a new market. It wouldn't impact our ongoing business at all. So a combination of the relatively low risk to the division and the symbiotic need of low cost and high interest in doing SMT occurred. It just all fell together.

When asked whether any detailed investigation of the costs or the returns associated with SMT was made prior to moving ahead, the division comptroller replied:

> To be perfectly honest, it came down to an emotional commitment at the lab manager's level. We showed reasonable cost estimates that supported what we said we'd be doing. And we showed reasonable market estimates for the sales revenue that we would generate. Also, I think there were a couple of other rationalizing arguments. One was, "If we don't do it, somebody else will."

The lead engineer who had championed SMT and who had been instrumental in setting up the interdivisional network smiled when I asked him whether he felt he'd finally been victorious:

> Look, I didn't do it by myself and I sure as heck didn't have all the confidence in the world that it would actually work. But I do have to admit a certain amount of satisfaction at finally getting some attention for what we'd been doing with our little pocket lab and no other resources than the things we could beg, borrow, or steal. More important than anything, it was the right thing for the company to do.

Thus, a grass-roots movement was built in support of a new manufacturing technology. It was stimulated, at least in part, by long-standing grievances about the second-class position of manufacturing and manufacturing engineers. But SMT was especially attractive because it enabled manufacturing engineers to be inventors—to turn a process into a product—and therefore to claim a status traditionally reserved for product engineers. A technology was transformed from just another technical possibility "out there" into a political symbol. But the process of movement building was made possible through the transformation of what were ordinarily weak ties into bonds of solidarity, the creation of a language with which to describe the innovation as a product, and the identification of the "process product" with real product needs. In a setting that seemed to be divided by many more barriers (e.g., in time, space, and product) than existed in the aircraft company, manufacturing engineers in the computer company managed to coalesce around a common candidate technology and to define a domain in which they could engage in "real engineering." Like the aircraft company cases, however, the choice between technologies was only the first step in the change process. The form of the change had been decided on, but not the content.

In this respect, it is important to recognize that while the official story portrayed the venture into SMT and a more centralized structure as a strategic choice, the people who brought SMT into view were doing so from a position far from the top of the organization and for reasons decidedly more complex than the official story implies. Their movement was as much a reaction to the existing structure and to their perceptions of an undeservedly unequal status as it was an effort to fulfill their formal obligations to the organization. Indeed, from their perspective, the new technology provided a means to alter the structure in the pursuit of what they believed to be real organizational and professional needs.

CHOOSING WITHIN THE TECHNOLOGY

With the increasingly open discussion of SMT, corporate manufacturing strategy staff began to ponder the implications of the new technology for the distribution of organizational resources and, as I will suggest, for the future structure of the organization itself. Here the pieces of the "official story" become clearer.

Corporate staff prepared a report suggesting that the proliferation of SMT equipment and engineering support, were it to mirror the existing pattern of through-hole shops, could be extraordinarily expensive—in terms of capital outlays, salaries, and production overcapacity. Serious questions, they claimed, confronted the company: Did it want to repeat the through-hole experience? Could it risk having the problem of over-capacity occur again? The corporate manufacturing vice president ex-plained:

> And so that [report] kind of made our mouths water. And we
> did try to get a lot of people to understand the numbers we were

talking about. At the same time, we did some studies that indicated that we had too many manufacturing facilities in general.

Ironically, the insurgency of divisional manufacturing engineers presented
an opportunity for corporate manufacturing staff to leverage off local
developments and use SMT as a vehicle for standardizing processes in
the organization. The corporate vice president continued: "So somewhere
along the line, surface mount appeared to be a pretty good opportunity
to kind of break that insidious chain." With manufacturing organizations considered low-status actors in the divisions, corporate manufacturing staff felt many of the same grievances that those "out in the trenches"
did. But divisional engineers and manufacturing managers were, according to corporate staff, too close to their own organizations to appreciate
the bigger picture. Thus, the insurgency provided an opportunity for corporate manufacturing staff not only to gain a measure of status but
actually to "lead" the movement.

Indeed, corporate manufacturing leaders were best served by the
specter of uncoordinated and expensive efforts on the part of the divisions. Corporate staff proposed a strategy of coordinated, standardized
and centrally controlled technology transfer. In other words, they offered to be two things at once: champion of divisional manufacturing's
insurgent effort and guardian of corporate interests.

THE GREAT INVESTMENT BAKE-OFF

Although presented as a relatively nonproblematic development in the
"official story," this situation offers an interesting insight on language
and politics in the large-scale corporation. Corporate staff sought to
build some degree of consensus about the process and the equipment
that would be sufficiently generic to serve quite varied divisional needs.
Their first move was to gain control over the membership of a committee to "oversee" the reorganization of the shops into "surface mount
centers." This move involved assembling a group of middle-level managers to serve as a policy-making body. According to the corporate manufacturing vice president who proposed the committee, participants had
to have both "technical capability and organizational clout. And I needed
people that had, you know, a fair amount of each. Although I was
willing to sacrifice technical capability to get the right amount of clout."
The second move was to acquire control over critical resources. The
corporate executive explained:

I wanted them to push the standard process. And I wanted them to limit the number of sites. So it was essential that we got our hands on the capital equipment budget. And it was passed by the Executive Committee that capital equipment spent on surface mount had to have our approval.

Given that this was a company built by and around engineers, corporate staff were well aware that the methodology for arriving at consensus would have to satisfy engineering criteria. After several inconclusive debates about the merits of alternative processes and equipment sets, the policy committee decided to set up a head-to-head competition among different machines. They called it "The Great Investment Bake-Off."

The Great Investment Bake-Off was a closely monitored series of experiments in which different machine vendors were given the opportunity to "strut their stuff"—to see which would perform the best. Despite what appeared to most participants to be carefully controlled conditions, disputes arose at virtually every turn. In one case, for example, proponents of different soldering techniques battled over the interpretation of the experimental results.

But debates about the "objectivity" of the Bake-Off and the "true" meaning of its results reflected the unresolved issue of who would determine the content as well as the use of the new technology. Manufacturing engineers who had already invested time, energy, and personal reputations in specific approaches (e.g., methods of soldering and types of equipment) felt they owned their particular inventions and did not relish the idea that, even though they might get a new process, it might not be their process. Many had sold SMT to their superiors as a resource that would serve specific divisional needs (e.g., speed, reliability, or cost reduction); suddenly they were confronting a group that called for generic applications. Although they appreciated corporate concerns about a repetition of the through-hole experience, most felt common goals were better served by optimizing the performance of the parts. Finally, the engineers themselves began to recognize that the impasse they faced was at least partly a product of their own success in pushing SMT—and themselves—into the limelight. One Midwest division engineer put it best when he said:

We finally had to face up to the fact that we got to that point through a lot of hard work and over a lot of opposition . . . and we had to decide either to declare the battle over and be satisfied, or to keep fighting. If we kept fighting, it would be against each other. That wouldn't do anybody any good.

Although the policy committee ultimately authorized a range of equipment and processes to constitute the approved approach to SMT, the Bake-Off did not really resolve the problem of coordination. In response to what was perceived as either slow or inappropriate action on the part of the committee, several divisions quietly acquired their own equipment. The corporate executive who had advanced the idea of standardization was sanguine about their actions:

> If you've got a group that's making mucho profit and you're talk-
> ing to their manager and he is talking about spending a couple
> million dollars and he brings in 300 million dollars a year and
> you try to tell him, "I'm not going to let you spend that money
> because I think you are making a minor mistake," you're going
> to have one unhappy camper!

Defections such as these and the threat of more forced the policy committee to stratify the choice process: a small group would be recruited to work on generic issues associated with SMT in a centralized location near corporate headquarters;[10] a new council made up of divisional manufacturing engineers would oversee the agenda of that centralized group; and the divisions that had already ventured into SMT would be allowed to continue, but their equipment purchases would have to be approved by the new council.

An uneasy compromise had been struck. Those who had formed and mobilized the engineers' network were authorized to pursue their inventions, but in exchange they would now sit in judgment of others who sought to join their ranks. In other words, the movement had succeeded, but it had also been effectively co-opted as part of a corporate effort to guide the spread of the technology. Each member of the council would somehow have to balance competing interests—for example, his own interest in being an inventor, manufacturing management's interest in process reliability and predictability, the divisions' interests in autonomy and specificity, and the corporation's interest in centralized control over technology development and transfer.

---

10. The group recruited to do central development work consisted largely of West Coast engineers who had pioneered the automated SMT line mentioned earlier.

Lacking a precedent to guide them, council members "stumbled along trying to figure out what the hell we could do to get us together on this thing," as one participant recalled. The uniqueness of their situation, in this company at least, was underscored by the insistence of several members, including one of the early SMT advocates from the East Coast division, that as engineers they ought to devise some way to analyze their task and ultimately express their solution in mathematical, indeed algorithmic, terms. If they could do that, one member argued, they could circumvent the politics that had "made such a mess of the Bake-Off." Council members searched for a methodology that would allow them to express interests as equations. They settled on a technique described in a major business journal as "quality function deployment" or QFD (see Hauser and Clausing 1988). From the perspective of the council, the virtue of QFD was that it assigned numbers to opinions and allowed them to be multiplied and divided to create a matrix of priorities. Mathematical procedures put distance between opinions and outcomes. What had appeared to be unmanageably political suddenly appeared rational and apolitical.

At this point in the history of the process, there appeared to be an intersection between the official and the unofficial stories of technological change. "Insurgent" manufacturing engineers had brought the idea of SMT into the company, and their network had helped sell the technology to higher levels of management. Their very success, however, appeared to corporate managers as both potentially very expensive and capable of undermining the efforts by the latter to elevate the status of manufacturing in the company. But the more fundamental debates only indirectly concerned SMT; rather, at issue was the question of who would engineer the future structure of the organization itself. Pronouncements about customer needs and creative efforts to devise rational or "apolitical" decision methods served only to recast what was essentially a political struggle as a technical one.

The significance of the conflict can be best appreciated by examining the subsequent process of implementing the chosen technology.

IMPLEMENTING THE TECHNOLOGY

The manufacturing engineers who had championed the adoption of SMT and gained notoriety for their achievement had little time to bask in the glow of their success. Their inventive abilities had been demonstrated, but as one West Coast engineer said ruefully, "Back at the ranch [i.e., the division], they were not about to let it go to our heads." Pressures to shape the form in which SMT would be used and the leverage that would be extracted from its use came from two directions. From one side, design engineers moved quickly to imprint their interests on the fledgling surface mount shops. Concretely, as I will show in the case of the East and West Coast divisions, the labs were organizing to ensure that the new technology did not upset the balance of influence between design and manufacturing: that is, the "driven" would not be allowed to become the "driver." From the other side, line managers from manufacturing moved quickly to domesticate the new process in order to prevent it from interfering with what they perceived to be their mission—making products routinely, reliably, and cost-effectively. Of particular interest here was the antipathy of manufacturing management in the West Coast division for an automated assembly line. The ensuing struggle over the organization and the operation of the new technology would have serious implications for the manner in which people, as well as technology, would be managed.

EAST COAST: FROM SLACK TO STRESS

The adoption of SMT in the East Coast division, it will be recalled, was hastened by the marriage of the new process with a new product. This arrangement provided ideal conditions for experimentation: the through-hole shop would remain in operation, servicing the product lines that already existed; the "blank slate" approach to product design offered an opportunity for manufacturing managers and engineers to be involved in the early stages of product development; and corporate sponsorship of SMT legitimated their endeavor. Most important, the undertaking was unusual in the amount of slack available to all participants. Time constraints were relaxed. Historical precedents were set aside. Money was available. And people were released from other responsibilities to devote their energies to testing the new equipment. Interviews with design engineers and their counterparts in production suggested that the "coevolution" of product and process fueled a departure from the traditional over-the-wall relationship. For example, the lab manager in charge of the undertaking praised the manufacturing engineers, going so far as to describe them as "creative" and "technically first-rate." Without saying so directly, he expressed a measure of surprise that such talent existed in the manufacturing: "Those guys keep a low profile over there. I mean, I certainly took them for granted before. Most of the time we just expected them to do what we think is reasonable . . . to go about their business and do what we want."

The lead engineer and early champion of SMT—promoted to manufacturing manager for the new area—used the ramp-up period to recruit select technicians, machine operators, and assemblers from the through-hole area and to engage them in bringing the new equipment on-line. His initial goal was to introduce a system of job rotation to achieve a greater measure of flexibility in work assignments. A production supervisor recruited from the through-hole area explained:

> There were a couple of things we were trying to do. First, we wanted to prepare for the day when we'd have a real mix of different kinds of boards coming through here. If we could shift people from hand-load to board test when we needed them, we could cut down on the bottlenecks we had in the through-hole area. Second, we looked at some of the jobs, like hand-load, and we knew that some of that was going to be really deadly if we stuck people there for too long. The parts were so small and the work is so tedious that we just knew we were going to have quality problems and ergonomics problems if people did that for too long. In the through-hole area it was different. People might do one of those jobs for ten years and it was okay. But like I said, it also made for bottlenecks. And then the third thing we wanted to do was rotate people so they'd get a sense of the upstream and the downstream of the process. That way, they'd be in a better position to understand the whole system. It would give them some more ownership of it.

Training, carried out largely by the manufacturing engineers, was intended to support this new and more flexible system of job assignments.

Early ("up-front") investments in training and selective recruitment were deemed important for two additional reasons. First, a great deal was riding on the success of the first products to go through the new process. Although the new product manager earlier discounted the risks associated with a product for a previously untapped market, he also admitted that

> a lot of people were looking on from the sidelines. There were plenty of skeptics in the lab and in the through-hole area and in

our sister divisions. If we succeeded, there'd be a lot of changes
made: a lot of rules rewritten, a lot of people moved around, etc.
If we failed, well, of course there'd be a lot of "I told you so's."

Added to the reputational risks was the unprecedented amount of money—
on the order of several million dollars—that had been spent on the new
equipment.

Second, training and selective recruitment were part of what a production supervisor characterized as an "insurance policy for the future."
The manufacturing engineers who had promoted SMT (and who were,
in turn, promoted to manage the process) envisioned the area evolving
into an automated system. Indeed, from their perspective, automation
would eliminate human-caused variability and defects, and it would crys-
tallize the process into a product—an invention on its own. An automated
system would require only a small number of highly skilled people. Thus,
given the company's informal pledge of employment security, it did not
make sense to staff the area with more people than was necessary.

Before their vision could be realized, however, the situation changed
abruptly. In anticipation of a smooth installation of the new SMT process,
salespeople began peddling demonstration models of the new low-cost
product that had been built by hand. Almost immediately they were
deluged with orders. Slack evaporated as marketing management insisted that production be geared up as quickly as possible. To make matters worse, a different product group in the lab announced its decision to
redesign an existing model using SMT. They would need the manufacturing organization scaled up for large-volume production within a few
months.

On the heels of the sudden increase in demand, two additional
complications surfaced. One complication was technical: the individual
machines were in place and workers had been trained in their operation,
but no one was sure how the different pieces might interact under normal,
much less high-volume, production or where bottlenecks in the flow of
boards might appear. Boards for the new products were reasonably
simple; but boards for the redesigned product were considered "ugly."[11]
Adding to the strain were frantic calls for design rules and documentation from the group redesigning their boards for SMT. If the engineers in
charge of the area did not fully understand how their process worked, how
could they advise others about how to prepare for that process?

11. "Ugly" boards contained a mixture of surface-mounted and through-hole components.

The other complication was organizational: the SMT area lacked sufficient numbers of workers experienced with the new technology to meet the dramatic increase in demand. The SMT area manager argued that he'd "already borrowed all the people we could from the through-hole area." Those who were borrowed were "plugged into the middle of the line," an area that consisted of two tedious and exacting jobs. One job involved hand-loading parts with a long, narrow tweezer and magnifying glass that the automated pick-and-place machines could not attach. The other was board repair: boards that failed functional tests at the end of the line had to be retested for lost, misplaced, or misoriented parts. A woman who had been hand-loading components in the through-hole area found the work both different and difficult:

> It was really different! I'd just gotten used to the job I'd been doing, but these new parts were really little and it was hard to put them on the right way. The color codes were all different. The designs and drawings weren't all complete. And there was a lot of pressure! Believe me, it wasn't pleasant. It still isn't.

The pressures of a new and incompletely understood process and inadequate time for training quickly took their toll. A first-line supervisor elaborated:

> Oh yeah, the stress went way up. I felt it on me and the people in my area felt it, too. We had some slack at the very beginning, but once we got those big orders, everything went crazy.

The East Coast SMT area was in a bind. They lacked detailed understanding of their process and adequate numbers of trained production workers. Adding full-time employees to cover the production forecasts was a double-edged sword: if new hires were made, they would have to be fully incorporated into the division; however, if the SMT advocates realized their vision of an automated system, not only would the new hires become redundant, but many veterans in the through-hole shop would become surplus labor, too.

THE TEMP SOLUTION

Convinced that both the technical and organizational problems were transient, the area manager decided to hire temporary workers ("temps") under contract with private employment agencies and to concentrate them in jobs that required the least training.[12] The temp solution held three major attractions for the SMT area managers: (1) it would provide a buffer against fluctuations in production volume;[13] (2) it would enable them to concentrate training resources on "regular" employees, in anticipation of a time when the line would be automated to a greater degree; and (3) it would keep down costs, especially overhead.[14] This last element was especially important, according to the area manager, because cost containment was the critical factor in the ability of the manufacturing engineers to claim that SMT represented not only an invention but also a contribution to the economic performance of the division. Overhead costs were allocated as part of the internal price charged for assembling circuit boards. Thus, by economizing on head count, recruitment, and training, the prices charged for assembling boards could be reduced, at least in the short term.

However, almost immediately after the hiring of the temps began, a two-tiered system of work allocation emerged: regular employees (those who were eligible for full benefits and access to training and promotion within the internal labor market) were allocated to the more skilled jobs; temps remained in the less skilled jobs. Temps were largely excluded from training, promotion, and participation in small group activities such as quality control circles, plant manager's briefings, and even company picnics. Two years after the practice was initiated, nearly 30 percent of the SMT workers were temps.[15]

Though aware of higher-level management's concerns about cost containment, supervisors and workers gave the temp solution a somewhat different appraisal. For them, the use of temps had at least three serious implications. First, because temps were given little training and were not socialized into the company, they were more likely than regular employees to adopt an instrumental orientation toward their work. A production supervisor remarked:

---

12. Temporary and part-time employment has grown as a form of labor market participation in the past decade—largely in response to employer efforts to economize on labor costs, especially benefits (see Abraham 1990). It has become especially common in the electronics industry in the area from which the East Coast division recruits labor.

13. As the area manager put it, "We can just ride the swings [in production demand] up and down with temps."

14. Overhead costs included salaries and expenses for supervisors, engineers, and other staff; internal inventory, equipment, and related expenses; recruitment and training; and accounting and bookkeeping.

15. Company policy prohibited temps for working more than one year. However, after a three-month "sabbatical," they could be rehired.

It's hard to explain but they really focus on finding out what they're expected to do. And then they do it. But then they don't do much more. I can understand it, actually, because I'd probably become a clock-watcher myself. It means that they don't worry about what's happening around them and, to be honest, I guess that we don't encourage them to, either.

For a company that prided itself on its dedication to individual development, clock-watching temps presented at best an anomaly; at worst, at least from the perspective of this manager, they contradicted historical norms.

Second, reliance on temps also seemed to restrict the ability of the area to improve its performance. For example, although no one had explicitly charted the relationship between levels of temporary employment and product quality, two different people—one from human resources and another from quality control—argued that temps were both less diligent and less productive than regular employees. They estimated that temps were between 60 percent and 70 percent as productive as regular employees and more prone to make errors. According to the quality control technician:

I've never really calculated it. But it's more than just a gut instinct I have: the cost advantage of temps gets wiped out by the fact that they're slower and less careful about their work.

A worker from the board test area denied that there was any overt hostility between regular employees and temps, but he did make two revealing observations:

The first thing is that they don't give them [temps] near as much training as they need. Hell, it's hard enough for me to get released for training and I'm running a machine that costs half a million bucks! But because they don't get training, they don't know what they're doing or what happens if they don't do their job right. It causes me problems because I have to try and figure out where the problem is with this board or that part. But worse than that, they're not paid to care about the whole process. . . . The second thing is that they're a bottleneck. . . . [I]t used to be that we could rotate through the jobs. You know, to get a little variety—it also helped us all understand the process. But these folks are just told to sit there and work because nobody knows if they're going to be here tomorrow or next week or next month.

Thus, process knowledge remained restricted to the engineers and the regular employees who populated the area.

Third, the disposability of temps indirectly encouraged supervisors to adopt a management style at odds with the culture of the company. Following corporate vision statements, all employees were to be treated with "respect, dignity, and integrity." Indeed, in the eyes of several managers I interviewed, the company's "Theory Y" approach (McGregor 1960) not only had made it a more caring place but also helped explain why it remained nonunion. However, with the advent of temps, some supervisors felt the door had been opened to a Theory X approach. A supervisor explained:

> I pay more attention to them [the temps] . . . because I have to look over their shoulders more to make sure they're doing what they're supposed to. It's not fun, either. I have to ride some of them. And the other thing is that if I don't ride them, then we have problems later on down the line. When a board gets into the test area, it's really tough and really expensive to be trying to catch the mistakes they can make. We could maybe deal with that by moving the temps around more. And we're doing that, but what that means is that the individual jobs can't demand a lot of skills because then we end up having to give lotsa training to people who may not be here tomorrow. So, yeah, I find myself getting a lot more hard-nosed.

Thus, not only did the use of temps encourage much closer supervision, but it obstructed investments—formal (e.g., in training) and informal (e.g., job rotation)—that would deepen the knowledge base of workers in the area. Ironically, it also made the entire process more reliant on the small and already overtaxed manufacturing engineering staff.

BACK TO CONVENTION

The persistence of the temp solution had another explanation—one that brings us back to the relationship between design and manufacturing in this division. After the success of the initial SMT product and the decision to redesign the older product, divisional management began to pressure the labs to shift to SMT. Although the manufacturing engineers were pleased by divisional management's embrace of their technology, the prospect of a large-scale shift was daunting at best. It meant that the

SMT area, its engineers, supervisors, and work force would face extraordinary pressure to meet an ever-growing and ever-widening set of demands from the labs for design rules, prototypes, and production orders.

In a very short time, the labs absorbed and then took control of surface mount technology and began demanding added capabilities—even as they produced boards that were, as one supervisor put it, "so ugly they make you want to cry." Thus, the new manufacturing management found themselves in a familiar position: "jumping through hoops" to meet production schedules; "putting out fires" in the existing process; and trying to fulfill lab demands for newer and more elaborate SMT capabilities. To make life more bearable, they used temps as a buffer—a source of slack in an increasingly conventional relationship.

After the funding for acquiring the original SMT equipment dried up, control over resources for completing their invention shifted back to the labs. And as had been the case in the past, lab groups were loath to invest in equipment, training, or process development for anything other than the immediate needs of their specific products.

In other words, the SMT champions had made their point. But they found it difficult—perhaps even impossible—to fully realize their invention. Strapped for resources, they clung to the temp solution in the hope that it would enable them to do what was expected of them, even as it forced them to pay a price of a different sort.

WEST COAST: LIGHTS ON OR LIGHTS OUT?

The West Coast SMT effort, it will be recalled, played a significant role in encouraging engineers in other divisions to mobilize their ideas, information, and arguments in favor of the technological insurgency. West Coast manufacturing engineers envisioned SMT to be a major contributor to the corporation's as yet unprofitable small computer line; they sold it to divisional managers on what it could add to the speed with which new products could be introduced and revised. A cornerstone of their pitch was the idea that SMT would enable board assembly to be *automated*. Moreover, an automated system could be modified and then transferred to any division within the larger computer group.

In several respects, however, the West Coast engineers had even more ambitious plans than their initial efforts implied. Most important, as a leader of the endeavor explained:

This company has never had a manufacturing research and development organization to speak of—much less one that was centralized and paid for out of corporate funds. But if you look at
[other major computer companies], they've all got a manufacturing development center or the equivalent. Here the culture has always revolved around the divisions and individual efforts in the
labs. We thought that if we could demonstrate that a new process
could be brought in and made to work—made to be transferable—we might strike a blow for a more centralized approach.

In other words, not only did some participants believe that they were
inventing a process, but they were also *inventing a new organization
through that process*. Automation—a lights-out factory—was critical to
their vision of both the process and the organization. The similarity in
both image and approach to the FMS and the RAC cases in the aircraft
company was striking. An automated system would be virtually self-
contained: a discrete entity whose parts would be computer-integrated
and controlled. A unique combination of robots, vision systems, and
self-diagnostic software (significant portions of which would be proprietary to the company) would make the process a product on a scale that
dwarfed most other divisions' plans, including those of engineers at East
Coast. Taking it a step further, their automated system would also be
integrated with the software and computers used by design engineers in
the labs—allowing, in theory at least, for a CAD-CAM solution of a sort
considered leading edge in virtually any manufacturing industry.[16] Once
perfected, the automated and integrated system could be installed in
virtually any site that needed it. Backers of this approach believed that
in one stroke they could eliminate the problem of incompatible production across the divisions *and* justify the creation of a centralized manufacturing R&D organization.

Before they could complete and fully install their creation, however,
the product that had served as the justification for their efforts (and the
principal source of its funding) was terminated by higher-level management. Still, a portion of their plans was fulfilled: a subset of the manufacturing engineering group was absorbed into the centralized team
chartered to do generic research on SMT under the direction of the council

16. In simple terms, computer-aided design (CAD) and computer-aided manufacturing (CAM) are intended to enable product designers to create digital blueprints and
translate them into electronic commands for driving manufacturing equipment, e.g., the
FMS described in the last chapter.

of divisional manufacturing engineers. Though less grand than their original aspirations, it nonetheless helped establish a precedent for process development as a corporate responsibility.

Their "process product," however, was transferred to one of the small computer divisions for actual production use. There it became the object of considerable controversy.

TOO MUCH TECHNOLOGY

An automated assembly line capable of rapid modification and self-diagnosis may have been the West Coast engineers' dream, but for those who had to make it work it resembled something different—not quite a nightmare, but certainly not a wish come true. The shop to which it was "bequeathed," as the manufacturing manager put it, seemed ideal for an automated system. The mix of products being served was relatively low, and the expected flexibility of the system could accommodate rapid revisions in the design and layout of printed circuit boards. Volume requirements at the time were expected to increase slowly. Thus, by contrast to East Coast (which was just beginning to realize its situation), the area could be brought on-line with careful preparation.

However, to the consternation of the SMT champions, divisional manufacturing management had a very different perspective on automation in general and on the benefits to be had from this invention in particular. Two key differences in perspective were important. The first difference had to do with the concept of the system itself. At one level the area manufacturing manager regarded the engineers' invention as inappropriate to his setting and his product line: "It's not a bad concept if you happen to be in a television or a walkman industry where you have a product that runs 24 hours a day, 365 days a year." Much more fundamental, however, was his objection that the system was an example of "automation for the sake of automation." He explained: "This is what happens when you give a bunch of very smart people a lot of money and no grounding in reality." In other words, the automated line not only did not fit the needs of the product but did not accord with the reality of production as he saw it. Thus, as the system was moved from its birthplace to the assembly shop, he instructed his own manufacturing engineering staff to remove some of the "bells and whistles":

> The original design was much more integrated than what you see here, and it had a lot more automatic controls and things. They

had robotics that . . . we had to pull out. There was much more technology than we needed.

THE CULT OF THE EXPERT

The second major difference in perspective between the engineer/inventors and manufacturing management concerned the distribution of knowledge about the process. Most concretely, the engineers' invention did not come packaged with instructions that would enable it to be used by the people who would be responsible for its operation. A production supervisor involved from the start-up of the new line elaborated his boss's concern: "The thing was not well-documented. It was out of their shop and into ours. Some of them were still chained to the machine . . . to help you understand it and run it." This predicament—what one of the inventors admitted to ruefully as the "Ph.D.-in-the-box" syndrome—made the transfer of knowledge about the new technology extremely difficult. The manufacturing manager went further:

> You have some Ph.D. in a certain technology trying to explain to an operator how to run this machine. And the operator is maybe high-school educated, very likely this is not their original culture, and things like that. If we could have found installable technology off-the-shelf and fully documented, that'd have been preferable to me.

The Ph.D.-in-the-box syndrome contributed to what several supervisors referred to as a "cult of the expert" that pervaded this and other company manufacturing facilities. The cult of the expert was best defined by one supervisor:

> Experts only have one way of doing things—that's how *they* believe it should be done. It's a belief system, not formal knowledge, not any documentation. It's a personal level of feedback.

Experts are created through the selective transfer of knowledge from the engineer/inventor to the operator, as the manufacturing manager continued:

> Our [pick-and-place, stencil, and soldering machine] operators are specialists. They were the ones that it was easiest to transfer that technology to on a personal level. And I think that's wrong

because those [engineering] guys are thinking: "I'm not documenting my process, so I'll just do a mind-meld with you because your culture and language skills are closer to mine. Well, I'll show you how to run this machine. You're the expert."

Although this was an expedient practice from the perspective of simply getting a piece of equipment up and running, a system of experts instilled rigidities in a production process that was intended to be flexible. A supervisor explained:

Traditionally, the expert is up here [putting his hand over his head] . . . the highest contributor because they were perfect. Literally, you are your own job description. Well, that's a very individual contributor, an independent type of work environment.

Without saying so directly, the manufacturing manager implied that experts formed a rigid stratum in the organization—one that resembled in its consequences the bureaucratic system of job descriptions and work rules about which managers complained bitterly in the aircraft company. When absent from work, an expert is difficult to replace, and unless experts voluntarily transfer their knowledge to fellow workers, the production process can be quickly brought to a halt—intentionally or unintentionally. Building a flexible system required area workers to have both breadth and depth in their knowledge of the SMT process.

Concern about the Ph.D.-in-the-box and experts might be written off as posturing or a badly handled example of technology transfer were it not for the insight it provides on the different experience of SMT implementation at West Coast. Both East Coast and West Coast were under similar pressure from higher levels of management to reduce costs, and each faced similar difficulties in extracting funds from their respective labs for such things as training, equipment, and additional people. West Coast, too, discovered it needed more people to meet production demand. West Coast's initial response, like that of East Coast, was to hire temporary workers to fill the gap.

However, soon after the temps arrived, a group of supervisors and regular employees sent a message to the manufacturing manager that problems were occurring. Specifically, as one technician told me:

We began to get real concerned that these folks were not really helping out. I had nothing against them. I had a couple of friends' wives working in the area. But the thing was, they didn't

know anything about what they were doing. It showed in the
back end [test and repair]. We weren't getting the job done.

Supervisors complained that they didn't know what they could tell the
temps and what they could not.[17] Another worker, a machine operator,
stressed that

> it was just so unlike anything we'd done before. This place is a
> good place to work because we're treated like equals. But the
> temps were just there for the short term and so nobody ever re-
> ally got to know them. And they never got to know us.

The temptation to "ride the temps," according to the manufacturing
manager, was great. But rather than do so, he quickly dismissed the
two-tier approach and went directly to counterpart managers in the labs
in search of funds to hire more regular employees and to train the ones
he had. In his words:

> I had to make a pact with the devil. Several pacts, actually. I had
> to threaten to delay some new products, too. I just couldn't
> allow my shop to become a place like you see on TV—you
> know, a factory where you have one group of people who sit and
> another who're busting their humps.

Although the transition took six months to accomplish, the gambit paid
off. The percentage of temps dropped from nearly 50 percent to less
than 10 percent. A wide array of training—from equipment operation to
statistics and quality control methods—was provided. Workers in the
area expressed pride in the fact that a system of job rotation had been
established and that, according to a survey, their SMT line had among
the lowest costs in the company.

Thus, both divisions implemented similar technologies but assigned
different meanings and purposes to them. For East Coast managers in
particular, SMT was an invention in which they had invested substantial
professional and political energy. SMT was, above all, a symbol of their
creative abilities and, as such, their claim to peerage in a company and a
culture dominated by "real" engineers. That they had not achieved true
parity in organizational power with the design lab was downplayed in

---

17. Temporary workers are expected to sign confidentiality agreements with the
company; however, in day-to-day production it is often difficult to tell what is proprietary
information and what is public knowledge.

the face of the opportunity, for a time at least, to be "real" engineers themselves.

More enduring would be the legacy of a production process organized around two distinctly different categories of worker. However, the creation of the two-tier system cannot be explained as the simple product of technological or market forces. Nothing in the concept of SMT required the establishment of one group of experts and one group of less skilled, temporary workers. The efforts of West Coast manufacturing management to achieve a flexible work process and a robust system of work allocation make that clear. Similarly, market pressures and, by extension, organizational efforts at cost containment cannot alone explain why temps came to be a durable feature of the work process at East Coast. Rather, the depth of engineers' conviction that their system would eventually be automated—that their invention would ultimately be complete—led them to create a category of disposable people.

CONCLUSION

The adoption of surface mount technology paid off quite handsomely for this company. As one of the early adopters of the process, the company was able to introduce a number of new products and to strengthen its position in several markets where it had faced considerable competition, especially from Japanese firms. In the short time from the first surreptitious experiments with beakers and hotplates to the creation of new assembly lines, the company successfully revised and improved the process to achieve unprecedented increases in board density and reductions in board size. Thus, there was grounding for the claims of the corporate "official story."

Yet what was most fascinating about the change *process* was the way in which engineers from the conventional side of the organization used unconventional means to bring a new technology into the company. Once again, political as well as technical factors played an important role in screening candidate technologies; but in contrast to the aircraft company cases, the candidate technology was carried in on the shoulders of a "social movement" composed of manufacturing engineers. Despite the barriers that separated them, the manufacturing engineers transformed themselves from a loose affiliation of people occupying similar positions into a cohesive voice for change—change in the physical process of production but, as I have tried to show, change in the status hierarchy of the company as well.

Three factors were critical to the movement. First, the "insurgents" selected a technology that was sufficiently common to their divisions' product lines that they could make a claim to serving general *and* specific organizational objectives. Second, the technology could be presented as both an integrated and an independent change: that is, it was certainly a process change, but when all the pieces were packaged together, it had the appearance of a product. It could therefore be comprehended and appreciated by the design labs. Third, the configuration of SMT as a "process-product" provided an opportunity to turn organizational values that had long been monopolized by designers into a claim to status for manufacturing engineers. It demonstrated that manufacturing engineers could be inventors, too.

The movement fell short, however, in one key sense: it did not substantially alter the status of either manufacturing or manufacturing engineers. Once it became clear that a change would be made, the design labs moved quickly to absorb the new technology and to reassert their authority in the determination of manufacturing procedures. By capitalizing on preexisting differences in product lines and stressing the historical importance of divisional autonomy to the success of the company, designers retained control over the allocation of resources for additional equipment and new variations on SMT. Both manufacturing and manufacturing engineers were reminded that their mission was to serve the labs, not to lead them: the "driven" would not become the "driver."

Although the movement may have failed to achieve some of its broader objectives, such setbacks did not dissuade some members from attempting to see their inventions realized on the divisional level. It is here that a focus on the entirety of the change process provides important insights—especially in explaining the contrasting "impacts" of SMT on the organization of work and workers in the East and West Coast divisions. Although the West Coast engineers had the more ambitious plans for change via SMT (i.e., a fully automated and transferable assembly line), it was the East Coast engineers who went furthest with their invention. However, in their zeal first to automate the process and then to salvage their invention in the face of pressure from the design labs, the engineers–turned–production managers resorted to a system of work organization that divided workers into two classes and centralized knowledge about, and control over, the work process. They clung tenaciously to the "temp solution" in the hopes that someday they would be able to complete their invention. Given that the design labs retained control over the core resources of the manufacturing organization, that someday would quite likely be a long time away. In the interim the "flexibility" of the manufacturing process would depend heavily not on the quality of the labor that could be incorporated into the line but on its quantity.

In the West Coast division, by contrast, manufacturing management was not nearly as invested in the notion of SMT as an invention. They felt no great loss in dismantling parts of the automated SMT line; and although they, too, resented the lower status accorded manufacturing in general, SMT did not appear to be an appropriate vehicle for addressing past grievances. Rather, what was critical there was the opportunity to create a flexible process by combining new technology with a *broader* distribution of knowledge and skill. That is, their working definition of flexibility gave a central role to the quality of the entire work force; instead of centralizing knowledge in experts and thereby erecting a barrier between regular and temporary employees, they sought to decentralize knowledge and thus create a higher average level of skill.

The different definitions of flexibility evident in these two divisions recall a key distinction between the cases analyzed in chapter 2. In both companies, when manufacturing engineers believed—or were encouraged to believe—that the only way they could do "real engineering" was through the creation of independent and self-contained inventions, they proceeded to define their task as one that effectively curtailed or eliminated human discretion in the work process. And even though the computer company did not make a fetish out of "losing heads," the practical result in the East Coast division was the same: heads might not have been lost, but the knowledge in those heads was devalued in favor of what were believed to be flexible machines.

It would, however, be a mistake to conclude that manufacturing engineers are somehow the villains in either company. Attributing to engineers a callous disregard for worker skills or a self-interested desire to control (or eliminate) people and their livelihoods would overlook both the manner in which political processes shape technological choices and the manner in which organizational and intellectual barriers can discourage collaborative approaches to change.

It is ironic that in both the aircraft and the computer companies lower levels of manufacturing management have proven the most open to collaborative efforts at technological choice and change. Long cast by labor process theorists as an undifferentiated part of "management" and intent on controlling work and workers, lower-level managers in the West Coast division and in the CNC case demonstrated far greater attentiveness to technologies that would work *and* that would enhance the knowledge base of the people they supervised. In both settings these same people were scorned for their shortsightedness and resistance to change; yet in both settings they sought to achieve a more productive combination of flexible machines and flexible people.

This counterintuitive finding has significant implications for the future of the industrial enterprise. However, before I can fully elaborate that argument, it is essential to look closely at what I describe in the next chapter as a *collaborative* effort at technological change.

FOUR

Collaborative Change

Technological Choice
in an Aluminum Company

The smelting, forging, and shaping of aluminum is an old and venerable industry. The major companies, as well as many of their plants and products, date back nearly a century, and their image, in the mind of the general public at least, is one of old-fashioned basic industry. Yet age and image are not accurate guides to the internal reality of the industry or the companies that populate it. Inside the aging brick and corrugated walls of eighty-year-old plants are state-of-the-art machines controlled by the latest computers and software. Alongside familiar cast and rolled products are high-tech alloys for airliners, spacecraft, and race cars. Not far from the smoke and fumes of the factory are corporate labs virtually indistinguishable from their counterparts in the Silicon Valley. Mining, manufacturing, and sales organizations are dispersed all over the globe, often in remote locations, but they are linked by a sophisticated network of satellites and computers. The combination of hammer, anvil, and expert system make the aluminum industry a useful point of contrast with the preceding settings.

Equally important for comparative purposes are differences in the role that process technology plays in the aluminum industry. Three dimensions of difference are salient. First, process technology is a key element in economic competitiveness. As in the steel industry, most products are commodity goods, and price competition is fierce. Efficiencies in manufacturing processes can yield significant competitive advantage. Process technology—and technologists—occupy a prominent position in the organization.[1]

1. See, for example, Graham (1990) and Chandler (1962; 1977).

Second, the manufacture of aluminum products more closely resembles a continuous process than do the batch processes that characterized the aircraft and computer companies. Fixed capital investments in plant and equipment are far greater (in both absolute and relative terms), and the exploitation of production capacity is, in many ways, far more critical to the financial well-being of the aluminum company. Thus, accumulated investments in an established process constrain the kinds of products that can be made. For example, if old products are to be made from new materials, they may require substantial investments in new capital equipment; by contrast, changing the functions of an electronic instrument may require only the addition or rearrangement of components on a circuit board, not an entirely new process for circuit board assembly.

Third, the aluminum industry has historically invested a great deal in *both* product and process R&D in order to remain competitive in mature markets and to open new ones (Graham 1990). In the company under study, the lion's share of that money has been directed to a centralized R&D department. By contrast to the aircraft and computer companies, this centralization offered the opportunity to examine technological choice and its consequences under conditions in which a central facility—a rather significant "technostructure," to use Mintzberg's (1979) term—is given direct responsibility to find and implement new technologies.

My initial discussions with representatives of the aluminum company centered on an instance of technological change in a small business unit that had been awarded a citation for technical achievement. Members of the unit had teamed with customers to improve the quality of one of the unit's major products, aluminum alloy wire.[2] However, as our discussions continued, I became increasingly interested in a story that predated and in many ways set the foundation for the quality improvement effort. That story involved the introduction of two new technologies over a period of five years (1984–89). One change consisted of a new system of hardware, computers, and jobs for making wire; the other involved a new set of "recipes" or operational procedures for running an array of alloyed metals through the new system.

A critical feature of both changes, I discovered, was the evolution of a collaborative approach to the change process—one that not only cut across functional and disciplinary lines but succeeded in bridging levels

2. The fact that an award had been given to the business unit suggested that this was a unique accomplishment. At first it made me wary; on reflection, though, I decided that studying an award winner would also provide an effective pretext for exploring how the process of change "normally" occurred.

in the company hierarchy. Though not without contention, the collaborative approach overcame what in this organization had historically been two rigid boundaries: between bureaucratically defined domains at the level of the plant and between the plant and the centralized corporate R&D organization. What emerged from my analysis of company documents and interviews with more than fifty participants (at plant, R&D, and corporate sites) was a picture of collaboration that evolved *despite* great external and internal performance pressures and a period of disarray when the new system seemed to have broken down completely.

Ironically, collaboration was only partly conscious or planned. Indeed, the most unusual part of the story has to do with the way in which conventional procedures were first used to acquire the technology and then transcended as participants devised a common language for describing the problems they faced and a common set of interests in solving them. In short, collaboration acquired a momentum of its own. And without that momentum it would be difficult to explain how an organization with a long history of guarding its processes from external view later opened its doors to collaboration with a customer.[3]

As in the preceding chapters, I begin with a brief depiction of the context and the technology and then move to a detailed analysis of the change process itself.

THE ALUMINUM PRODUCTS COMPANY

The company from which this case study is drawn is one of a small number of vertically integrated producers of aluminum and aluminum alloy products, such as ingots, rolls, and cast products. Its major customers include the aerospace, automobile, and container industries, as well as a host of producers of other finished goods. The company is structured by different phases of the manufacturing process (e.g., smelting, forging, and casting) and by product line. The principal units are product-based divisions that operate as relatively autonomous businesses that range in size from those (e.g., in sheet aluminum and containers) with annual revenues in excess of a billion dollars to those in specialty or low-volume products with only a fraction of that income.

---

3. An additional irony deserves mention: although the division's quality improvement achievements were substantial, if this analysis is correct, the award should also have been made to division and to the R&D center for their collaboration in introducing and refining the new technology in the first place. However, to have done so would have rewarded the two groups for *doing what they are routinely expected to do.*

Like its major competitors, the company has historically invested a great deal in the development of new materials and processes, many of which it has patented. R&D is largely a corporate function, funded out of an accounting "tax" levied against the business units. Special projects may also be underwritten by the business units.[4] The advantages to such a division of labor have been debated in the R&D management literature,[5] but two points deserve specific mention. First, separation from the business units insulates R&D from short-term pressures of budgets, quarterly production goals, and deadlines, and it allows scientists and engineers to work on developing future generations of both products and processes—to "pull" new technology into the organization as well as to create technologies that will provide proprietary advantage. Second, centralization enables R&D to work on issues that cross-cut lines of business with funding that reduces dependence on any single source. In theory, at least, the R&D organization can then serve as a conduit for the transfer of knowledge from one part of the organization to others.

There are, however, potential disadvantages to this approach as well.[6] Chief among them is the fact that housing R&D as a separate administrative unit can create barriers to the flow of knowledge. For example, the absence of direct accountability to a "bottom line" may make R&D appear (and be) detached from the rest of the organization. R&D may become unequally attentive to the needs or the situations of the business units—depending, for example, on the latter's ability to pay for R&D services or to provide R&D with interesting problems to work on. Under such circumstances the R&D organization may be inaccessible to, or uninterested in, small business units. Going "outside" for help—for example, to an external equipment vendor or consultant for

4. One aspect of corporate history deserves special mention since this case study takes place in one of the smaller divisions. This basic structure has been in place for many years, but the independence of the divisions has fluctuated over the past two decades. In the 1970s the company shifted a substantial share of profit-and-loss responsibility to the divisions; with that autonomy came greater divisional control over the expenditure of resources on R&D. The larger divisions moved quickly to influence the research agenda of the R&D center, and some began, at the same time, to build up their own R&D capabilities. Smaller, less profitable divisions found themselves hard-pressed to support R&D and staffing expenses, and according to several people I interviewed, many began to lose ground to their competitors. In the 1980s some controls were recentralized, and corporate-wide functions such as R&D were rebuilt. However, one legacy of the restructuring is a continuing debate as to the "true" charter of the R&D organization.

5. See, for example, Tushman and Moore (1988), Bower (1970), Abernathy, Clark, and Kantrow (1983), and Cohen and Zysman (1987).

6. See, for example, Hayes and Clark (1985) and Allen (1981).

equivalent services—is difficult precisely because technology is a critical element of organizational competitiveness. Finally, the organizational separation of R&D from the businesses is often accompanied by a physical separation. In this company the differences are rather striking: production facilities are hot, noisy, and often dirty places; R&D facilities resemble college campuses, with air-conditioned buildings interspersed among rolling lawns, trees, and recreational spaces.[7]

For the most part the production labor force in this company is unionized. Although company and union have begun to talk about the need for a new style of industrial relations, there have only been small pockets of change in what has remained a traditional, adversarial relationship. By contrast to the experience of the automobile industry (H. Katz 1985), the process of downsizing some operations and modernizing others has not resulted in greater flexibility by either management or the union with regard to traditional dimensions of labor relations: for example, job descriptions and wage grades remain a dense thicket of rules and formal contract language; seniority systems continue to structure the movement of people between jobs and shifts; and most production managers conceal their business and technical plans from the union. The union supports company efforts in such areas as quality improvement and worker participation, but progress to date had revealed few significant changes in day-to-day affairs or in the collective bargaining process. In a study of one aluminum manufacturer, Pavadore (1990) chronicled the ups and downs of quality-of-work-life programs and concluded that without serious and sustained support from middle managers and elected union representatives, change would be slow in coming. Her conclusions apply, I would suggest, to this company as well.

THE TECHNOLOGY

At first glance the technological change under study in this chapter is neither as dramatic nor as exotic as the use of robots to build airplanes or the manufacture of high-tech instruments using printed circuit boards. The development of a new process for making wire for things such as window screens and high-voltage lines may appear a bit droll. However, both the process and the product acquire a certain cachet when we recognize two things. First, continuous casting technology was

---

7. Even though many of the plants have been modernized, it is impossible to wash away the years of grime attached to everything, including the chain-link fences that surround the industrial gray and green buildings.

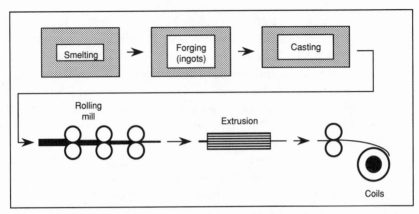

Figure 8. Segmented wire-making process

one of the key devices with which Japanese and Korean producers bludgeoned the U.S. steel industry in the 1970s and 1980s (Hoerr 1989; Dertouzos, Lester, and Solow 1989); this company's move into the technology put it at the forefront of aluminum producers globally. Second, adoption of the technology enabled the company to capture and hold a dominant market position after years of being on a par with its major competitors.

The prevailing technology for casting and drawing aluminum wire is easily fifty years old, and it is in many respects derivative of even older casting practices. Prior to the introduction of the new system, the casting and drawing of wire were segmented, not continuous, activities (see figure 8). In centralized locations aluminum would be smelted from ore and cast into ingots in separate stages. Often ingots would be stockpiled in inventory to await further processing.[8] To make wire, ingots would be pulled from inventory, reheated, and then cast as smaller bars. These bars, in turn, would either be set aside for later processing or sent directly to rolling mills, which would reduce the hot metal to long, narrow rods. Then, if the rods had not been returned to inventory, they would be reheated, drawn to narrower diameters (e.g., three-eighths of an inch in diameter), and coiled around giant spools for shipment. To make continuous spools, lengths of wire would be welded together end to end.

Each stage of the process was organized as a separate unit, with workers, supervisors, technicians, and engineers assigned discrete responsibil-

8. Alternatively, ingots would be shipped directly to customers for use as raw material in their own production processes (e.g., auto companies would cast transmission housings from remelted ingots).

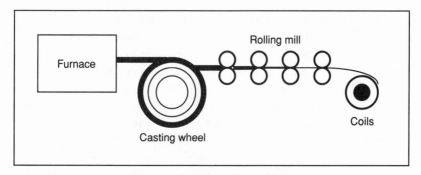

Figure 9. Continuous wire-making process

ities within those units. These units served as "natural" breaks in the overall process; they also acted as bookkeeping units and anchors for the seniority system.

Continuous casting, as implemented in this company, dramatically consolidated wire production in both time and space (see figure 9). In the simplest terms, molten aluminum is now poured in at one end, and seconds later, finished wire emerges at the other end. To be more precise, aluminum and alloys are delivered in a molten state to the casting operation and kept liquid in an adjacent furnace. Hot metal is channeled directly to a vertical casting wheel, which shapes and cools the metal and delivers it to the rolling mill before it has a chance to solidify completely. The rolling mill, in turn, squeezes the rod into a cylindrical shape and reduces its diameter in a series of steps. The progressive extrusion process accelerates the metal from a speed of roughly one-third mile per hour as it leaves the casting wheel to nearly twenty miles per hour as solid wire is wrapped in five-thousand-pound coils around enormous spools.

Continuous casting and rolling does more than eliminate the physical and temporal separation among production steps. It reduces the need for stockpiles of inventory and the physical transfer of ingots and other materials, preventing bumps and scratches that can scar the surface of the metal.[9] It also eliminates the need for transport labor and for inspection between stages in the production process. Because wire is produced in continuous strands, there is no need for welding together pieces to make a complete coil.

The hardware and work reorganization are, however, only a part of what makes continuous casting and rolling different. As I noted earlier,

9. Surface scarring can weaken the metal when it is later drawn to a smaller diameter.

a key feature of the new system is its ability to produce a variety of what are referred to as hard or "mechanical" alloys. These combinations of aluminum and other materials (e.g., magnesium or silicon) are used to produce wire with different properties, such as greater resilience or higher strength at lower weight. Hard alloy wire was produced under the earlier, segmented system, but the real innovation was the creation of a casting and rolling process capable of making a wide variety of wires continuously. Thus, this part of the technology involves the ability to mix materials, deliver them directly to the casting and rolling process, and have them come out the other end with the desired physical properties— and to do it consistently. I use the term "recipe" to simplify what are actually extremely complex procedures for monitoring and controlling the array of variables that govern the process (e.g., heat transfer, molecular structuring, deformation, etc.). Each alloy requires a different recipe.

CHOOSING BETWEEN TECHNOLOGIES

Once the continuous caster was agreed on as the focus for my research, I was given a copy of the original funding proposal. The proposal seemed fairly standard: it announced the wire division's intention to spend several million dollars to acquire a continuous casting process. The new equipment would enable the division to gain advantages in cost and production flexibility over its competition. Payback projections were good but not so extraordinary as to raise eyebrows. Given the time I'd already spent poring over similar documents from the aircraft and computer companies, nothing seemed particularly unusual in either the form or the content of the proposal.

Yet as I reread the proposal, two aspects began to make me wonder. First, the division was proposing to buy the equipment from an outside source, have it installed, and bring it "on-line" without any assistance from the corporate R&D center. Given that I had sought a case in this industry in order to study how centralized R&D departments influenced the process of change, I was a bit surprised (and disappointed). But equally important, I was surprised that a turnkey system would be purchased in a company that prided itself on its own internal capacity to develop new process technologies. How could the division gain competitive advantage by acquiring technology that was available to any one of its competitors?

Second, buried in the proposal was a notice to the effect that the division was planning to take on an outside partner for a substantial role in the financing of the purchase. This aspect was equally surprising: I knew that many companies were moving to strategic alliances and joint ventures as a way to share expertise and financial resources, but such a move on the part of a small division seemed unusual. Two questions nagged me: How could the division make money on this kind of a deal? And how could it avoid "exposing" its methods of production to a customer that was in a position to share that knowledge with those competitors?

Although I had pushed initial impressions and questions into the background in the other case studies, I found these sufficiently perplexing to use them as opening questions in my early interviews with division managers. Those interviews revealed that interest in continuous casting technology had been high for at least five years before formal efforts were made to acquire it. Two issues were seen as important: for some time the division had been looking for a way to break out of what one marketing manager referred to as a "boring horse race" with its major competitors in the wire business. Market leadership was passed back and forth annually, and according to the marketing specialist, "Nobody was making a lot of money in the process." A new technology for making wire was the common answer to the problem. A general manager who had just conducted his own review of the business situation concurred:

> It became very clear that if we were going to survive . . . we had
> to bring in new technology. We couldn't continue to compete
> with what we had. The technology we were using was very high-
> cost and had very long lead times.

Not just any technology would do, however. For the company to break away from the other horses, the new technology would have to gain a significant advantage over the existing process; in particular, it would have to enable the division to make *both* aluminum wire and the much more complex hard alloys with the same process and at a substantial reduction in cost. Precisely which approach to take was the object of debate among division-level and R&D center engineers. No one had developed such a process, and the potential expense seemed considerable. Thus, as a division general manager lamented, "The debate just kept cycling back on itself, and the business went nowhere."

By this point in my research, having completed two major studies in the overall project, I did not consider it unusual to find a problem and a solution (or a set of solutions) waiting in the wings for a decision opportunity. I did, however, question why a company with such a high-powered technostructure should shy away from the challenge of bringing a new process into a division that, by its own admission, was stagnating technically and economically. According to a divisional engineer, the situation seemed all the more ripe for change given that, in his estimation,

> none of the pieces to the technology were all that new. I mean, we already did casting and rolling and drawing, and we had a redraw shop [for making fine wire]. It seemed to some of us that all we had to do was put the pieces together.[10]

Added to that was the awareness at all levels that continuous casting technology was decisive in the successful move of Japanese and Korean firms into the U.S. steel market.

However, two major obstacles hindered bringing the technology into the division. First, corporate management flatly refused to fund the effort—as either a straight purchase from an outside vendor or as a subsidy to the R&D center for doing the development work. According to a divisional manager, cash was in short supply, and even if it had been available, the wire business was not considered all that good a bet: "The company was really not that interested in investing a lot of money in this business without a little more tangible evidence that there was going to be a market for this stuff." Second, there was reason to believe that the R&D center did not rate either the problem or the solution as particularly important. The divisional manager put it bluntly:

> This is a small business by most [company] standards, and this is one of the things we've had to fight. This was a small business that could take a lot of time and resources, and so is it worth their time and effort to do it? . . . So it was a matter of not having higher-level support—and without that support, R&D's not going to feel compelled to listen to you.

Confronted by both financial and organizational roadblocks, divisional managers reviewed their alternatives and concluded that going ahead with the new technology was the only way to expand their business.

---

10. He went on to admit that putting the pieces together *and* making a wide variety of alloy products from one system was unprecedented. Nonetheless, as I argue later, confidence in locally available skills helped keep the technology at the forefront of investment discussions.

Incremental changes in other facets of the operation were deemed safe but likely to offer only marginal gains in profits or sales. Technical challenges and business opportunities brought managers and engineers back again and again to the continuous caster. The divisional manager described the process as one in which he sought consciously to "uncouple the technology debate and get back on the business objectives . . . and then circle back on the technology again." A department manager close to the process described it differently:

> It seemed like we all wanted to go with the new technology but nobody was willing to shoulder all the responsibility. But at some point, I don't remember when, it seemed like we got into a different kind of game—a game like liar's poker. We were all under pressure to come up with reasons why we *could* do it, and pretty soon I'm hearing from one guy that he can install it in this short a time and another guy says he can sell X amount if the guys in production can just produce it. . . . It was easier to sign my name to something when I saw other people—cautious people usually—making equally outlandish promises.

In relatively short order, all other alternatives were abandoned.

The choice process was capped by news from several of the division's customers that a European competitor was marketing alloy wire from a continuous caster. Reports of this development had appeared before, carried by marketing representatives, but had been received skeptically by both divisional and R&D engineers. A marketing staff member recalled that

> there were two things that kept the news from being taken seriously early on. First, nobody trusts marketing. They call us the "Chicken Little" department. Second, they figured that if our engineers couldn't do it, nobody else could.

Having convinced themselves that the technology was not only necessary but feasible, engineers now took the news seriously.

Lacking corporate funding and the resources to underwrite the R&D center, divisional managers elected to try creative financing. Getting a partner to help pay for the equipment was unprecedented, but in an environment of scarce resources, it seemed the only alternative. Besides, as one manager reflected back on his thinking at the time, there was a political point to be made:

We had to go outside of our own resources and funds just to prove that this was something that would pay off in the long term. Being a small business, isolated from [corporate headquarters and the R&D center] and everything, you have to find a way to make things work.

Much to the division's delight—and to the surprise of corporate management—they did find a customer willing to share in the cost.

Finding a partner cemented the choice between technologies, but it also raised a set of thorny questions that had been obscured in the earlier debates and maneuvers. The customer-partner was attracted by the prospect of acquiring the production capacity and price break from its supplier; however, it could also appropriate knowledge about the new technology and pass it along to its other suppliers. Such a move would enable it to reduce the cost of all its wire and avoid the dependency associated with buying from a single source. Equally important, the wire division (like the rest of the company) jealously guarded its processes and equipment from prying eyes. Opening its doors would, as one engineer put it, "meet with profound disapproval from our corporate fathers and our big-brother divisions."

As part of the agreement, therefore, the customer-partner got a share of the product but not of the knowledge. A divisional manager described the agreement this way: "In other words, all they bought was so much time on that caster. We weren't going to tell them anything about the technology. We weren't going to tell them about how it was working. We didn't even tell them we'd bring them in to look at it unless it was something we wanted them to do." Given their success in funding the caster and protecting knowledge about it from capture by the customer-partner, divisional management received corporate blessing for the project. Corporate "fathers" may not have believed the scheme would work, but at least the company's financial risks had been minimized.

At this point in the process, the caster project not only had funding but represented a business challenge, a technical challenge, and, in the context of this company, an opportunity to do something that small divisions did not routinely get to do. For some individuals, it was an opportunity to thumb their noses at corporate management and their bigger "brothers." For others, scoring points in the corporate political arena was less important than the chance to do a conventional thing—bringing in a new technology—even if it meant doing it in an unconventional way.

The unconventional carried with it, however, serious implications for the choices to be made within the technology and for the manner of its use.

CHOOSING WITHIN THE TECHNOLOGY

By going "outside" for funding, the division constrained itself on two sides. On one side, it was under pressure from its customer-partner to put together a process that was neither too exotic nor too expensive. Engineers in the customer-partner company preferred to go with a wheel-type caster because they felt it was better understood and cheaper. It would keep risks to a minimum and hasten the production of aluminum and alloy wire. They (and some technical staff members inside the aluminum company) thus argued for the purchase of a replica of the European system.

On the other side, the division had to be wary of outsiders. Going outside to an equipment vendor for selected pieces of equipment or to a consulting firm for answers to specific questions was not unusual for any division; proprietary knowledge could be kept under cover by, as one technician described it, "getting them in and out as quickly as possible and keeping our mouths shut while they're here." But going outside to contract with a single vendor for an entire system raised the possibility that valuable knowledge would be drained in the process. An engineering manager put it bluntly:

> The fine print in these technology agreements says that it's a two-
> way street . . . that the supplier gets to use what he learns from
> us, as well as we get to pick his brains. But if he just listens to the
> questions we ask, he'll learn a lot more than we will.

Balancing the fear of losing in the exchange was a suspicion among some engineers that no one—including the company that had pioneered the equipment—had mastered the "recipes" for producing hard alloys on the continuous caster.

Ultimately, price and pride forced a compromise. The division would purchase the same system as the one employed by its European competitor, but it would not buy the recipe for making alloys. Participants in the process suggested that price was the most important factor, and, given that the European system was the least expensive alternative and looked like a turnkey operation, the division could get up to speed quickly. Pride in local metallurgical and engineering talent suggested that the division could concoct the recipes once the equipment was in place.

IMPLEMENTING THE TECHNOLOGY

As the aircraft and computer cases showed, the choice process does not end with the decision to adopt a new technology. Critical dimensions of a technology's "impact" are determined in the configuration and implementation of equipment, jobs, and social relations in production. This point is given further support in this case. However, the conduct of the choice process differs in fairly dramatic ways, for reasons that a cursory overview would not reveal.

Descriptions provided by a wide array of respondents suggested that in the past, new technology introductions in the division had resembled the approach taken in the FMS case presented in chapter 2. That is, decision making was a closed process. Lower-level engineers, production supervisors, and hourly workers were kept in the dark until equipment arrived. An engineering supervisor argued that

> normally this is how we do things: we put equipment in and then we stand back and say, "Okay, construction's done. We've debugged it. Blow the whistle and bring on the five guys who're going to run it!"

Such recollections were even more emphatic when people were asked about new technology introductions that involved the R&D center. An operator put the matter succinctly:

> It was like a caste system around here. An [R&D center] engineer would come along, and you didn't speak to him unless he wanted you to speak to him.

A divisional engineer described the traditional approach:

> In the past, we'd try to make sure we had the thing nailed before we turned it over to production. You know, everything would be set up the way we wanted it. Everything would be programmed to the nth degree so nobody could screw it up.

In this instance, however, the people I interviewed described the implementation of the caster as a dramatic break with the past. Even the financial risks, the newness of the technology, and the pressures faced by the division cannot explain the overwhelming enthusiasm with which operators, supervisors, technicians, engineers, and managers described the rollout of the new system.[11] Enthusiasm was expressed as much about the *collaborative* nature of the process as about the outcomes of the effort.

The collaborative approach was rooted in both conscious and unconscious apprehension on the part of divisional management. At one level managers spoke openly about their concern that they satisfy their customer-partner and vindicate their own decision to bring in the new technology. Those concerns dictated careful preparation and the engagement of all the parties involved. Careful preparation was also politically expedient: divisional management felt it could ill afford a negative reaction from workers or the union.[12] In the words of one staff member, "A few well-timed grievances could have killed us."

At another level, however, what loomed in the background was an unspoken apprehension about the things that could go wrong but could not be anticipated. Engineers talked repeatedly about the fact that their plans were ambitious, and each pointed to things they thought might go wrong. For example, a metallurgist said:

> There's always going to be things that you're overly optimistic about. You just look at what you're doing and you informally assign probabilities: there's a 40 percent chance that this will goof up or there's a 20 percent chance that this won't work, etc. You build a little slack into your schedules and your budgets.

What caused most apprehension, however, was what aircraft designers refer to as the "unk-unks," the unknown-unknowns, the problems you cannot anticipate because you don't even know they exist. The potential danger of unk-unks was brought home to the divisional engineers when they encountered a sobering reality: simply because the division had experience in segments of the wire-making process, segmented expertise did not easily add up to a collective understanding of continuous casting technology. Representatives of each process met before the equipment arrived only to find that the consolidation of activities introduced interactions with which no one was completely familiar.

11. For those who have had the opportunity to visit "showcase" plants, especially those that have accomplished a major innovation, it is not uncommon to hear glowing reports from articulate and carefully prepared representatives. The glow usually makes me squint skeptically. However, I spent enough time unsupervised in this setting to be convinced that what I was hearing was genuine.

12. The impending change might have been kept quiet for a long time because plans did not call for any jobs to be eliminated. Moreover, the division was facing tough economic times, and an argument could be made that the new system would bring a measure of stability to jobs that already existed.

Some knew about casting but didn't understand thermal dynamics. Some understood thermal dynamics but didn't understand crystallography. Some understood crystallography but didn't understand rolling mills. No one understood how all the pieces fit together. Thus, up-front investments in preparation and in knowledge sharing would hasten the rollout of the new system and would provide an insurance policy against unk-unks.

The first real test of management's commitment to a collaborative approach came with the decision to build a team around the caster. Group efforts among members of the technical staff were not without precedent, but they usually meant that team responsibilities were added to regular duties or that a fraction of each individual's time would be dedicated to the undertaking. In this case part-time involvement appeared far from sufficient: if the complex technical issues were to be mastered quickly, a group of engineers would have to be turned over to the caster on a full-time basis. Moreover, they would have to be pulled out of their functional homes (and budget lines) and relocated to an organizational place where they could devote themselves to learning about the technology. What might have seemed a simple chore in many organizations—freeing people from other responsibilities in order to create a task force—strained bureaucratic boundaries in this setting. Accomplishing it required approval from top divisional management. Once the decision was made, however, it helped build momentum for even further collaboration.

Building a team of hourly workers was in many ways a far greater challenge. Union officials were advised in advance of the division's plans and assured that this was a special undertaking. No jobs would be lost in the process, union leaders were told, and equally important, this was not an effort to assault long-standing agreements and customs around work organization. After lengthy discussions the union agreed to give some ground in the determination of precise job descriptions and wage levels until the new system was operational, but it held fast on the criteria for bidding onto the jobs (i.e., higher seniority applicants were given priority) and for the general job types that would adhere to the new system—that is, dividing the work among furnace workers, casting process operators, and rolling mill operators.

The establishment of a full-time technical staff and the selection of a core group of supervisors, operators, and maintenance people not only provided a public signal that the caster was a different kind of technical undertaking but also gave the participants the sense that they were engaging in a different form of social undertaking. For example, I asked a production manager who had been close to the planning of the team efforts how he approached his task differently from past assignments. His initial response was revealing:

> Honestly? Well, I didn't really know what I could do or couldn't do. I mean, it was like entering a new territory. I didn't know what the limits were . . . so I decided to do what I thought made sense and wait to see if anybody clobbered me for doing it.

One of the first moves was to introduce hourly workers to the concept of the new technology before it arrived. He went on:

> Oh yeah. Operators were involved. God, the operators were assigned to their positions before the caster was even on site! We had the crew selected and sent a number of people down to [another company site] to watch the caster down there. . . . So many days a week they would do their regular job, and the rest of the week they were assigned to the caster, where the caster was just being installed. The same thing with the maintenance mechanics and electricians. They were assigned, or bid on the job, before the caster actually was up and running. So they got to see it being installed, so they understood what you can't see and what you can see. We had in-house training programs for the operators, and . . . we had the people go down to the wire drawing area to understand what the product was going to be used for. If you take somebody from down in the ingot plant, they really may not have any idea of what wire drawing—what's involved in the wire drawing. So we had them spend time with the cable mill and wire-drawing operations.

Beyond the initial training, the two teams began to meet weekly to share information on the operation of the system. At first, one of the operators told me, those meetings were one-way exchanges: "Engineers would tell us what they thought we should know." Workers responded passively at the outset, but as time wore on and the complexities of the undertaking became clear, the meetings changed tone:

> The engineers started off telling us what they thought we needed to know, but pretty soon we could tell they didn't know every-

thing. So we'd tell them we didn't think they knew everything. Or we'd ask 'em questions we knew they didn't have the answers to. Part of it was we wanted to show them we knew some things, too. Those were sort of bitchy gripe sessions. But eventually we made a truce.

In other words, once it became clear that no one had a monopoly over knowledge of the system—and all sides were willing to admit it—the caster became a collaborative undertaking with a momentum of its own. The feeling of commonality and exclusivity was heightened when meetings were shifted to an assembly hall away from the noise, dust, and fumes of the factory.

The attention and the challenge strengthened the commitment of the workers involved. One operator, nearing the end of his thirty-fifth year working at the site, showed me with great enthusiasm a set of original blueprints he'd saved from the "early days" and described the way his job had changed:

You've now got to have a little bit of computer jock in you, you've got to be an electronics-type person, a metallurgist to a degree. You have to understand what everybody is talking about.

Another worker admitted that the hourly members of the team were probably "special" in that they had bid for jobs on the caster because of the challenge it promised. Yet he also suggested that the promise of a challenge could not by itself account for his enthusiasm:

For the most part you've got guys here with a lot of seniority and a lot of experience with doing things in the old, traditional way. If we felt that management wasn't serious about giving us a chance to do things differently, you can bet we'd have gone back to the old rules very quick.

His sentiments were echoed by the other operators as we talked during one coffee break. Afterward I was shown numerous alterations to the existing equipment that they attributed to their recommendations. A metallurgist who described himself as "an old-timer" offered his own sense of surprise at the level of operator enthusiasm:

I remember a guy on the caster. His kids and my kids happened to be taking piano lessons together. We'd chit-chat about that and see each other at these little piano recitals. He'd be talking shop out there! He wasn't highly educated but he was curious. You could tell because he'd bring up something and say "Well, if we changed this. . . . "

In short, divisional management responded to the combined pressures of "getting into production" and "going it alone" by preparing the ground for a collaborative approach to implementation. They need not have done so; indeed, the inertia of tradition was not overcome in a single moment. However, once collaboration was legitimated formally and informally, it began to build a momentum of its own. Most important, the gradual development of a commitment to knowledge sharing—a recognition of the need to consolidate activities across space and time—convinced all participants that the process would proceed much more smoothly with a greater *breadth* of process understanding than anyone had previously anticipated.

UP AND RUNNING

By all accounts, the installation and initial operation of the new caster went far more smoothly than anyone had anticipated. Of course, the only reference point available was the team's own schedule, but even that was surpassed. Part of the achievement was accorded to a strategy of beginning production with well-known materials, mostly pure aluminum and soft alloys.[13] But the teaming effort was raised repeatedly as an explanation for the rapid move into production.

Efforts to begin standardizing operating procedures were accelerated by a level of trust that had been established among operators and among operators, engineers, and metallurgists. Working closely together, experiencing common successes and failures, and jointly solving problems discouraged the traditional tensions between these groups. As one operator told me emphatically, this was the only time in over twenty years of working on site that he'd *not* kept a "little black book" that detailed the tricks he'd used to run a particularly difficult operation but that he'd concealed from supervisors and engineers. Instead, he argued, there was no reason for a black book:

13. According to one metallurgist, there was nothing new in the casting of their principal product: "The stuff we began with was very well known. I mean, hell, we'd been doing [soft alloy] for a long time. Everybody knew how to do it. You could give an Amazon monkey five minutes of instruction and he could do it!"

I'd gotten to know those guys in our trial by fire and I'd come to
have more respect for what they brought to the problem. So,
yeah, I didn't hide what I knew like I used to or the other guys
used to.

The sense of common mission and joint learning carried over to other
practices that had traditionally generated tension. Supervisors who had
traditionally been excluded from hands-on involvement in running the
machines were allowed to get their hands dirty. A veteran furnace
operator recalled:

We cut those guys a lot of slack. . . . We let them tinker around
because we were all trying to make this work. It was new to all
of us and they needed to learn, too.

Similarly, metallurgists and engineers anxious to experiment with running hard alloys were able to get time on the system. Their sense of
excitement grew with each opportunity and the freeing of time on the
system allowed further progress to be made.

At the same time, the process of translation was a process of discovery. For example, earlier tests of sample products from their European
competitor revealed that *both* hard and soft alloys could be run through
the rolling mill at far greater speeds than had been deemed possible.
Higher speeds translated into lower costs, greater productivity, and potentially reduced response times to customer orders. Equally important, as
engineers became more familiar with the equipment, they began to
uncover and correct flaws in the manufacturer's design, adding functions that were not included in the equipment they bought (e.g.,
in-line inspection), and making myriad adjustments to optimize the
system.

HITTING A BRICK WALL

Roughly a year and a half after the equipment was installed and after a
period of successfully producing soft alloys, the entire system, in the
words of one observer, "hit a brick wall." To be specific, a combination
of new business pressures and knowledge constraints brought the process
nearly to a halt. The shutdown of one of the division's major customers
dramatically reduced the demand for soft alloy products. The division
was forced to accelerate its efforts to produce large volumes of hard alloys
in order to keep the caster running and to help sustain sales revenue. Yet it

soon became clear that the local knowledge base necessary to accomplish the transition simply was not adequate to the task. What had appeared to be a small intellectual hurdle—a stepwise increment in sophistication—loomed as large and as impenetrable as a brick wall.

Despite early efforts to increase the breadth of process understanding, the shift into hard alloys revealed limits to the *depth* of process understanding. In the early stages of operation it seemed sufficient for operators to know their individual jobs and to understand the relationship between their part of the overall system and adjacent activities. There was no need, in the words of one engineer, to "make scientists out of a bunch of blue-collar guys." A similar assessment carried over to divisional engineers and technicians. An engineering manager summarized his sentiments at the time this way: "We figured our hammer-and-anvil techniques were more than good enough for doing the harder stuff." Doing the "harder stuff" turned out to demand a greater depth of process knowledge; it required from both technical staff and operators a more fundamental understanding of the "science" that underlies the system— that is, going beyond the hardware to include properties and dynamics of the raw materials as they went from melting, mixing, casting, and rolling to coiling, and then the interaction of the two.

Ironically, sophisticated sensors built into the system—in the hopes that someday the entire process could be automated—compounded the confusion the engineers and technicians faced. They were, in the words of one team member, literally awash in data. Computers cranked out numbers (about heat, rolling speed, etc.), and tests of sample wire spewed out analyses of composition, grain size, and physical structures, but very few of the numbers made any sense. There were far too many variables and far too little understanding of what they meant.

Breakdown in the operation of the system forced divisional managers and technical staff into a choice situation. Experimentation could continue in the hopes that a breakthrough would solve the breakdown, or outside help could be solicited to arrive at a solution. The choice was neither obvious nor easy. Recalling the equipment vendor would resuscitate negotiations over the cost and the ownership of the "recipes." Going to the corporate R&D center to get help was appealing, but that was not a simple matter either. As noted earlier, this was a small division without a great deal of cash to spend at the R&D center. Moreover, fears about time lost in "educating" the R&D center about the system and memories about the relative inattentiveness of the R&D organization to business pressures and deadlines argued against looking to it as a white knight. Worse yet, divisional technical staff recognized that the problems they faced were complex and bedeviled by physical interactions that cross-cut disciplinary boundaries. An adequate response on the part of the R&D center would thus require not only concentrated attention—something that would be expensive and would require dedicated personnel—but interdisciplinary attention—that is, a "team" effort at least an order of magnitude greater than had been employed to implement the caster at the plant level.

Less obvious, but equally important, was the requirement that a dedicated, interdisciplinary effort be able to communicate across differences in *knowledge bases, time horizons,* and *status and class lines.* Even if a team could be created and resources made available, translation would have to be accomplished between the science of the R&D center and what was described as the "hammer-and-anvil" techniques of those who worked at the level of the plant. Although operators' black books had been eliminated, a tremendous amount of tacit or working knowledge resided in the heads of operators and technical staff members; unless and until it could be translated into terms, variables, and relationships that made sense to R&D center staff, it would be largely invisible. Conversely, if the knowledge of the R&D center could not be translated to plant-level people, R&D's solutions would largely be opaque: they might work and they might be codifiable as new standard operating procedures, but they would provide only limited insight as to the underlying dynamics and principles of the system and therefore would be difficult to extend to new materials or to analyzing operational problems that occurred once the R&D center staff returned to headquarters.

Time horizons would have to be bridged to allow R&D center staff adequate opportunity to adjust to the pressures of production while still thinking in more fundamental terms. Equally important, the operational time frame of the plant would have to be extended from a day-to-day or week-to-week orientation to allow for the likely slow and fitful progress of R&D research.

Status and class lines posed subtler but more formidable problems. In this as in the other cases described in this book, historically entrenched distinctions between "professional" engineers and their manufacturing counterparts and between engineers and hourly workers formed a significant part of the organization's culture. Though perhaps not as extreme as described in the aircraft or computer company cases, the distinctions among engineers were real in terms of compensation, promotional opportunities, and perceived intelligence. The situation was underscored by one R&D manager:

> It's not pleasant but you have to face it. Many people here [at the R&D center] think of themselves as scientists, a better class of people. Going out to the plants and talking to the guys in white socks is not easy. They think they know everything and obviously they don't; otherwise, why would they be calling us to get their nuts out of the fire?

Equally important, an extended focus on plant-specific problems—however challenging they might appear to some R&D center staff who saw a need to support the business units—carried the risk that a problem might be solved, but valuable time would be lost in the process. In the currency of the R&D center, the "real" challenges came from opening new domains of knowledge to scientific and professional inquiry and generating data that could be published in the right journals. One staff member put it bluntly:

> If you had your choice of working on the next generation of aerospace materials for supersonic transports or working on something that's going to be used for hanging a car muffler, which are you really going to want to work on?

Not only were such accomplishments rewarded financially, but they also brought attention to those who were professionally recognized. Getting bogged down in a plant-level problem that arose from decisions made without the advice of the R&D center staff was seen as professionally counterproductive and, at best, unhelpful in terms of career progression.

Class lines represented an important source of confusion and apprehension. Several of the R&D center staff I interviewed imagined the plant as a dark and dirty environment pervaded by mystery and, in some ways, danger. Relations between workers and managers were mysterious: things never ran as smoothly or as efficiently as they could. Lacking a better understanding of the social system of the plant, engineers were apt to attribute the mystery to characteristics of the workers themselves. For example, one engineer gave this impression of how R&D staff were perceived:

> These guys on the floor, they see some crazy researchers coming and they think, "Here comes trouble. They're going to ruin my

life and I have to go to a ballgame after work and I'm going to get all screwed up."

Nothing of great value could be gained by participating in that world— much less by trying to understand it fully—and therefore even those who felt it necessary to "talk to" the operators in order to do their work did not actively entertain the idea of becoming intimately familiar with the social life of the plant. Some were actively discouraged from crossing the line:

When I first got into the position I'm in, . . . my boss told me, insisted on, that I do not talk to hourly people.

Workers for their part expressed little open animosity for the scientists and engineers, but several noted suspicions as to their motives and willingness to really try to understand production "life" as workers experienced it. One operator argued that for most of his twenty years in the plant:

The doctors from [the R&D center] would strut around here like they owned the place. They might talk to you once in a while, but they'd never really care what you thought. They could come in and leave and we'd be stuck trying to make sense of what they wanted us to do.

COMMUNICATING ACROSS BOUNDARIES

Divisional management chose to go "outside inside," but they pursued a very different strategy than they might have in the past. First, they set aside far more money than they had ever expended on R&D. Second, they sought explicitly to use those resources as a lever to encourage R&D to dedicate a core group of specialists to the caster project. The first tactic could be accomplished by divisional management fiat. However, the second could at best be stage-managed with incentives structured around things that mattered to the R&D center.

At root was the relative power of the two sides to define the problem. In the early stages of caster operation, there was no problem, and thus the division pursued its traditional approach to the R&D center. As described by a divisional manager:

We tended to walk by all these technologies that people [in the R&D center] were working on and say, "Oh, geez, that one

looks like it's got some merit. How about if we give them
$35,000 and they keep us posted on what they're doing. Let's see
if we can get a tenth of a man-year of his time, or her time."

In other words, money would be spent in the hope that, at some unspeci-
fied future date, there would be a payoff. In this case, however, seed
money would not do the job. The division was desperate for solutions to
what it perceived to be its problem.

The attention of the R&D center had to be captured *and* focused on
real, pressing problems. Yet the division could not attempt to define the
problem; it had to leave open the nature of the problem to definition by
the R&D center. The latter's diagnostic capabilities were clearly not to
be underestimated; but allowing them to conduct the diagnosis was
equally critical. In the words of one divisional manager close to the
process:

You don't tell them what they can do for you. You tell them
what problems you're having and they tell you what they have to
offer.

His assessment was quite accurate, especially when paired with the
following remarks expressed by a research scientist from the R&D
center:

Most of the plants I have dealt with . . . they tend to be a bit con-
fused. You have to spend several months trying to find out what
the exact problem is.

The analogy of doctor-patient relations is not too far from the mark
in describing the situation. That is, the patient (division) suffered from a
variety of ailments, some of which it believed it could understand and
relate to an underlying cause. But to entice the doctor effectively, it had
to refrain from suggesting too strongly that it had its own diagnosis of
that underlying cause. Moreover, this patient knew that, although its
ability to pay was an inducement, more important would be its ability to
present the doctor with an interesting case.

The complexity of the situation was multiplied by the recognition that
the problem did not reside in the intellectual or the professional domain
of any single R&D discipline. Put differently, several language barriers
would have to be crossed: between engineering disciplines (e.g., mechanical and electrical), between engineering and metallurgy, and between
the R&D center and its counterparts in the division. This dimension of

the problem was best described by an R&D center metallurgist when asked about his experience of working with other plants. He argued that

> you talk your own language essentially, but there are lots of
> times when you look at people's faces and find very little under-
> standing of what you're talking about.

This comment reveals a critical juncture: if R&D center personnel don't feel they need to find alternative means to communicate, they can withdraw, write off the confusion to ignorance or lack of "real" interest on the part of the audience, and go back to the lab. If the division is "serious" (i.e., the patient really wants to be cured), then the staff scientist may, in his words,

> struggle to find a common ground . . . make the effort to learn
> their language and then figure out how to say what I know in
> that language.

In this case, divisional managers took great pains to structure their relationship with the R&D center (the doctor) without appearing to dictate the content of that relationship. Several referred to this technique as an explicit extension of the collaborative approach to problem solv-ing and implementation they had experienced in the caster area. That is, they spent considerable time convincing R&D center managers that their ailments were real, urgent, *and* interesting. They offered the plant as a subject for experimental treatments. They paid for an airplane to shuttle R&D center personnel from the lab to the plant and back in the same day. And they gave R&D scientists and engineers ample opportu-nity to define the plant's problem. But they also stressed that the teaming approach they had nurtured in the plant was something they wanted to continue.

For their part, R&D center staff responded enthusiastically to both the situation and the inducements. The R&D manager given responsibil-ity for composing a team played a pivotal role in relating the divisional situation to his staff and in convincing them of the benefits to be had from cooperation with the plant. He assembled his own team and then coached its members on how to respond to plant-level personnel. For example, one younger team member recalled being advised to be as blunt with certain plant staff as they were likely to be with him. As a plant-level engineer who was alleged to be a "hard case" later told me, this approach paid off:

> I didn't know these guys from Adam and you can bet that I'm
> not an easy guy to get along with. But, I'll tell you, they stood up
> and said what they knew and that earned my respect.

The success of the liaison role depended on the ability of the R&D
manager to interpret across organizational boundaries. As one of the
divisional operations managers argued:

> He can walk into a meeting and speak the same language
> whether he's on the floor with the operators or back at the R&D
> center with a bunch of Ph.D.s.

Even more critical than the inducements and the efforts to construct
a viable relationship was the creation of a common language and a
shared commitment among members of the expanded project team.
Neither communication nor commitment was easily achieved, and at least
from the perspective of those I interviewed, one was not sufficient without the other. Commitment to a common goal or enterprise was essential
to people making the effort to translate their own discipline- and function-
based interests into a common vocabulary. Conversely, continuing efforts
to achieve familiarity with one another's perspective, principles, and
experience cemented a sense of common benefit in the research process.

A good example of this escalation of commitment involved an attempt by R&D engineers to define and then model the parameters
influencing the performance of the caster. Plant-level engineers could
describe the operation of the system in terms of what they could see,
hear, smell, and feel, but they suspected that things were going on that
affected the casting process that they couldn't measure or track with
human senses. R&D engineers interpreted what they heard in terms of
mechanical, electrical, and chemical processes, but they could not immediately translate their thoughts into words that made sense to non-
initiates. After several false starts, the R&D engineers began an
interrogatory with plant personnel from which to build a mathematical
model of the process. The interchange continued slowly until one engineer suggested that they translate their equations into a series of computer drawings and then videotape the "operation" of the caster from
the screen of a workstation. Suddenly the visual image became an
intellectual link between what the R&D engineers "saw" mathemati-
cally and what the plant-level engineers saw physically. One production
supervisor suggested that

not everybody has the same background, and the videotapes
were a way to show results without having to go into the mathe-
matics of the thing. Something people can see and understand.

The videotape became a vital part of the emerging common language.

The benefits of achieving a common language might have remained
exclusively at the level of the "peer" engineers had it not been for the
teaming effort that had preceded the effort to run hard alloys. But in
large measure because the earlier effort had helped forge mutual respect
between operators and engineers at the plant level, R&D center engineers and scientists were encouraged to share their findings much more
broadly. The payoff, as described by both engineers and operators, was
a *deepening* of the knowledge base of all those involved with the caster.

For example, one R&D engineer marveled at what he learned from
the collaboration: "It gave them [operators] a pretty good process
understanding. Before, they knew they had problems but they didn't
know why." Likewise, he argued:

> I didn't have much reason before for really trying to explain
> what I was doing. But the more I got to respect what they
> knew—and what they could do—the more I got to recognize
> that learning was a two-way street.

A veteran caster operator described what he'd learned in similar terms:

> When you're working on something that looks like a black box
> and you just do things from the outside, you don't know what is
> happening. All of a sudden you're able to see what's going on in-
> side. For me that was a real eye-opener.

In other words, collaboration left behind a *deeper and more detailed
process understanding at the level of the plant* that was made possible by
efforts to devise and sustain a common language that cut across intellectual and bureaucratic boundaries. Moreover, it enabled the overall team
to carry their lessons learned to other efforts: the members of the R&D
side of the team—especially those who aspired to managerial ranks—argued that their future goals included teaming activity of the sort they
experienced in the rod caster project. At the level of the plant, the
teaming experience and the respect for the benefits to be gained from
communicating and learning across boundaries were later employed in
the quality improvement effort. This undertaking earned the division the
corporate award for technical achievement—but as I noted at the outset

of the chapter, the real achievement was the creation of a collaborative process for assigning meaning and purpose to new technology.

CONCLUSION

Like the preceding chapters, this one has provided a window on technological change and its "impact" on organization. And once again the choice of technology was shown to be filtered through political, technical, and economic screens. Managers and engineers used their group and individual interests to define a situation in which a new technology was required, and then they selected among possibilities in light of those interests and objectives. The choices they made embroiled them in dependencies and constraints that were unprecedented, certainly in their own experience, but that, once established, encouraged further departure from "normal practices"—especially in their approach to the configuration and implementation of the new technology. Although this entire process might be written off as a product of extraordinary circumstances, it is also worthwhile to recall that of the three companies studied thus far, this is not only the oldest but easily the one most encrusted with a history of bureaucratic rules and relationships.

The innovation they initiated was at least as impressive a social process as a technical one, but the implications of the former were far more difficult to predict. Collaboration and knowledge sharing clearly were not explicit objectives at the outset when managers urged preparation for the new technology. But once initiated and once grasped as a legitimate approach, collaboration yielded a powerful social process for identifying and solving problems. Most important, it resulted in a breadth of information sharing and process understanding that enabled engineers and workers to get the system "up and running" rapidly. Moreover, it helped establish a social system of production that was remarkably flexible and robust in the face of what appeared to be a catastrophic breakdown in the technical system.

Collaboration yielded another powerful but unanticipated consequence—a sort of positive organizational "unk-unk." It served as a template for dealing with what had been perceived to be an aloof and rather recalcitrant resource in the form of the R&D center. Engaging the R&D center involved an elaborate and politically sophisticated set of inducements. It built from what could perhaps best be described as an ethnographic approach to the problem. That is, managers and engineers devoted considerable energy to analyzing the social system of the company, especially that of the R&D labs, in search of a better understanding of the worldviews that made up the company. The collaborative approach, based on this understanding, effectively transformed a hierarchical "doctor-patient" relationship into one defined by common interests and facilitated by a common language. The process understanding that had been broadened as a partly conscious goal of the first stage of collaboration was deepened as a result of the second stage.

A critical feature of the collaborative approach to choice and change was a conscious and *public* recognition that the knowledge necessary to make the technology work did not reside in any one functional department or level in the organizational hierarchy. Though the perceived centrality of this technology to the future of the business unit might have made it easier to admit, the admission itself required, for lack of a better term, a kind of courage not often found in organizations such as this—or the aircraft and computer companies already studied. As in the prior cases, managers and technologists were both directly and indirectly discouraged from admitting incomplete knowledge: promotion and reward systems encouraged either *bravado* (e.g., in the form of claims built on shaky data or rhetorical images of "modernity") or *docility* (e.g., refusing to push the boundaries of knowledge about a process for fear of angering the design organization). Rigid barriers between functional and professional groups encouraged knowledge hoarding, jealousy, and suspicion—leading manufacturing engineers to covet opportunities to do "real engineering" and other departments to lie in wait preparing to ambush change proponents at the first sign of vulnerability. Moreover, hierarchy and concerns about the legitimacy of managerial authority discouraged the possibility of trusting subordinates—especially those at the point of production—or admitting that they might have knowledge or capabilities that higher levels did not have or did not productively employ.

Managers and engineers in this case walked a fine line when they admitted that their process was not well enough understood. R&D center engineers were quite prepared to rush in to save the patient—a practice from which they historically derived considerable influence over the process of technological choice. But by transforming a situation in which they lacked knowledge into a situation in which knowledge sharing was based on trust and commitment, business unit leaders effectively engaged all parties, including workers, in a process of joint learning. Equally important, they helped establish very different grounds for legitimating managerial authority: no individual or group was given an opportunity or a reason to claim sole proprietorship over the technology, to employ it as a hammer to bludgeon anyone else, or to withhold information as a hedge against being blamed for its failure.

More fundamentally, perhaps, the collaborative approach changed the rules of the game. It broadened the search for solutions beyond the purely technological fix, and it legitimated the idea that investments in the social system of production could have impacts as dramatic and as positive as investments in the technical system. In fact, it legitimated two levels of investment in the social system: first-level investments in skills and abilities necessary to accommodate the technological change; and second-level investments in the *capacity to change*. Most organizations, including the pair studied in preceding chapters, routinely make the first-level investments. They are necessary simply to make a process work: whether the new equipment or system is invented in-house or acquired from the outside, training is included as part of the purchase price. Second-level investments, by contrast, are not routinely made because they are difficult to describe, much less to justify: how can you justify investing in the breadth and depth of the knowledge base of production workers, for example, when the purchase of new technology is predicated on the idea that heads will be "lost" and that people will "go away"? Yet in this case it was the second-level investment that enabled the area to recover from catastrophe and, more important, to set the stage for continuous improvement and change.

In the final case study, we encounter another collaborative effort at change, one that takes place in an equally old and venerable setting—the auto industry. Like the aluminum company, it is a study of an organization struggling to define a new self-concept and new ways to structure the relationship between people and technology. From it we will catch another glimpse of a possible future for the industrial enterprise.

FIVE

A Contest over Content

Technological Choice in the Auto Industry

This chapter is best begun with a story:

In trying to arrange a case study in the U.S. auto industry, I called a contact I had in a parts manufacturing plant. I explained my objectives and, although I thought my much-practiced introduction was fairly clear, he kept asking, "But what do you want to see?" I repeated that I wanted to study how the company makes decisions about new technology and mentioned several examples, including a flexible machining system that had been installed recently in his plant. Finally, in a tone of exasperation, he said:

> Look, we've got two tours we can give you. One is what I call
> the "human relations" tour and the other is the "factory automa-
> tion" tour. One gives you the warm and fuzzy and the other gives
> you the bells and whistles. Which one did you have in mind?

My initial, unspoken thought was to protest that I was after more than just a tour. But after a moment's reflection I realized that his remarks suggested three very interesting hypotheses: (1) The same technology could be represented in very different ways (e.g., as a social or a technical innovation), and I was being asked which script I wanted to hear. (2) This person (and perhaps others in the site) had been visited often enough to actually script tours. And (3) people who visited either wanted or received only one of the two possible scripts.

Later, as I reread my field notes and interviews, I found that initial interchange to be a revealing commentary on technological change in this setting. New technology, in the form of a sophisticated machining cell, had been given two scripts: one authored by the engineers who designed it initially and oversaw its implementation; the other by those who used it. In an earlier era factory automation alone would have been showcased; there would not have been a human relations script. However, the equal billing now accorded the two suggests that a new approach to technology and work organization might be emerging: one in which users play an expanded role in the choice of technology and, therefore, in organizational structuring.

In this chapter I will argue that the story of the FMS offers an important window on changes being experienced and debated in the auto industry at large. Those changes have been hypothesized in the literature as a transition from mass production or "Fordism" to new approaches depicted in evocative phrases such as "flexible specialization" and "lean production."[1] Fordism, the archetype of mass production, consisted of long production runs, standardized parts and standardized jobs, a detailed division of labor, enormous inventory buffers, and, at root, an infatuation with control—over people, processes, and products. Flexible specialization and lean production, by contrast, feature shorter production runs, an emphasis on the versatility of people and processes, the elimination of slack through minimal inventories and careful attention to quality, and, of necessity, greater organizational flexibility in responding to environmental change.

Despite a growing sentiment that Fordism is indeed being rivaled and, in some instances, supplanted by new approaches, a pivotal issue has yet to be resolved: how will control be exercised? Or more appropriately, *who* will control the lean and flexible production system? Inside the auto companies, as this case will demonstrate, the debate is intense, even if it is rarely made public.

For the sake of introduction, two sides can be distinguished. One side acknowledges change in the competitive environment but adheres to a Fordist conception of engineering and management. From this perspective, flexibility may now be a key objective, but the exercise of control remains one of detecting and eliminating unwanted variation—a major source of which remains the human "variable." Thus, computer con-

---

1. See, for example, Piore and Sabel (1984), Sabel (1982), Krafcik (1988), Krafcik and MacDuffie (1989), Womack, Jones, and Roos (1990), Clark and Fujimoto (1991), and Dertouzos, Lester, and Solow (1989). For a somewhat less optimistic assessment of the nature and direction of changes taking place in the industry, see Parker (1985), Parker and Slaughter (1988), Wells (1986), Hyman (1989), and Thomas (1988).

trols and information systems are seen to be modern replacements for the mechanical pacing of the conveyor belt or the time and motion study.

From the other side, control is no longer the property of the technology or the policing function of a management hierarchy. It is instead a responsibility shared among those who design, deploy, and operate the physical apparatus of production. Proponents of lean and flexible production systems presuppose *both* understanding and commitment on the part of the people who make the system work. This approach requires greater skills, not diminished ones, and greater commitment, not an instrumental orientation toward work.[2] More important, the tight coupling brought about by just-in-time inventory controls, in-process inspection, and the cost of engineering changes makes lean production extraordinarily reliant on the willingness and the ability of people to monitor and correct technology.

To date, at least, few opportunities have been provided to study in detail the emergence of a new approach to production.[3] This case offers a unique opportunity to examine the way in which meaning and purpose are attached to technology during an era of organizational and environmental change.

THE AUTO COMPANY

The setting for this case is a parts manufacturing plant in a U.S.-based auto company. Along with several other plants, it forms the core of the company's engine and fuel systems division. The bulk of the plant's products are consumed by the corporation's major car and truck lines. A small but growing fraction of its output, however, is produced under contract with other companies, including major competitors in the world auto industry.

Like many parts-producing plants in the company, this facility had been buffeted severely by the combined forces of global competition and business cycles. In the period under study (1984–1989), the plant had

---

2. Adler (1986; 1987) provides one of the clearest statements of this perspective.

3. This is not to deny the insights to be gained from research that seeks to document and then explain differences in outcomes, especially performance outcomes, associated with traditional and "lean" (e.g., Womack, Jones, and Roos 1990) or "robust" and "fragile" production systems (e.g., MacDuffie 1990). Indeed, as I argue throughout this book, it is essential to *complement* outcome- or impact-oriented research with studies of the processes through which those outcomes are created.

come under considerable pressure from corporate headquarters to achieve cost competitiveness with outside suppliers. The pressure reached a peak in the early 1980s, when the plant faced a complete shutdown ("mothballing"). From a peak of nearly four thousand hourly and salaried employees in the 1960s, employment dropped to fewer than two thousand in 1980 and climbed slowly to twenty-three hundred in 1990. A series of divisional and corporate reorganizations in the decade of the 1980s only added to the flux. At the time of my research (early 1990), hourly workers averaged fifteen years of seniority. No new hires had been made in nearly eight years.

From the outside the plant would be difficult to distinguish from any of a thousand industrial sites, but its interior exhibited a curious combination of the old and the new, the used and the abandoned—leaving the distinct impression of a system in transition. For example, adjacent to a cluster of bright yellow and chrome machine tools stood decrepit lathes and punch presses leaking oil and clattering with noises that betrayed their age. Off to one side and cloaked in dusty plastic sheeting rested a large metal panel studded with gauges and switches; this, I was told, was the heart of an automated machining system that had been partially installed when the company decided to "outsource" (subcontract) the parts and abandon the equipment. While the loading docks were largely empty as trucks arrived promptly to cart away finished goods, several million dollars of raw materials and semifinished parts lay scattered throughout the plant.

The same impression carried over to the organization of the plant. On one hand, the plant was structured along very traditional lines. Each of the major areas (e.g., assembly, fabrication, maintenance) contained three layers of management—superintendent, general supervisor, and supervisor—in a structure largely unchanged for forty years. Outside the plant, hourly and salaried employees parked in lots separated by a fence topped with barbed wire. A traditional union hierarchy paralleled the management structure. Several elected union representatives complained openly that their main job was handling grievances and engaging in lengthy preparations for the next round of contract negotiations. On the other hand, however, plant managers and union leaders pointed to a long list of joint committees and innovative work practices that they claimed to be decisive breaks with tradition in the domain of industrial relations. Union officials regularly attended the plant manager's staff meetings, where they received updates on the business climate, plant performance, and corporate plans for upcoming product lines. Next door to the plant cafeteria, finishing touches were being put on a million dollar training facility formally dedicated to preparing workers and supervisors for new generations of manufacturing and information technology.

Although the transitional nature of the plant's physical and social organization must be understood in terms of its specific history, an important part of the story resides in developments at the level of the company and the industry. During the period in which the FMS was being developed and implemented, two distinct strategies of organizational restructuring and change were unfolding in that larger context. One strategy, endorsed by corporate management in this and the other U.S. automakers, emphasized technological "renewal." Specifically, the company set aside an unprecedented sum of money for repairing aged capital equipment and acquiring advanced manufacturing technology in the form of robots, information systems, and the latest in computer-controlled machines. The other strategy involved efforts to reshape the social organization of production. It focused directly, though not exclusively, on reform of the system of union-management relations. Kochan, Katz, and McKersie (1986) characterize it as an effort to move from an adversarial relationship focused on collective bargaining and a legalistic governance process to a multilevel process of cooperation featuring programs of employee participation and information sharing between the company and the union.

These two strategies roughly coincided with the sides taken on the internal debate over control. Although not subscribing publicly to a technological "fix," ardent supporters of technological renewal were far more comfortable investing in machines and computers than in new forms of social organization. Conversely, those who favored reform in the social system of production did not (and in many cases could not) oppose investment in new technology; but they did question whether technology could work without skilled and committed employees.

Given the complexity of the companies and the relatively long time horizons associated with both renewal and reform, each side had substantial opportunity to pursue its strategy/definition in isolation. As indicated in previous chapters, the choice between and within technologies often takes place over a period of years. The same applies to the engineering of change in the social relations of production. Both are further insulated by functional and hierarchical divisions within these giant organizations themselves. However, as this case will show, they do ultimately intersect and interact. When they do, the outcome is far from predictable.

THE TECHNOLOGY

The technological change at the core of this chapter concerned the installation of an FMS in the machining area of the plant. It is a larger and somewhat more sophisticated version of the cell described in chapter 2. From a novice's perspective, it certainly lives up to its "bells and whistles" billing. The cell (depicted in figure 10) consists of nine machining centers or tools connected by wire-guided transfer shuttles (or automated guided vehicles [AGVs]). The machines and shuttles are linked to a computer-controlled storage and retrieval system. The machining centers form two sides of a large horseshoe, at the base of which stands inspection equipment that combines laser and other optical equipment to gauge the dimensional accuracy of finished parts.

When operating according to plan, this FMS is almost fully automated: humans "assist" the system only at the beginning and end of the process. To be more precise, rough castings are delivered on pallets from a nearby casting facility, hand-loaded onto tooling fixtures, placed atop a waiting shuttle, delivered to one of the machine tools, and then retrieved for movement to the inspection station. After inspection, parts are transferred by hand to small wire baskets; these are in turn whisked away to an automated storage and retrieval system or, if needed immediately, stacked in containers for shipment to the assembly area.

The machine tools at the heart of the FMS are of a sort that puts them somewhere in between the two types discussed in the aircraft company cases. They are CNC machines, like the shop-programmable equipment in chapter 2, and can be programmed and operated as stand-alone machines. However, they are also wired into a central computer that can either drive them individually or control all nine via an integrated electronic network. Thus, by contrast to the FMS in the aircraft company, this system has the flexibility to shift from complete computer control (e.g., for long runs of a small number of different parts) to individual, machine-level control (e.g., for small runs of a large number of different parts).

Surrounding the FMS is what one engineer described as an "envelope" of software for monitoring operations. Sensors enable supervisors and engineers to "dial up" and monitor any part of the system as it

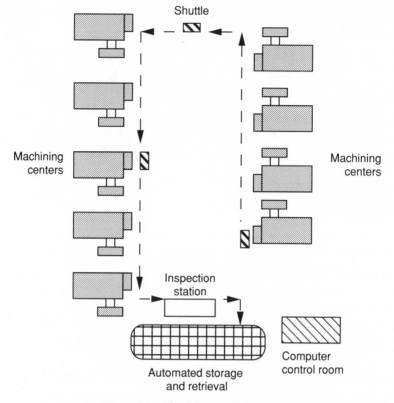

Figure 10. Flexible machining system

operates (in real time) or to collect data for later analysis. For example, an engineer can sit in her office and call up a screen to tell which machines are running and how fast or to get a summary of actual versus planned performance of each machine. Other software ties the system into an inventory data base to track the arrival, storage, and departure of individual parts.

Although the engineer who gave me a tour of the area boasted that the addition of robots at both ends of the cell would enable it to run in a lights-out mode, the FMS was a hive of human activity for much of the time I was on site.[4] In addition to the pair of loaders, there were three machine operators, three set-up workers, one quality control inspector,

4. This was one of three tours I eventually received. A manufacturing engineer introduced me to the "bells and whistles." A union steward teamed with a salaried trainer to give me the "warm and fuzzy" tour. And a machine operator, having seen me get my two other tours, insisted on taking me through to see "how it really works."

three maintenance workers, two manufacturing engineers, and two production supervisors in the area.[5] Apart from the manufacturing engineers assigned to support the FMS on a half-time basis, all others were dedicated to the area. Operators and set-up workers were each responsible for three machines. Set-up workers adjust the machines for cutting and grinding different parts and are given limited authority to modify computer programs; they must clear any changes they make with their supervisors before proceeding. Operators who have not been qualified through classroom training and on-the-job testing are prohibited from "touching" the software. Maintenance workers, divided by specialty into electrical, hydraulic, and pneumatic systems, perform routine servicing and make emergency repairs.

CHOOSING BETWEEN TECHNOLOGIES

As I began to study the process through which new manufacturing technology arrived in and "impacted" this organization, I was torn as to whether the plant was the right level from which to start. A long history of sociological studies in the auto industry had focused on, and extrapolated from, the plant level.[6] Not only were auto plants, especially assembly plants, treated as distinct and autonomous entities, but they also provided the most recognizable image of factory life, the modern example of the "hidden abode" about which Marx wrote so passionately.[7] However, I also knew from my own research (Thomas 1988; 1989) and from earlier critiques of "plant sociology" (Burawoy 1979) that factories are not isolated entities. In large, multiplant companies the factory is quite often subject to pressures and dictates far beyond its control.[8] If decisions about the placement of new product lines and the future of individual facilities were made at some distance, it would be risky to limit my analysis of technological change to the plant level—much less to focus on only the "impacts" of new technology at that level.

My suspicions were confirmed almost immediately on the initiation of the research. In questioning the plant manager and members of his

5. This count applied to the day shift. At the time the FMS was running on two shifts and cleaned and repaired on the third.

6. See, for example, Chinoy (1955), Walker and Guest (1952), Gartman (1989), and Blauner (1964).

7. See, for example, Garson (1975), Braverman (1974), Rothschild (1973), and Marx (1967, esp. chaps. 11–14).

8. General Motors and Ford combined operate more than two hundred manufacturing facilities in North America alone.

staff about the decision to invest in a multimillion dollar FMS, I was repeatedly stopped short and told that I needed to understand "the context." I was tempted to interpret their concern with context as special pleading or as a prelude to the finger pointing that occurs when things go wrong in bureaucratic organizations. However, it soon became clear that most were quite enthusiastic and proud of "how the FMS turned out." Understanding this context, I discovered, was essential to explaining what they felt to be the success of the FMS.

Context, I was told, consisted of several critical elements. From my notes I collapsed them into three principal elements: corporate control over the fate of the plant; the plant's limited autonomy in choosing technology; and the state of union-management relations.

CORPORATE CONTROL

The extreme economic turbulence of the 1970s and early 1980s shocked top company executives into rethinking some of their core assumptions about organization and organization structure. Internal studies and external (academic and business) analyses suggested not only that the industry and the company suffered from substantial overcapacity—especially given the shrinking market share held by U.S. firms—but that they also failed to match the competition when it came to the cost and the quality of their products.[9] One major explanation for both dilemmas was the historic practice of insulating organizational subunits from direct competition with external firms: for example, engine or fuel system plants were virtually assured of a steady stream of orders as long as they met the performance objectives set out for them.[10] Because those objectives were usually established with only passing reference to other potential suppliers or to estimates of what competitors were doing, plants were exposed only minimally to market forces. Thus, parts plants might be "captives" of their corporate parents, but in many respects the corporations were also captives of their in-house suppliers.

In the depths of economic crisis, executives in this company decided to undertake a systematic and centralized review of how and where they

9. See, for example, Harbour Associates (1989), Cole and Yakushiji (1984), and Abernathy (1978).

10. Vertical integration was, of course, a central part of the auto companies' strategy in the 1920s for protecting themselves against fluctuations in the supply of components and even raw materials (Chandler 1962). However, in "buffering" (Thompson 1967) their core production processes, they also created enormously complex bureaucratic structures—within which it was possible for suppliers to operate as virtual monopsonists.

allocated contracts. The goal, according to a top executive I interviewed, was to "expose the divisions and the plants to market discipline." This goal was accomplished by informing the divisions that future work would be allocated on the basis of cost and quality improvement. Units that failed to achieve parity with—and ultimately surpass—the competition would stand in danger of losing product lines. At the same time, the corporate executive told me that "adequate performance would not be a guarantee of survival. If we have too many plants with redundant capacities, we're going to consolidate them. Plants will be shut down."

The parts plant's first exposure to the change in corporate thinking came in the form of an intensive review, conducted by an outside consulting company and paid for by the corporate engineering organization. According to the plant manager, the review was conducted as a preliminary to any discussions about investment in new technology. It involved

> a systematic audit of the whole plant. Everything was looked at very closely: our equipment, our physical infrastructure, our relationship with the union. They even inspected the cafeteria, for godsakes!

Referred to in several interviews as the "hit squad," the consultant's team had been commissioned to determine the suitability of each plant as a site for future investment. In a later interview with one of the corporate executives who had sponsored the hit squad, I was told that

> we [the corporate engineering organization] wanted an objective review of our strengths and weaknesses. It wasn't so much that we didn't trust the plant people to tell us the truth, but face it, they're going to show us only the positive things and we needed to know where the warts were, too.

If judged suitable, he explained, a plant would qualify for consideration as a recipient of technology "renewal" funds. The review, from the perspective of its sponsors, was believed to be a rational and necessary extension of the strategic planning process—and nothing more.

From the perspective of plant management and union officials, the review had an additional objective. A plant engineering manager put it this way:

> On top of everything else, they wanted to put the fear of God in us—especially those of us who had been in this plant all our lives

and didn't have much chance of moving downtown if they
boarded up this place.

The union local president agreed:

Hell, we'd been up and down like everybody else, and we'd
pretty much convinced ourselves that this plant was here to stay.
I think they really wanted to rattle our cages. And they did, let
me tell you!

If these assessments were any guide, managers and workers emerged
from the experience awakened to the real possibility of the plant's demise.
The net effect, according to the plant manager, was a resolution not to
take their future for granted. These sentiments were strongly stated even
though five years had passed since the review.

PLANT AUTONOMY

The second contextual element involved the plant's ability to actually choose
the equipment and systems in which it could invest. Here, especially, the
limited autonomy of the plant was underscored—by both local and corporate managers. When I queried plant-level managers and engineers about
the manner in which they invested in technology, I was told emphatically
that although the plant ultimately has the right to choose, their choices
were more likely to be made "within" a given technology than "between" technologies. Several reasons were offered in explanation:

1. Plants are actively discouraged from making changes in core
processes without clearing those changes with product and manufacturing engineers at the divisional and corporate levels of the organization.
If, for example, designers are planning to alter the shape or the attributes
of a future generation of engines or fuel systems, the plants cannot
arbitrarily change their manufacturing technology in ways that could
conflict with those designs. Equally important, the product engineering
organization made very clear that only under exceptional circumstances
could new processes be introduced simultaneously with new products.
Again, as in the aircraft and computer companies, the hegemony of
product engineering was well established in this company.[11]

11. See Abernathy (1978), Hayes, Wheelwright, and Clark (1988), and Clark and
Fujimoto (1991) for a further discussion of the evolution of this hierarchy and current
efforts to reshape the organization of new product design activities.

2. Corporate and divisional manufacturing engineering organizations are supposed to serve as technology "gatekeepers" in the company.[12] As in the aluminum company, R&D engineers see their role as one of developing and then transferring new processes to the plants and, in addition, promoting uniformity in processes across plants, so that, for example, products might be shifted among plants. The manufacturing R&D engineers I interviewed argued that they were much more likely to succeed in "selling" new technology if they first convinced product designers to accept it than if they attempted to go directly to the plants—even though under most circumstances the plants must ultimately pay for the new technology. Thus, the "transfer" of new technologies like the FMS may appear more like an imposition on, rather than a choice by, the plants.

3. Many plants, including this one, lack sufficient engineering staff with which to independently plan for, much less design, major new processes. While assuring me of his confidence in the staff he had, the plant's engineering manager made clear that it was "difficult enough to put out the fires we have without trying to develop whole new systems." Where the plant could act independently, he told me, was in the purchase of off-the-shelf replacements for equipment that had worn out but for which the plant could project a continuing need. This situation suggests a set of constraints quite similar to those experienced by plant management in the aircraft and computer companies. In the aluminum company, divisional managers had sufficient authority and resources to be more aggressive; even then, however, there were implicit limits on how much new technology they could bring in without corporate approval or without clearance from the central R&D staff.

The auto company's division of labor thus made the centralized manufacturing engineering organization sensitive to the needs of the product developers and relatively insensitive to the plants.[13] As one top plant manager advised me, "You have to understand that in engineering terms, the plants are at the bottom of the food chain." To that he added:

The plants don't have a great deal of authority when it comes to new technology, especially when it comes to big ticket items. We

12. For a more thorough discussion of the gatekeeping role, especially in product R&D organizations and development teams, see Allen (1981).
13. See Abernathy (1978) and Womack, Jones, and Roos (1990) for a history of this relationship.

can buy bits and pieces of what we might want or need. But when it comes to making major changes—changes that we still pay for—we have to sign up the [R&D] people to get their okay. They're supposed to see to it that we don't do something stupid, and I can appreciate that. But once they're involved, you lose control over your own destiny.

UNION-MANAGEMENT RELATIONS

The third contextual element raised in the interviews involved the relationship between new technology and union-management relations at the plant level. Although, as I suggested earlier, technological renewal and industrial relations reform appeared to be quite separate strategies unfolding at the level of the company and the industry, they intersected at the level of the plant. In the "salad days of the 1960s and even the 1970s," as one manager put it, new processes might have challenged long-standing agreements about skill and compensation levels, but the union did not intervene in the process of technological change. Of course, he added, they weren't invited to participate either. People could be shifted around, or, as tended to be the case, increases in demand made it possible for new hires to be foregone in order to retain workers displaced by new technology. Beginning in the early 1980s, however, old traditions came under tremendous pressure, and as both plant managers and union leaders attested, new technology could no longer be separated from union-management relations.[14] Concretely, union officials were warned that the combined pressure of international competition and the company's own plan for technological renewal meant that jobs were going to go away.

At the same time, plant management and union representatives began exploring the possibility of joint efforts at quality improvement—partly in response to what they perceived to be a need in the plant, but also because both sides felt it would enhance the plant's image in the eyes of corporate decision makers. It was not long, however, before probing discussions turned to active debate about the potential consequences of technological change. The assistant plant manager described it this way:

We started talking about the future of the plant and these people's jobs, and it was hard to avoid the fact that the union was

14. It should be noted, however, that U.S. unions were (and largely remain) ambivalent about the benefits to be gained from involvement. See, for example, Solomon (1987), Hershizer (1987), Cornfield (1987), Sorge and Streeck (1988), and Thomas and Kochan (1992).

being put in a corner. Mind you, I didn't have any great sympathy for them at the time; a lot of those guys I considered SOBs then. But I knew that the union wasn't going to go away, and therefore we had to work with them. When we discovered that we were all rational people, we began to recognize that whatever affected them was eventually going to affect us. If they decided to dig in their heels because they thought that new technology was going to hurt, they could make damned sure the stuff would never work. Like we say around here, "Did you ever notice that the machines that don't work on Thursday always seem to work on Saturday—when we're paying time-and-a-half?"

A skilled trades representative (in a separate interview) made a similar assessment:

When we started meeting with them, it was pretty clear that those guys downtown meant to hammer us with new technology. We knew we could kick and scream about it, but we also knew what was at stake. A number of us got to realizing that it might make more sense to see if we could minimize the damage. For us in the trades, we're not afraid of new technology. Hell, we love it. But we also wanted them to do things right for once.

Thus, interests were converging at the level of the plant to mitigate the impacts of technological change.

From the perspective of the plant, these three contextual elements explained a great deal about how choices were made *between* technologies. With its centralized review and its threat of closure to recalcitrant plants, the corporation sought to reestablish control over its subunits. The promise of funds for new technology did not come without strings: plants would not only have to comply with corporate edicts about cost and quality but would also have to submit to the technology choices made by central engineering staffs. However straightforward and necessary these moves may have seemed to corporate management, they had the effect of challenging plant managers, hourly employees, and union leaders either to accept technological change in whatever form the corporation deemed appropriate or to mitigate the impacts of those changes by putting themselves at risk of closure.

To complete the analysis of context, however, it is necessary to look more closely at what was going on in the central engineering staffs—the part of the organization assigned to make choices between technologies.

MANUFACTURING RENAISSANCE
AND REAL ENGINEERING

While the "hit squad" was conducting its review and plant-level interests began to coalesce, corporate manufacturing engineers were busy
preparing for the enactment of technology renewal. Renewal represented a prelude to what one vice president described as "manufacturing's renaissance after the dark ages." That is, he explained:

> The manufacturing side of this company has been treated like a
> stepchild for many, many years. Manufacturing expertise and
> common sense were ignored while we fiddled around making
> cars more and more complex. And manufacturing just did what-
> ever the car guys told us to do. You can see the results: we've got
> parts on our cars that look great, but they're a nightmare to pro-
> duce. That's how Honda and Toyota have beaten the pants off
> us . . . . You look at their cars and you see that what it takes us
> nineteen operations to do, it only takes them three. Are you
> going to tell me that it doesn't cost us six or seven times as much
> to make that part as it does Honda?

Technology renewal was expected to contribute to manufacturing's
"renaissance" in three ways. First, it promised not only to loosen
company purse strings but also, as one R&D engineer speculated hope-
fully, even to ease the "stranglehold the bean counters had us in." He
explained:

> In the past when we had a chance to meet with the finance peo-
> ple, they just preached to us. Financial decisions came from on
> high, and up till now nobody could tamper with those things.
> Twenty-one percent return on investment is a decision that was
> made by the company, and nobody, but nobody, will differenti-
> ate from that. Even if you identify a 21 percent ROI, you need a
> payback within a twelve-month period. If you couldn't show
> that, forget it. Maybe, just maybe, that'll loosen up now.

In other words, having money to work with was important, but much
more exciting was the possibility that the rules about *how* it could be
spent might change as well. Decision criteria such as ROI and payback
periods were not rejected as inappropriate, but as in the aircraft company case, many engineers saw them as arbitrary and artificial and a

symbol of the power of the financial side of the organization. One equipment designer described the situation in terms that recall the enormous effort expended to finesse the ROI in the earlier FMS case:

When you come right down to it, these restrictions can force you into making outright lies in order to do something that you know is right but you don't have the numbers to defend. It's hard on us engineers because you know something will work as a professional engineer. But that doesn't carry weight with the bean counters. They aren't professional engineers.

Second, technology renewal offered the opportunity to do "real engineering" work. In this company, as in those visited in prior chapters, real engineering consisted of creative activity, not simply repairing or fixing something already in place. Creativity could take the form of completely new inventions, or it could involve putting known elements together in an unprecedented way. In either case, real engineering resulted in unique and identifiable achievements that were recognized as such by professional norms and by professional peers. To be recognized, however, the products of real engineering had to be put into practice. This is where technology renewal came to have special meaning for the corporate manufacturing engineers—on two levels. On one level, the company-wide push to develop (or acquire) and then install new production technology was expected to turn the manufacturing R&D engineers from "salesmen" into technologists. Referring to the "hit-squad" review, a corporate engineering manager said bluntly:

That process was necessary for a whole lot of reasons, but it had one clearly positive benefit for us: it softened up the plants to the idea that things had to change. Up to that point—and I hate to admit it—we were pretty much stuck in a sales mode. We had to sell new equipment and new ways of doing things to the plants. It was really incredible. Here we were with this enormous warehouse of ideas and new technologies sitting on the shelf, and, damn, we couldn't sell them to the plants. Well, [renewal] gave us leverage, as well as money.

On another level, technology renewal promised to give those who designed the process for making cars a measure of standing—if not an equal standing—with those who designed the cars, that is, those whom the vice president earlier referred to as "car guys." Although not as pronounced as in the aircraft or computer companies, the gulf in status and influence between process and product engineers in this company was real and long-standing. From the perspective of the "manufacturing guys," technical artifacts such as FMSs and robots are the devices through which claims to engineering peerage are made: they are the coin of the realm.

The third and most expansive contribution expected from technology renewal was its service as a platform for promoting design for manufacturability (DFM). The vice president who earlier compared his company's design practices with those of its Japanese competitors offered an apt summary of both the technical and political problems DFM was intended to address. The technical problem, he explained, was clear and simple: cars were designed to conform to criteria and aesthetics that often made them difficult, expensive, or even impossible to manufacture. DFM, as detailed in a growing technical and managerial literature,[15] addresses the technical problem by codifying knowledge about manufacturing processes and using it as a basis to critique and amend product designs. In the vice president's words:

> DFM takes the practical wisdom and common sense of the manufacturing guys and plants it in the heads of the car guys. That's KISS: Keep It Simple, Stupid.

The political problem is not, however, quite so tractable—nor is it openly addressed in the literature. The political problem revolves around the relative power of the "car guys" and the "manufacturing guys" to make and enforce the rules for designing and building cars. The aspirations that manufacturing engineers attached to technology renewal were themselves evidence of an asymmetry of influence. The relative salaries and promotional opportunities of the two provided further evidence of the inequality, at least as perceived by manufacturing engineers.[16] In other words, beneath the framing of DFM as a "commonsense" solution to a technical problem resided a far more ambitious agenda for realigning the engineering status hierarchy and, by extension, the distribution of power in the organization at large. Renewal would provide the funds, the tools, the raw materials, and the leverage for that undertaking.

15. See, for example, Hayes, Wheelwright, and Clark (1988), Liker and Fleischer (1992), Clark and Fujimoto (1991).

16. See, for example, El-Hout (1990) for a more detailed discussion of pay and promotional paths in the auto industry.

FROM CONTEXT TO CONTENT

Immediately on announcement of the renewal fund, a group of corporate engineers was established to investigate flexible machining processes. According to company documents, flexible machining was de- fined as "processes capable of rapid changeover between products or sets of machining routines." Flexible machining was deemed to be the solution to a pair of problems. One problem, as explained to me by the manager in charge of the group, derived from marketing considerations. In short, the company wanted to increase its capacity to vary the products it offered and to penetrate smaller market niches in order to counter the competition. To do that, it needed manufacturing processes capable of design shifts within and between product lines.

The other problem was stated in more conventional language: flexible machining would help reduce the labor it took to manufacture parts (i.e., it would "get rid of heads"). Even though I persisted in asking whether labor costs (both direct and indirect) would go down with the introduction of flexible machining processes, the engineers with whom I spoke thought my questions silly. According to their calculations, overhead would be more than offset by reductions in head count. In one case, my persistence so irritated one of the engineers that he replied:

> Look, the numbers are there! It's not a game we're playing here.
> The point of the matter is that our DL [direct labor] costs are
> over forty dollars an hour and that's just ridiculous. Even worse
> is the fact that we're paying guys forty dollars an hour to sit on
> their asses while they're waiting for somebody else to set up their
> machines and forty dollars an hour to make believe they're work-
> ing while the machine is just cutting air! Come on!

Despite his obvious concern that I share his conviction, he would not share the numbers to which he referred.

When the flexible machining group was told that the parts plant would be a candidate for renewal, a subset of engineers was tasked with designing a specific FMS. The lead engineer on the project described his goals in language reminiscent of *Hot Rod* magazine and Tom Wolfe's *The Right Stuff*:

> We had some ambitious plans in the early stages. We felt we
> could put something together that would push the outside of the
> envelope. It was a dream machine.

They proposed an FMS that would be: (1) completely integrated by computer with parts inventory and tracking; (2) capable of remote monitoring and, eventually, remote control from a single station; (3) relatively impervious to anything but very limited operator input; (4) equipped with modular tooling to simplify setup dramatically; and (5) equipped with self-diagnostic software that would identify actual and impending electrical and mechanical failures. The last feature would reduce the job of machine repair to one of "swapping" printed circuit boards when called for by the machine itself. It was, as the lead engineer put it, "what a factory should look like."

Thus, the choice between technologies was made—apart from the plant and before plant managers, engineers, union officials, or workers were aware that the choice had even been commissioned. Corporate engineers had sketched their dream machine, and, emboldened by the promise of funds and a smooth path into practice, they prepared for the "real" task of bringing it to life.

CHOOSING WITHIN THE TECHNOLOGY

News that the hit squad had recommended a longer lease on life for the plant was received with a mixture of excitement and apprehension. Obviously, all parties were pleased to see work and jobs stay in the plant, and no small amount of rejoicing occurred. As the manufacturing manager reported: "We were thrilled at the time. I mean, we thought, 'Would they spend that kind of money and then shut us down?'"[17]

However, when word came that the principal machining area was going to be removed (or as one person put it, "become just so much landfill") and replaced with a state-of-the-art FMS, apprehension took the edge off their excitement. According to the manufacturing manager, this wasn't the first time the corporate group had approached the plant with an advanced system like the FMS:

> There is example after example in this plant where they have this
> vision of new technology, . . . where automation coming into the
> plant would offset the labor cost. We pay the price for that now.
> They bring in new machinery and new equipment to displace
> people and then don't take into consideration the tremendous
> cost of the engineering people that have to be assigned to those

17. Having said that, he stopped and then shook his head, saying, "Now we know that they would. But we didn't know that then."

areas, the skilled tradesmen that have to be assigned to those areas, the tremendous training that has to be done with your operators and your staff.

A skilled tradesman made a similar point but approached it from a different angle:

The problem on the upper level is that people in those positions worked in a plant twenty years ago. They leave this kind of environment, they go uptown, and they're predispositioned. They say, "Twenty years ago I got fucked down on the floor by somebody," and they still remember twenty years ago. And that's the problem: getting them the hell out of twenty years ago!

This time, however, the fact of a review, combined with funding by the corporation, left plant management little room to reject the FMS. Still, the plant manager set up a "reception committee." He explained:

Because we wanted it to work and because we wanted it to work fast and because we wanted to prevent another case of what I would call "technology overkill," I wanted to have my people in there as early as possible. I sent a delegation, my reception committee, to find out what they had in mind. No surprises.

What they found, according to a member of the committee, was "more bells and whistles than you could imagine! I was surprised they didn't want the damned thing to talk!"

The reception committee convinced the plant manager to convene a meeting of his staff and to invite the local union president. The union president recalled what he heard:

Basically he told us that we were in a tough situation. He saw this thing [the FMS] as an indication of what we could expect in the future. If we wanted to bet that it'd work as advertised, then we should just sit back and let them do their thing. Otherwise, we should draw a line in the sand and say we wanted a say in this thing.

The assembled group chose the latter course, and it was in this meeting that an alliance was formed between plant management and the union. The union president went on:

He and I agreed that we had to use whatever muscle we could to get a say in this thing. He wanted something that would work, and I wanted to save jobs for my people. We had that as a common ground.

With that as their conclusion, the plant manager sent a message to manufacturing R&D:

I told them that I'd love to have their toy, but since we were going to be left holding the ball, they ought to let us in on the design stage.

He proposed a joint development effort, one that would include representatives from the plant's manufacturing engineering, maintenance, and quality departments. The request was justified, he argued, by "the spirit of participative management that we'd heard from the big bosses." His request was accepted.

CONTESTED TECHNOLOGY

Early in 1985 the newly christened "FMS team" convened for the first time to discuss the project. Before more than a few minutes passed, according to those participants I interviewed, emotions exploded. The manufacturing R&D engineers, it seemed, expected this "teaming" enterprise to take a traditional form: the corporate group would lay out its ideas, suggest a timetable for the effort, and then throw the meeting open for questions. However, the plant representatives had other plans. They insisted on talking about objectives and priorities and, in the words of one participant, "politely warning them that this was not going to be a rerun of past fiascoes." An equipment designer from R&D offered his perspective:

It got pretty ugly pretty fast. One of their guys was practically standing on the table, yelling and telling us, "You can't do this and you can't do that!" I thought we were going to be mopping up blood soon!

A plant manufacturing engineer who considered himself "caught in the middle between my engineering cousins and my plant cousins" intervened to try to clarify the lines of difference between the sides.

What he described in form, if not in content, resembled the first round of a traditional collective bargaining process. The R&D group laid out a list of attributes that they intended the FMS to have (most of which I described earlier). The plant group listed their objections: too many sensors; remote monitoring only if it could be made invisible to the operator; modular fixturing was too expensive and risky; and modular repair was acceptable but would probably be undone by the skilled trades. Most aggravating to the plant group, however, was the issue of the programmability of the system itself—in other words, how control over the FMS would be distributed.[18]

As I questioned the engineers and managers about this issue, I was initially puzzled as to why they should be so upset about a system that would wrest control over machining processes out of the hands of machine operators and setup workers and put it squarely in theirs. I received two responses: for some the issue was not *who* would control but *how* control would be exercised. For this subset the real fear was that the software would simply fail to do what was advertised. For the others, however, programming was a land mine waiting to be tripped: some years earlier the older machining system—an NC system—had been the object of considerable controversy. When installed, programming had been purely the domain of manufacturing engineers; they input data, modified programs, and oversaw the operation of the punches that made the tapes for running the machines. However, over time, setup workers, machine repair specialists, and even some operators had learned how to read the tapes and had worked out informal agreements with supervisors and engineers to allow them limited opportunity to modify existing programs. Apparently, the informal agreements held until a new supervisor discovered the practice and filed a disciplinary report against the worker he'd caught altering a program. Before long the issue spiraled into a full-scale grievance.

Although the grievance was resolved without arbitration, it did not exactly bury the issue. According to the union local president, the supervisor was given a new assignment, but the question of job jurisdiction was left hanging. That is, an agreement was reached that "things would go back to where they were," but, he added, "We didn't put down on paper 'what were' and therefore no precedent was set . . . except for those of us who remembered it." Thus, even though the R&D group's plan to lock out programming might have been attractive to plant managers and engineers, it also threatened to trip the land mine.

The first session adjourned in a stand-off, and no future meetings were set. Each group returned to its home base with the apparent

18. The maintenance superintendent put it this way: "We told them: bells are okay, but no whistles. Period."

conviction that it needed to marshal its forces for the next encounter. The R&D project manager described his first reaction simply:

> I figured we'd just go back about our business and in a few months' time we'd have our specs finished. In the meantime I'd talk to my boss and see about getting a message through to the plant . . . a message that they really didn't have all that much influence on this one.

Meanwhile, the plant group confirmed the earlier fears of the reception committee to an audience of managers, engineers, and union representatives. Without mentioning the details of the programming discussion, the message got through to the union president. He proposed the addition of a skilled trades representative and another member of the union to the plant "team." The proposal was accepted by the plant manager. He later explained his reasoning:

> I went out on a limb. I saw we were heading for a fight, and frankly, I wanted this guy and his people on my side. I also looked at what we were doing *in* the plant, around employee and union participation, and I thought that this kind of collaboration fit with that philosophy. So maybe I was being a little Machiavellian. But I was also trying to do the right thing when it came to cementing change in the way we relate to the union.

A LANGUAGE OF COMMON INTERESTS

The FMS project lay dormant for nearly a year as the R&D group continued to elaborate its plans and the plant was preoccupied with manufacturing engine parts. But when word filtered in that the R&D group was ready to unveil its specifications, both sides prepared for action. Prior to a scheduled meeting of the joint team, the plant manager reported receiving a call from his boss to the effect that "there should not be a repeat of the last meeting." He interpreted the message as a warning ("Somebody got to him, and he got to me") but not an explicit prohibition against the team approach. In what several people described to me as a stratagem bordering on genius, he ceded to the wishes of his boss but proposed, again in the spirit of participative management, that the meeting not be a "show-and-tell" dominated by the R&D group. Instead, he offered, why not conduct the meeting in the style of consensus decision making that was taught to the burgeoning quality control circles? The plant would provide process consultation from its own externally trained facilitators. His proposal was accepted.

The meeting, according to participants on both sides, was a remarkable event. The R&D engineers confronted a room populated by pressed shirts and ties *and* greasy overalls.[19] There was an agenda, but it did not include a heading for "R&D presentation." Rather, the meeting began with introductions, and the facilitator then proceeded to break the participants into small groups for a role-playing exercise. One R&D engineer recalled being flabbergasted: "I thought, 'What the hell? Are we going to hold hands next?'" The role playing called for each member to describe what he thought were the most interesting and the least interesting parts of someone else's job. The parts were distributed so that plant people portrayed R&D roles and vice versa. According to a plant engineer who had been through a similar exercise before, "The looks on those [R&D] guys' faces were worth the price of admission." Though the exercise proved cumbersome, it had a substantive effect. For example, one member of the R&D group remarked:

I thought it was phony like everybody else did. But I had to admit when we got done that I really didn't understand what life was like as a hydraulics repairman down on the floor. I learned something. And I think they learned something, too.

Indeed, by the time the assembled group finally began discussing the FMS, the ice had been broken. Hidden agendas were not suddenly disclosed, but they were brought closer to the surface. At minimum, they could be discussed without accompaniment by threats of bodily harm. More important, as far as both sides were concerned, the FMS came to be seen as a common interest as well as a factional one. The plant engineering manager said it best:

We reached a real milestone when we agreed on two things: One, that no matter what they wanted to achieve for themselves in this, we were going to be the ones who would have to make it work and to keep it working. Two, that they had to be able to meet the major objectives set out for them by the big bosses.

19. The skilled trades representative explained, "Nothing we do is without some meaning! We wanted to show them that what you see is what you get."

The principal outcome of the meeting was a plan for dividing the task of translating the R&D objectives and designs into a new set of specifications for circulation to potential equipment vendors.

Over the next nine months, subgroups composed of R&D and plant representatives visited nearly two dozen machine-tool and computer vendors. Each vendor was asked to address a list of questions devised by the team as a whole. Those questions were extensive and included items concerning options for allocating control over programming. The issue had not been resolved by the team; instead, it was decided to see what vendors had to offer before a solution was proposed. In regular meetings following site visits, the team reassembled to compare notes. These meetings were not always pacific—differences in interpretation continually threatened to revive old prejudices—but slowly a common understanding of what was desired, what was possible, and what was affordable began to emerge.

In attempting to reconstruct the history of this change, I managed to gain access to the company that successfully bid to supply the machining centers for the FMS.[20] According to vendor representatives, the FMS team was an enigma. Never before had they seen some of the questions forwarded to them (e.g., "How does your equipment support a philosophy of participative management?"), and never before had they heard hourly workers explain what a company engineer "meant" in a technical question. As a vendor engineer recounted:

> I was stunned, to tell you the truth. I thought it was a joke when they said they'd be bringing some union guys along. I figured it was their way of saying they were going to be hard bargainers.

20. Technology vendors are an overlooked source of insight on the behavior of technology buyers. Three aspects of their role in technological change as a process of translation deserve further attention. First, the vendor's marketing and sales organization is expected to be a source of information for its product developers; therefore, it should not be unusual for that organization to be very knowledgeable about the way that potential customers are organized and where the power or authority to make decisions actually resides. Second, equipment vendors may advertise themselves as "selling solutions" (as Wang used to in its ads), but in many ways they actually sell problems. That is, they cannot sell a solution until they've convinced a buyer that he or she has a problem that only the vendor's solution can fix. And third, whether they are aware of it, vendors also sell new organizational designs when they sell their products. That is, assumptions about how a product can or should be used are often designed into the product itself, and therefore the instructions, training, and directions that vendors provide can also be very influential in how the buyer organization structures use of the product. Some of these considerations are touched on in Von Hippel (1988) and Workman (1991); however, they are in need of much further elaboration.

After the visit, and convinced that it wasn't a joke, the vendor engineer told his manager:

> I told him this was going to be different. We'd make money, but it was going to be very different. . . . A collaborative exercise is what they called it. I warned him that this was not going to be easy or simple.

"Crunch time," as several team members called it, came when the team had to draw up specifications from their various visits. It was a critical time for the collaborators: each had achieved a measure of comfort with the others, and as in the aluminum company case, a common language had been built atop common interests. Now, however, each faction—R&D engineers, plant engineers and managers, and union members—had to translate common understandings back into the native languages of their respective groups.

The process was difficult for all participants. An R&D engineer said that he was literally afraid to tell peers at the corporate center what he'd been up to, much less what the team had concluded: "I knew they'd laugh at me if I did." A skilled tradesman felt he had to choose his words carefully, adding:

> It wasn't so much an issue of the union president. It was my workmates, guys who I respected and who respected me. If they figured I'd copped out or knuckled under, they'd never let me live it down.

Finally, a plant engineer claimed it was the toughest thing he'd ever done:

> Put yourself in my place. Here I'm trying to make sure everything works, and if I fail to walk that tightrope. . . . Well, let me put it this way: the next plant manager's not going to understand.

The joint proposal was, in the eyes of the R&D group manager, "nothing if not a beautiful piece of wordsmithing." Most of the bells remained, but few whistles survived: the inventory software, remote monitoring capability, and a small segment of the modular repair options remained. Gone was centralized control and the self-diagnostic software. Left intact was the capability to lock out programming. That

would be the subject of later discussion between the company and the
union.[21]

Despite concerns about how their various constituencies would receive the proposal, team members felt both pride and confidence in what
they had accomplished. The R&D engineers described the joint proposal as a real technical achievement: the plans they devised for integrating the system were, in their eyes, equal to anything they had seen in
their site visits. The plan was so good and, in their estimation, so
economical that they prepared to do the system integration themselves
rather than hire an outside software vendor. Moreover, their exhaustive
review of machine-tool options led them to conclude that less expensive
machines could be modified to perform functions that even the vendor
had not anticipated. One R&D engineer insisted that credit be shared
with the plant engineering staff and one of the hourly electricians:

> He [the electrician] really knew what he was doing. I didn't re-
> ally take his suggestions seriously at first. But later I got to think-
> ing, "Why not?" We ran some experiments at the vendor's
> plant—and, what do you know, it worked!

The electrician in this case said he had been reluctant to share his ideas
with the R&D group, largely because

> here's a bunch of educated guys who are probably thinking I'm
> an idiot. I kept my mouth shut for a long time. But, hey, when I
> get around those machines, that's my turf. I know those things in-
> side and out. So I tossed my two cents in—and they listened.

In looking back on the proposal, all sides claimed to see a positive net
benefit. The R&D engineers felt they had achieved a technical breakthrough. Their apprehension about admitting that the achievement was
a collaborative one showed only that the ethos of their home organization had not changed in the interim. As far as they were concerned, the
FMS would ultimately be recognized as a feat of real engineering. Plant
engineers and managers felt they had fulfilled their goal of packaging a
system that would work and therefore would not become another white
elephant. Union representatives spoke proudly of their technical contributions. Those contributions affirmed a point they felt needed repeating.
In the words of one of the setup workers: "We may be factory rats. But

21. According to the vendor, programming could be either locked out or enabled
without a change in the machines themselves.

that doesn't mean we're dead between the ears." Equally important, the proposal they helped construct resulted in the displacement of less than half the people that had been projected in R&D's initial plan.

GETTING TO "YES"

Much to the surprise of the team members present, the corporate analysts and managers to whom the proposal was presented virtually yawned through the "pitch." A participant complained later, "I think we caught them after a big lunch." The fact that the plan was approved prompted cheers from the team, but the lack of comment and the few questions that were asked left the team with mixed emotions. They had been prepared to fight for their ideas; several admitted that they thought the team deserved some sort of an award. The plant manufacturing manager shook his head slowly and told me: "That's this company through and through. You can never figure out what they're thinking."

Thus, a protracted negotiation over the meaning and the purpose of this new technology came to an end. Careful to recognize the fact that all sides had group and individual interests to protect, the team nonetheless demonstrated that it was possible to find common interests and common purposes and to construct a solution that could serve many masters. The ho-hum reception accorded the final proposal indicated clearly that, despite the accomplishments of this diverse group, the principal evaluative criteria remained the "numbers" they promised to achieve. In that sense, the FMS story is only one among thousands in a huge company—an organization slow to recognize, much less to adapt, to change.

The final moment in the process—implementation—might be predictable, given the high level of agreement and enthusiasm that accompanied completion of the proposal itself. However, context reemerged to influence the content of the change.

IMPLEMENTING THE TECHNOLOGY

In the period immediately following approval of their proposal, the plant-based members of the FMS team met to discuss how the new technology would be implemented. During the creation of their proposal, the team had consciously chosen to ignore the question of implementation, in large measure because issues relating to the selection and training of staff and integration of the technology into the work

flow of the plant seemed too distant and complex. Moreover, representatives from the personnel and labor relations department had actively
discouraged staffing plans that did not accord with the existing job
descriptions and seniority system. Traditional practices, they warned,
should prevail: that is, questions about, for instance, who should work
with the FMS and how they should be paid could wait until everything
was "bolted down."

Success in getting funding, however, encouraged the team members to
consider a different approach to staffing and managing the system. One
member in particular, a setup worker, had visited another, newer plant
that had begun experimenting with self-managed work teams. He persis-
tently urged the team, the union president, and others to consider this as
an approach to the FMS. As he later told me:

> The big revelation for me [from being on the FMS team] was just
> how easy it was to understand this system. It's complicated,
> don't get me wrong. But, hell, if I can learn how it works and if
> we could put together the right group of people with the right
> skills, we could run this thing in a very different way.

At his urging, and with the blessing of both management and the union,
the team visited the "sister" plant and held long and frank discussions
with workers and supervisors there.

OWNING THE TECHNOLOGY

What emerged from those discussions was a single, powerful concept:
"ownership." In virtually every interview I did with team members (and
with workers in the FMS area as well), ownership was employed to
describe what was different about the FMS area. The team member who
eventually became supervisor for the area gave me one explanation of
what ownership meant. I quote him at length because the examples he
provides are helpful in understanding the local meaning of the concept:

> You work all your life in a plant, even in one small corner of a
> plant, and every day you come in and you're reminded that
> you're just a cog in this great big machine. You're just another
> tool. Oh yeah, every once in a while you get an "attaboy" from
> the plant manager or somebody, but for the rest of the time
> you're a rat like every other factory rat . . . and you know how

much attention rats get. Well, if you take a guy or a gal—and not everybody, but most everybody—and you say, "Okay, this here is a brand-new lathe or a brand-new punch press and you're going to run it." If you just walk away, he or she's just going to say, "Well, this here machine is new but nothing else is changed. So I'm just going to do what I've always done." And that's just treat the thing like it's somebody else's machine. It's like the difference between your car and a car that belongs to somebody you don't know. You wash your car, you change the oil . . . you do all these things because it's yours and you want it to look good and last a long time. You're proud of it. That's ownership. These machines and all don't belong to us personally, of course. But what we do with them *does* make a difference. If we take care of them and if we do good work, then we make good parts and the plant does well. The plant does well and we keep our jobs, our houses, our boats, etc.

A machine operator from the FMS area echoed those sentiments but added that newness of the equipment alone does not make the crucial difference:

The real key to ownership is having the resources and the reasons to do a quality job. If you got a brand-new car but you can't afford gas or insurance, sure you got a brand-new car, but what good's it do you? If I got a brand-new machine before but then I was told that I couldn't do this or I couldn't do that or, as happened a lot around here, they told me to make only quality parts and then gave me lousy stock or not enough time to do a quality job, then I'd just say to myself, "They're not really interested in quality. They just want the output." So I'd give them exactly what they wanted: output. Now, though, we've got the resources and the reasons to do a quality job. The resources are good stock and people who know how to work with it. The reasons are, one, that we're responsible: . . . if it blows up, we've got nobody to point to but us. And it's our jobs that are at stake. So, yeah, ownership is the resources and the reasons to do a quality job.

Ownership meant control over resources, responsibility, and pride, as the quotes above explain, but it also meant the opportunity to engage in a creative act on the order of what the R&D engineers alluded to in their quest for the chance to do real engineering. No one argued that engine parts were, in and of themselves, creative artifacts—although several said they made it a practice of going to the car show every year to see what the competition did differently. Rather, engine parts were the output of a *creative process*—one that could be altered and improved when people had the resources and the reasons to understand it. In that sense, just as the R&D engineers recognized that real engineering was incomplete without the opportunity to see a concept into practice, the FMS team members and workers in the area argued that "real work" was incomplete if it did not allow them to affect the concept as well as the output of the process.

Bringing these ideas to fruition was not, however, an easy task. For workers, supervisors, and engineers in the FMS area to "own" the process, they had to attach meaning and purpose to it and to one another through it. Though the idea was certainly not articulated this way, the team members recognized the problem and sought to devise a strategy of implementation that would emphasize ownership and pride as key objectives to be achieved in the roll-out of the new system.

After lengthy discussions with both plant management and the union, agreement was reached that the usual process for bidding into the area would be augmented by a battery of interviews to determine whether candidates had the proper attitude to be a part of a self-managed work team. The union president explained:

> In doing that, we tried to use the dictates of common sense. I'm not going to say we violated the contract . . . but we did extend above and beyond the realm of the contract because it was the right thing to do to get this stuff off the ground the right way.

This temporary suspension of the rules was not a popular undertaking with everyone in the union, but as the president recalled:

> Well, I'd just been reelected and I figured I had some breathing room. If everything went well, there'd be no memory of this by the time the next election rolled around. Or better yet, if it worked out well, people would have a positive memory.

The plant manager suggested that his biggest obstacle resided in his own personnel and labor relations department:

> I had a director of personnel who came up through the labor relations ranks, and for him, this was a little bit much. I'm not going

to say he was Attila the Hun. Let's just say he grew up in the "old school." Over the years he'd gotten to where he was by being the meanest son of a bitch on the block when it came to the union and all. For him, it was like the inmates were asking to take over the asylum . . . and he couldn't tell if I was the warden or the biggest loony in the bunch.

When I asked how he finally got around the personnel director's objections, he smiled and said, "I helped him find a more suitable position."

Thus, before the new equipment arrived and long before the FMS was up and running, a new FMS team was formed. With assistance from the hardware and software vendors, area workers and supervisors were given training on simulators and in some cases taken to vendor sites for practice in running the machines. Classes in technical fields (e.g., statistics, problem solving, electronics repair) and in team building (e.g., dispute resolution, communications, and even managerial accounting) were alternated with regular work shifts to minimize expense. Outside consultants were hired but kept in the background: the team was to own its own process as much as possible.

UP AND RUNNING

When the equipment began to arrive, workers were assigned permanently to the area. When not bringing the system up to operational level, team members were encouraged to rotate between jobs in order to become familiar with one another's duties. The goal, as described by the area supervisor, was to enable team members to cover for one another in the event of an absence and, more generally, to "set in place from the very beginning the idea that we jointly own the process."

Ownership required both familiarity *and* responsibility, however, and this is where the issue of programming resurfaced. After skirting the question formally, plant management and union leaders met to discuss who would be allowed to "touch" the software. Both sides were aware that their decisions were not going to be made in isolation: the rest of the plant and other parts of the division and the company were watching. If programming were formally opened to hourly workers in the FMS area, similar claims could be made elsewhere. If programming were denied, the union representatives argued, the concept of ownership would be seriously undermined.

After lengthy and closed discussions, the question was resolved by tying programming to a new approach to compensation. Three wage grades would be built into the FMS area. Though traditional job classifications would continue to apply, the three grades would be distinguished by unique qualifications. FMS "operators" would be qualified to operate but not to program. FMS "technicians" would be qualified to operate and to program with the approval of area supervisors. FMS "setup" workers would be qualified to operate, program, set up, and do minor repairs on the equipment. Qualification required classroom certification and demonstrated competence. Thus, workers would be paid for knowledge but, once qualified, would be paid at the highest qualified rate, independent of what work they were doing at any given time. Programming was therefore woven into ownership but made a major accomplishment as well. For the rest of the plant, the FMS solution did represent an important precedent, but replication beyond the FMS area would require substantial rewriting of existing contract language and informal practice.

A year later, when I began my research, the FMS was finally in full operation. Much to the disappointment of the area team, however, production orders remained unclear: the parts line originally slated for the system had been curtailed severely, and it was unknown what would replace it. Divisional managers assured the plant that it would get a product, eventually, but turmoil in the higher realms of "car guys" left them unsure what product would be announced or when.

Though everyone involved was aware of the ups and downs in the industry and that the ripple effects of market shifts were felt most acutely in the plants, how corporate management made decisions remained a baffling mystery and a source of irritation to team members. Contract allocation, investment decisions (such as the one to build an FMS in the first place), and approval procedures seemed arbitrary, capricious, and almost totally without logic to those who "owned" the FMS. The irony, from the perspective of the FMS team, was that ownership—for all the vagueness of its legal status—had come to have far greater meaning to those at the bottom of the company, at the lowest link of the "food chain," than to those at the top.

CONCLUSION

Near the end of my human relations tour—the "warm and fuzzy" side of the FMS—I asked my guides why there were two tours. The question prompted hesitation, an exchange of glances between the company man and the union steward, and then a bit of laughter. The steward replied:

Well, we've found that there aren't many people interested in both sides of the story. The big shots from downtown—*and*, by the way, the MIT professors and the Harvard professors—like to see the bells and whistles. They never ask about what it really takes to make all the gadgets work. The warm and fuzzy folks like to hear about employee involvement, but they don't really want to know about the gadgets.

Clearly implied was a third point: neither really wants to believe that both sides are essential to understanding what the FMS represents to people in the plant, or to the people who brought it into being. Thus, in advance of their visit, people are asked what they *want* to see, and that is precisely what they are shown.

The FMS story is a revealing one at several levels. First, it draws conspicuous attention to the influence of context—contemporary and historical, organizational and economic, technical and social—on both the process and the impacts of technological change. The explanatory significance of contextual factors has, of course, been pointed to repeatedly throughout the book, but here especially context could not be flattened analytically to mean only market conditions or external pressures. Rather, context involved both objective conditions and subjective interpretations of those conditions. In particular, the competing interpretations of organizational strategy, of real engineering, and of real work were critical to understanding how and why the technology took the shape it did.

Second, the FMS story is remarkably revealing about the way in which the meaning and the purpose of the technology came to be negotiated. Corporate engineering management envisioned technology renewal as a tool to refashion both the technical and the social systems of production, much as the operations manager did in the FMS case in the aircraft company. From their perspective industrial relations reform was restricted to the level of the plant and therefore did not intersect with (or constrain) time-honored management rights to organize production or contravene unspoken assumptions about who had the knowledge and the ability to choose among technological possibilities. Corporate and divisional R&D engineers saw the FMS as a means to demonstrate their inventive prowess, much as did R&D engineers in all the other companies studied. And as in the other cases, their working definition of real engineering did not require them to understand, much less to accommodate, the social system of production at the level of the plant. The higher levels of manufacturing engineering (above and beyond the plant) interpreted the strategy of technology renewal as a vehicle for equalizing (or at least recalibrating) the status and the influence of the manufacturing and design sides of the organization. They did not, however, envision an organic link between DFM and either plant-level knowledge or industrial relations reform. Thus, for all intents and purposes, DFM would be a practice defined by and pertaining to engineers.

Plant management, in a fashion similar to that in the aluminum company case, redefined a crisis as an opportunity and drew leverage from common interests in the plant's survival to force consideration of their interests—although it was accomplished by a number of deft political maneuvers rather than a direct confrontation. The burgeoning industrial relations reform turned out, in fact, not only to unite local plant management and union leaders against the corporation and the division but also to encourage workers to begin to articulate largely unspoken assumptions about the meaning of real work.

In an important sense, therefore, the two distinct organizational strategies—technology renewal and industrial relations reform—ultimately intersected at the boundary between the plant and the rest of the company. Technology renewal, which was envisioned by most people as a top-down forcing of modernization and change, ran headlong into industrial relations reform, which was initially defined as a shop-floor program but which, in the hands of local management and union leaders, became a means for giving expression to plant interests and, more fundamentally, to plant knowledge and plant power. Had plant management, union leaders, and, ultimately, workers themselves adopted a passive stance with respect to the FMS and the company's grand plans for technology renewal, it is quite unlikely that they would ever have been able to influence the shape and the impacts of the system once it was installed, much less to feel or to act like they owned it. The irony, of course, is that if they had failed, the system would very likely have been installed anyway—but it is an open question as to whether the FMS would have achieved anyone's goals, least of all those of the R&D engineers.

Finally, the FMS story offers a caution about predictions of the demise of Fordism and the emergence of a new approach to production. Neither the technology itself nor the strategy of technology renewal implied a need for the creation of a flexible, skilled, and committed work force in the plant. Indeed, left to their own devices, corporate engineering management would very likely have accomplished its goal of bringing technological flexibility into the plant, and R&D engineers would have realized their vision of real engineering. In the process, however, their issue would have trampled over the burgeoning plant-level efforts to define a flexible combination of machines and people.

SIX

Politics and Technology

"What distinguishes man from the rest of the animals is his
ability to do artificial things," said Paul. "To his greater glory,
I say. And a step backward, after making a wrong turn, is a
step in the right direction."

Kurt Vonnegut, *Player Piano*

At the outset of the book, I suggested that, despite the apparent incompatibilities between the different sides to the debate on technology and organization, it ought to be possible to bridge the competing perspectives. I explicitly targeted a domain of study that had been overlooked in prior research—that is, the process of technological change broadly conceived—and suggested that detailed empirical study might provide the foundation for a theoretical bridge between perspectives. The power-process perspective sprang from the idea that the relationship between technology and organization was dynamic and interactive, not static and unidirectional as it had been portrayed in prior research. To "test" that hypothesis, it would be necessary to set up a research effort that differed from prior studies in four distinct ways: (1) it would take history into account (theoretically, in terms of its influence on the structure of activities and perceptions, and methodologically through the use of longitudinal research designs); (2) it would pay greater attention to the manner in which the dissimilar logics underlying an organization's technical and social systems were coupled; (3) it would make the process of organizational choice an explicit focus of investigation; and (4) it would assess the role of power and conflicting worldviews in each stage of the process of change.

The case studies provide ample evidence that any effort to understand how technology affects organizations requires explicit attention to organizational process, that is, how conceptions of what is possible (as well as what is necessary) are formulated and translated into specific choices. They make a compelling argument that it is not enough to claim that technology "impacts" organizations; it is essential also to ask how and why particular technologies are chosen (or refused or missed entirely) such that they have the impacts they do. Likewise, these case studies demonstrate that it is not enough to claim that technology is the simple product of social or strategic choice; it is essential also to ask how technological alternatives are themselves framed, how the worldviews of different organizational actors shape the range of possibilities considered, and, most important, how differences among worldviews influence the outcomes of change. In other words, the case study findings do more than simply confirm my initial hypothesis: they suggest that the power-process perspective on technological change could both serve as a bridge and inspire much more fundamental change in the way we think about the relationship between technology and organization.

This chapter is divided into five sections. In the first two sections, I review what the case studies tell us about the limits on both the technological determinist and social choice perspectives. I argue that neither perspective should be dismissed or devalued completely; however, in each review I go to some lengths to indicate what would be missed in the analysis if the case descriptions were limited to a study of the "impacts" of change. The third section elaborates the power-process perspective and highlights its unique contributions to the study of technology and organization. At one level the power-process perspective *diverges* from both the technological determinist and the social choice perspectives—particularly in its emphasis on the mediating role of history, structure, and power relations in the process of technological change. At another level, however, the power-process perspective *bridges* the other perspectives by recasting the relationship between technology and organization as dynamic and interactive. In the fourth section I take a key idea from the power-process perspective—that political action can be viewed as a stimulus to technological change—and use it as the basis for a reconsideration of the role of politics and political mobilization in the broader process of organizational innovation. The final section considers the implications of the case study findings and the power-process perspective more generally for research and theory in related fields, such as industrial relations and comparative industrial organization.

THE LIMITS OF TECHNOLOGICAL DETERMINISM

There can be no denying that new technology had real and in some cases quite significant "impacts" on the social and the physical organization of work in these companies. Many of these impacts can be related directly to the unique characteristics of the technology involved: that is, each technology established a particular design space that limited the array of possible ways it could be used. However, the case studies also point out that organizations—more precisely, people in organizations— exercise influence over the choice between technologies and within technologies and over the manner of technology's use. Not all of these choices are obvious—even at the time they are being made—and not all of them are recognized as choice opportunities, in large measure because the factors influencing choice may not be evident or even present at the point of decision. Still, choices are made, and it is only through detailed analysis of technological change as a *process* that we are made aware of the *"impact" of organization on technology,* that is, the way technology is employed to reinforce or to change organization.

In this section I draw three points from the case studies that indicate critical limits on the utility of the technological determinist perspective.

THE IMPACT OF ORGANIZATION ON TECHNOLOGY

If we extend the temporal and the organizational context for analysis and thus expand the study of technological change beyond a narrow focus on outcomes, it becomes very clear that one of the most critical limits on a technological determinist perspective is its inattention to history, especially organizational history, and to the embodiment of history in organizational structure. History matters in the sense that prior technological choices directly influence what organizational actors perceive to be the range of possible technologies and organizational forms. However, history's influence is not limited to physical constraints (e.g., in the form of fixed capital investments that cannot be ignored); it also takes the shape of formal structures, rules, and interests that get built up around physical technology. These social system features may, as Nelson and Winter (1982) have argued, enable an organization to function in a routine fashion, but they can also act to limit what people in organizations are capable of seeing or are willing to see as technically and socially possible.

Thus, although it might be appropriate to characterize new technologies such as FMS cells or robotized assembly equipment as exogenous developments, it is also very clear that in each case the technology was chosen from among a number of competing options; they were not "forced" on the organization. Moreover, the choice between and within technologies was materially affected by both the structure of the organization (i.e., who or what groups had the authority, resources, and expertise to define problem and solution) and the interests and ambitions of those who had access to the decision process. R&D engineers, for example, were more likely to "see" (and be attracted to) an FMS than a new storage and retrieval system or a new social system in the shop (especially one that originated in the shop) because it fell within the rules that defined their department's distinctive mission or role. *Thus, technology may, as the technological determinists argue, affect structure, but it is evident that structure and the interests embedded in it also affect technology.*

It is testimony to the influence of history and structure that in nearly every case the process of identifying and evaluating problems and solutions was oriented in the direction of technologies that reproduced or reinforced existing relationships. In the aircraft robotics case, for example, the search for ways to employ the new technology was quickly narrowed to a problem over which the R&D project team thought it could exercise complete and unilateral control; the negative reaction on the part of other departments clearly demonstrated an equally great concern that the new technology *not* be a vehicle for altering existing relationships. The net result, as we saw, was absolutely no change in the status quo—a failure from the perspective of its proponents but nevertheless quite telling as an example of the limiting influence of existing structure. In a similar vein the cross-country tour of FMS users revealed an extensive array of alternative approaches to configuring and staffing the machining cells; but almost instinctively the R&D engineers ruled most of those alternatives "out of bounds," explaining that they didn't fit with "the way things worked" in the company. This sort of self-censorship or pruning of alternatives spoke volumes about the potency of precedent and the inviolability of unspoken assumptions in the company.

Indeed, the cases that provoked the greatest contention and the most visible anxiety were those in which attempts were made to breach traditional practices and understandings by means of new technology. In the CNC case, for example, the shop managers' effort to gain control over their work flow—a seemingly minor event in the larger scheme of things—erupted in boundary disputes with adjacent departments. What seemed to shop managers to be a reasonable undertaking (i.e., one that would reinforce relationships *internal* to the shop) revealed just how important lines of demarcation were to other organizational actors. Most revealing, of course, were the battles that ensued when end users dared to question the assumptions that others—internal as well as external to the organization—had employed in their definition of the problem and then built into the technologies they had chosen to solve those problems. Divisional engineers in the auto company, as well as engineers in the equipment vendors, were clearly unaccustomed to having their plans challenged (except in marginal ways); they were totally unprepared to have their assumptions about technology questioned by those "at the bottom of the engineering food chain."

In emphasizing the constraining influence of history and structure on the process of technological choice, I am not denying that dramatic technological innovations can shock organizations (or entire industries) and force them to respond. Furthermore, the case studies offer no reason to believe that organizations cannot "engineer" their way off one historical track and onto another. However, what the case studies do suggest is that the longer a particular coupling of technology and structure is in place and the more deeply held interests and assumptions are about the appropriateness of that coupling, the more likely it is that a given structure and its associated interests and assumptions will become *institutionalized*—that is, possessed of a measure of legitimacy based as much (if not more) on its longevity as on its consistency or "fit" with environmental conditions or, for that matter, its economic value.[1] In other words, technology and structure can become so deeply intertwined that together they acquire an inertial quality—one that does not disallow improvement or refinement within limits but that does, over time, ensnare participants in a circular logic of cause and effect.[2] At the level of the organization, this inertial quality can be manifested in various

---

1. This point has become increasingly central to the sociology of organizations—particularly in the institutionalist perspective on organizational structure and goals (e.g., Fligstein 1985; Zucker 1983; DiMaggio and Powell 1983). The extension of the idea to technology is a unique contribution of the case studies.

2. Allen (1981) among others has characterized this as the NIH syndrome: "not invented here." NIH, evidenced quite clearly in the opening stages of the aluminum company case, need not be a particularly debilitating syndrome (e.g., it may reflect a justifiable pride in the inventive capabilities of a particular group or organization). How-

ways, including the censorship of propositions that violate historical norms (to such an extent that people unconsciously but unstintingly rule out unorthodox propositions) as well as in the contraction of the range of possible technical and social systems to linear extensions of existing systems.[3] The net effect is a reduction in both the ability and the willingness of an organization to recognize, much less respond to, ideas, innovations, and opportunities that fall outside the bounds of an existing coupling. Thus, new technologies as well as new approaches to social organization may, as the technological determinists argue, emerge as exogenous developments, but *they will attract attention only to the extent that they can be assimilated within an interpretive framework already resident in the organization.* Or if they are recognized by some faction or another, they will be assimilated only to the extent that they can be imposed or insinuated by other means.

The case studies provide evidence for this argument from another and, in many respects, much more provocative angle: they suggest that the idea of technology—and more specifically, the idea of automation as a labor-saving device—can itself become institutionalized. In these companies as in much of American industry, the presumed benefits of automation have become so taken for granted that in the absence of overwhelming proof that other alternatives are possible, automation becomes the default option.[4] Indeed, so deeply ingrained is the idea that in virtually every case I studied, managers and engineers jumped almost

---

ever, to the extent that it *insulates* a group or organization from the interchange of knowledge or insights from other potentially inventive sources (including other parts of an organization), it reduces the opportunity for the breakthroughs that result from efforts to account for anomalous findings or the creative friction that often accompanies confrontations between different worldviews. In particular, Allen (1981) and Von Hippel (1988) have demonstrated the significance of these interchanges for the performance of product development groups and R&D organizations. As I suggest in this and a later section, however, their studies tend to focus on innovation in *one* part of an organization (e.g., product development) while assuming that other parts will (or should) follow the sanctioned innovators' lead. That is, those who are not sanctioned to innovate are expected to forgo the effort to innovate themselves, especially when their efforts might conflict with those from the group that has been granted the right to innovate.

3. This circularity can also lead potential innovators to abandon the organization altogether in order to pursue an idea or innovation. For example, the proliferation of computer and software firms in the Silicon Valley in the 1970s is in many ways a story of frustrated engineers who fled corporate bureaucracy, rigid accounting and costing rules, and historical constraints in order to realize their ambitions (see Rogers and Larsen 1984).

4. This attitude may help explain why, as Cole (1989) has suggested, many American managers have taken so long to seriously entertain the idea that global competitors, especially Japan, have achieved their strengths not through technology but through very different approaches to such things as training, human resource management, and management style.

immediately to technological solutions for organizational problems—
and in at least one instance, a technological solution set off a search for
organizational problems. The unusual cases (e.g., the auto company
FMS and the aluminum rod caster) appeared to be those in which a
social or nontechnical solution was entertained, much less given priority. Even more telling was the ability of some actors to finesse the
economic evaluations of a new technology—and others to accept (or at
least not question) the cooked numbers—rather than undertake a social
system change that might have been no more risky or uncertain.[5] Thus,
the case studies suggest that it may be more appropriate to argue that
technology is not determinant of organizational structure but that,
instead, the *idea of technology as the only legitimate alternative* is
determinant.

BREAKING INSTITUTIONAL MOLDS FROM WITHIN

It is important to reiterate that these points do not deny that technological innovations are often experienced and represented as exogenous
developments or that organizations are not capable of engineering
changes in their technical and social systems.[6] However, those points do

5. As Johnson and Kaplan (1987), Kaplan (1984; 1986), Gold (1983), and others
have argued, traditional measures of return on investment (ROI) often grossly distort the
present (or future) value of technology. In particular, the use of direct labor costs as the
principal determinant of ROI results in an overemphasis on "losing heads"—even in
situations where it is known that other heads (usually salaried ones) will have to be added.
However, despite the efforts of accountants, especially those working in the field of
behavioral accounting, to generate new measures and methods (e.g., "Activity-Based
Costing" as described by Johnson and Kaplan [1987] and even the more extensive reforms
suggested by Kofman [1992]), no one has yet come up with techniques for estimating the
net present value of what I will later refer to as "nontechnical" investments, e.g., in
training, upskilling, expanded systems of communication and knowledge transfer, and so
on. Such metrics may prove, by definition, impossible; still, the lack of effort in this
direction suggests that traditional distinctions between physical and human capital remain
very much in force.
    6. In this respect I would underscore Clark et al.'s (1988) argument that the "techno-
logical baby" should not be thrown out with the "determinist bath water." Indeed, their
study, classic works in the sociotechnical tradition (e.g., Emery and Trist 1960; Emery and
Thorsrud 1976), and recent work by Zuboff (1988) suggest that organizations *can*
accomplish large-scale shifts in the way they couple their technical and social systems.
However, it is important to recognize that efforts of that nature require long-term and
widespread support at all levels of the organization. In the absence of sustained support,
many well-intentioned efforts devolve into "programs," that is, periodic campaigns to
improve or alter one or another aspect of an organization's functioning (e.g., quality, cost,
cleanliness) that may have a legitimate purpose and appeal but are known to virtually
everyone *other than* their proponents to be finite in duration and episodic in nature. For
detailed examples of this phenomenon, see Thomas (1988), Walton (1981), Hammer and
Stern (1986), Parker (1985), and Parker and Slaughter (1988).

raise interesting questions about the capacity of organizations that have institutionalized particular beliefs about technology and social organization to recognize, much less to initiate, changes that break these institutional molds. For example, Tushman and Anderson (1986) and others have shown, in a broad sense, that organizations that are quite adept at incremental innovation within a particular technology can still fail miserably when confronted by radical innovations. In a similar vein Henderson and Clark (1990) demonstrated in their study of the semiconductor industry that firms that generated one technological breakthrough often failed to repeat their achievements in the future. If the case studies described in this book are any guide, it may be that *the structure adopted to conform to a technological change in one time period can come to operate as the principal constraint on an organization's ability to innovate (or to recognize an exogenous innovation) at a later time.* In other words, between shifts in technology, organizations may be able to achieve incremental improvements, but without knowing more about technological choice and change as an *organizational process*, it is impossible to explain (much less to predict) under what conditions incremental improvements lead to new breakthroughs (or the capacity to recognize them when they occur) and under what conditions incremental improvements lead to the narrowing of horizons and to the institutionalization of a particular coupling.[7]

Critical under these circumstances are the mechanisms or the processes through which institutional molds are broken. Unfortunately, from a technological determinist perspective—as well as from the perspective of studies limited in scope to outcomes or purely structural features of organization—we can do little more than infer what differentiates organizations that create or adapt to radical changes from those

---

7. An example from a different locale—"total quality management" (TQM)—further illustrates the point. TQM has been adopted in two distinctly different forms in U.S. industry. One form is consistent with the broad philosophy of its advocates and emphasizes continuous improvement and learning at both the individual and the organizational levels. Although advocates of this approach don't use these terms, their conception of TQM is one of unrelenting scrutiny, criticism, and improvement—a conception that is reminiscent of Mao's "self-criticism" (cf. Mao Tse-Tung 1976; Schurmann 1970). The intent is to prevent the institutionalization and ossification of any organizational process. The other form involves a routinization of TQM in narrow (and in some cases ridiculous) activities: for example, the tightening of quality standards without any change in or greater understanding of the processes that lead to quality problems; increased penalties for defects; and the application of both tighter standards and higher penalties to activities for which they have little apparent meaning or benefit (such as typing errors per page). In the first form, TQM techniques are intended to facilitate change; in the second form, they are used to prevent change.

that don't. However, the case studies strongly suggest that it is *purposive action inside organizations to alter structure by means of technology* that separates organizations that create or successfully adapt to radical new technologies from those that don't.

In this regard, purposive action can apparently take one of two forms: one that is sanctioned by upper management as a legitimate activity (e.g., reflecting a recognition of the inertial tendencies of technology and structure); and the other that is *not sanctioned*. The former, at least according to the literature on organizational innovation and change (cf. Nadler and Tushman 1980; Kanter 1988; Marquis 1982; Van de Ven 1986), is a prerequisite for organizational survival, and it is quite often designated as the raison d'être for R&D departments. Yet simply having an R&D organization (for products or for processes) and having an incentive to innovate will not by themselves lead to innovation—as industrial organization economists and political economists from Schumpeter (1950) onward have shown. Thus, the addition of structural features (e.g., the size or location of an R&D organization) to a technological determinist model might bring us closer to an understanding of what differentiates organizations that recognize or create innovations, but it would not tell us why in one organization improvement efforts lead to breakthroughs, whereas in another organization they lead to stagnation.

Equally important, neither the technological determinist nor the structural arguments can shed much light on the role that *nonsanctioned* purposive actions might play in challenging or even dissolving institutional molds. At one level, of course, such actions would be virtually invisible to these approaches. But even an investigation based on official sources might not be adequate as a guide to understanding the influence of nonsanctioned or unconventional efforts, such as I found in the computer, aluminum, and auto cases. All three of those cases, I suggest, involved efforts to transcend the bounds associated with an existing structure and historical precedent, and each traveled a considerable distance *outside* sanctioned procedures to do so.[8] The point remains: if nonsanctioned action *does* occur and if it is a vital part of the process of technological innovation and change, then it ought to be incorporated into our explanatory framework.

---

8. That all three were considered, at least by their major participants, to have been successful did not necessarily mean that *new* precedents had been set. For example, the scripting of two distinctly different tours of the auto plant FMS suggested that the corporate hierarchy may have blessed the outcome but not the process that led up to it.

HOW INDEPENDENT IS TECHNOLOGY?

The case studies also show that there is real reason to question whether we ought to ascribe universal characteristics to any given technology. This is most aptly demonstrated in a comparison of the FMS cells adopted in the aircraft and automobile companies. On the surface both shared certain basic characteristics: for example, they were intended to "link up" machine tools that were formerly operated independently into a computer-integrated system. Yet on closer examination the FMSs differed in very important ways: in the aircraft company the engineers designed the cell to be run from a central control station (originally to be staffed by a managerial employee); in the automobile company the FMS was designed to be operated by a manufacturing "team" made up of machinists, setup workers, and maintenance technicians. Part of the difference, as I suggested in the case study analysis, can be accounted for by the distinctive processes through which each FMS was designed and implemented; but more important for the argument I am making here, the differences in the FMSs that were constructed suggest that it is unlikely that we could arrive at a definition of a "pure" example of FMS technology.[9]

A much broader implication flows from this comparison: many of the studies that propose to compare the organizational "impacts" of a "given" technology may be starting from a very shaky foundation. That is, it may be quite inappropriate to assume that there is a "pure" form to a given technology that can serve as an independent variable in empirical analysis. Given the large number of studies that operate from this premise, the implications are substantial. At minimum, the findings from this research suggest that far greater attention must be paid to specifying adequately and accurately the shared as well as the divergent features of any technology before it is employed as an independent variable in the analysis of organizational structuring and change. At the extreme, the case studies call into question whether it is possible even to adopt arbitrarily one or another definition (e.g., what engineers themselves might use as a definition for a given technology) without undermining the premise that technology can be detached from the context of its use. Only under conditions in which researchers are confident that

9. Jaikumar (1986) and Jones (1982) both make similar points when they find that technologies that are quite similar in name are configured for operation in dramatically different ways. Still, they and most others engage in comparative analysis *as if* the technologies *were* identical.

the *identical* technology has been chosen for implementation would it make sense to conceive of that technology as analytically independent.[10] To date, at least, few researchers have attempted such an approach. Instead, they have tended to assume that similarity in the labels attached to a given machine or process—such as Kelley's (1990) study of CNC machine tools—is sufficient reason to treat that technology as a single variable. However, as the CNC case in the aircraft company showed, what might appear to be a narrowly defined technology can be configured and used in very different ways (e.g., allowing or disallowing operators access to machine programming in the *same* piece of equipment).[11]

In sum, the case study findings do not completely devalue the technological determinist perspective. They leave intact the idea that physical objects and their relations do exist "out there" and that they do constrain the range of possible forms of production. But they strongly suggest that the logic that governs them cannot be understood independently of the social setting in which they are deployed. Physical reality, in other words, remains a social construct; that is, its meaning cannot be divorced from the worldviews or interpretive frameworks that get applied to it. And as the case studies demonstrated repeatedly, the social construction of physical reality often involves considerable contention as to which worldview or interpretive framework will be employed to guide the definition and choice of technologies. Thus, we can argue, in order to have an impact on organizations—much less to be defined as an exogenous force—technology must be made to accord with particular worldviews. The dominance of one worldview over another cannot be understood independent of power relations in organizations and in society at large.

One possible way to salvage the insights to be gained from the technological determinist perspective is to focus, as I have tried to do, far greater attention on both the realities and the possibilities of a given

10. A research design that compared the structural changes associated with a technology designed and sold by a single vendor to multiple customers might provide a partial solution to this problem. The closest example would be Barley's (1986) study of the changes occasioned by the introduction of identical imaging equipment in a pair of hospitals. However, research designs of this sort should also extend the temporal and organizational context in the ways I suggested in chapter 1.

11. Mike Parker, a skilled electrician with considerable experience in machine control systems, reminded me of this point in comments he made on an earlier draft of chapter 2.

technical process. That is, social scientists have tended to be far too insensitive to (or reticent about exploring) the actual workings of the technologies whose impacts they have studied. This oversight has led, as I noted at the outset of the book, to generalizations about technology that have obscured significant differences in what machines can and cannot do. It has also led to searing criticisms and, far too often, to dismissal from the engineering and scientific audiences with whom dialogue desperately needs to be established. If, however, we are to continue to unravel the complex relationship between technology and organization, it would seem essential that we gain that kind of working knowledge and establish that kind of dialogue. Two significant benefits could rapidly follow: (1) we would be in a better position to understand why apparently similar technologies have dramatically different impacts or get used in dramatically different ways; and (2) we would be far better positioned to understand the paths that were available or were possible but were not taken. This latter point, as I argue in a later section, applies far beyond the boundaries of sociology as a discipline.

THE LIMITS OF SOCIAL CHOICE

Although findings from the case studies point up serious limits on the applicability of technological determinist arguments, they do not necessarily suggest that the opposing view—from social choice—ought to be embraced without reservation. Indeed, they suggest rather strongly that social choice arguments—especially the notion of strategic choice advanced by Child (1972) and the assertion of a managerial "control imperative" in labor process theory (e.g., Braverman 1974; Edwards 1979)—provide an equally partial depiction of the process through which technological choices are made and implemented.

WHOSE STRATEGY? WHOSE CHOICE?

The concept of strategic choice as laid out by Child (1972) and applied to the study of technological change by Buchanan and Boddy (1983), Child (1985), and Clark et al. (1988) draws explicit attention to the active role that top managers and executives play in influencing, if not directly determining, organizational structure. It portrays strategic choice, and strategy formation in general, as an *interpretive process*: organizational leaders may gather and assess information from a wide variety of sources (external as well as internal to the organization), but the strategies they formulate and the choices they make are interpretations of the world that surrounds them. As Child argued in his seminal article (1972), the world—whether it is defined as the environment, history, or the organization itself—is no more real or immediate to those at the top of an organization than it is to anyone else. What distinguishes those at the top, however, is the power they possess to *enact* their interpretations as plans and directives that structure the organization. In this sense Child makes an important but often overlooked point: the behavior of organizational leaders is as likely to be affected by broadly normative, ideological, and political considerations as is that of any other group. In this formulation he builds into the concept of strategic choice a conception of politics that goes well beyond simple self-interest to include distinctive perspectives or beliefs about how people and organizations *should* work.

Given this conceptual base, we might expect analyses rooted in a strategic choice perspective to be far more sensitive to the mediating role of organizational process and politics in relation to technological choice. Yet we find instead that those studies have, for the most part, taken *a* strategic choice—or, more accurately, a formal decision to adopt a given technology—as the *starting point* for analysis. As a result, all that remains to be explained is the effect of the people and groups who occupy the layers between the top and the bottom of the organization on the manner in which "strategic choices" are *implemented*. We may be alerted to the existence of substrategies and to their ability to attenuate strategic intent, but the process of change is rendered analytically static: that is, the only interaction is that which is occasioned by the technology as it passes from one layer to the next. Politics is once again reduced to narrow self-interest, and substrategies are engaged only in reaction to hierarchical orders.

However, the case studies suggest that although this conception of strategic choice may apply in some situations, the process of change is on the whole far more dynamic and interactive than prior work would lead us to believe. Moreover, they show that politics is far more central to the choice of technology than has been recognized to this point. Three points from the case studies are relevant here.

First, choices between and within technologies—and by extension, choices between and within structures associated with those technologies—are not limited to the higher echelons of management. They may, in fact, originate at some distance removed (in time and space) from the top of the organization. Such choices and the activities that go into the framing of alternatives *prior to* the formal decision represent a critical part of the process of technological change that is all but invisible when one begins, as the strategic choice perspective does, with the formal decision to proceed with a change.

For example, the adoption of the FMS and surface mount technologies in the aircraft and computer companies, respectively, could be presented as outcomes of top-level strategic choice. After all, top managers' approval set each change in motion. But characterizing these changes as the outcome of strategic choice would seriously understate the significance of activities that preceded formal decisions. The decision to pursue the development of the FMS was made *in substance* in the middle of the organization, where the divisional operations manager resided. The choice was *ratified* or approved by top management, but little of the content of the change or the full range of its purposes or intended impacts was revealed in the process. Arguably, the choice was linked to organizational strategy, but given that, as the divisional manager explained, strategy consisted largely of the admonition to "cut costs, improve productivity, and lose heads," it would be difficult to argue that strategy was an explicit guide to choice. Rather, the FMS option was chosen on the basis of a particular *interpretation* of that strategy, the organization, and its environment and on the way each fit with that manager's world views. Thus, the divisional manager and his staff may have lacked the formal power with which to enact their choice, but they did exercise considerable influence in the *framing of the decision* to be made by higher-level executives. They exercised this influence by carefully constructing a story about the FMS that would, to all appearances, speak directly to broader organizational strategy—even if it required finessing the ROI.

The computer case makes the same point from a different angle. On the surface the "official story" about SMT seems to be a classic example of strategic choice. Yet detailed examination revealed that the official account told at best half the story. Missing was an explanation of how (or why) SMT came to be sufficiently strategic to warrant corporate action. Overlooked entirely were the arduous and in many ways quixotic efforts of manufacturing engineers to *make* SMT a strategic choice. Once again the point is not that top managers were uninvolved or that the organization lacked a competitive strategy; rather, it is that the choice alternatives *presented to* top management were the outcome of a complex set of events that took place long before and far away from the moment of strategic choice.

Second, the "substrategies" employed by different actors in the choice process are not just passive filters, nor can they be easily reduced to simple self-interest or structurally defined objectives. Instead, the case studies suggest that organizational actors—both in formulating proposals for change and in choosing how to respond to changes initiated by others—engage in no less complex a process of interpretation than do those to whom a strategic choice perspective pays greatest attention (i.e., top decision makers). In other words, subordinate position in an organizational hierarchy does not preclude the possibility that people harbor or even desire to enact objectives they feel to be important; nor does it mean that those objectives will be limited in scope to immediate self-interest or to the specific domain in which people work.

In fact, as the case studies demonstrate repeatedly, much of the overt contention that surrounds the process of technological change derives from differences in the interpretive frameworks—the worldviews—of the actors involved. Although often derided as "just politics," contention and conflict emanated from differences in what people believed to be important or necessary not only for themselves or for the positions they occupied but *for the organization as a whole*. Thus, even in what seemed to be the least ambitious or expansive example of change, the CNC case in chapter 2, shop managers saw in the new technology a means by which to achieve what they believed to be vital organizational objectives, as well as what might be viewed as specific positional objectives. Similarly, the actions of the divisional manager in the aircraft FMS case, the manufacturing engineers in the computer company, and the plant and union leaders in the auto company could very easily be dismissed as extensions of narrow career or economic interests; but such an explanation would overlook the way their actions also reflected visions of *the way things should work*. In the absence of formal power or the authority with which to impose their interpretations on the rest of their organization, each sought—albeit in different ways—to influence the premises on which decisions were made. Failing that, they sought to imprint on a decision already made their unique interpretation of the way it ought to be implemented.

The third and in many respects most significant limit on the utility of a strategic choice perspective involves the role of strategy—or *lack thereof*—in the process of technological choice. In short, in none of these organizations, and certainly in none of the cases, was there anything that could be identified as a technology or a manufacturing strategy. This is not to say that these companies did not routinely create elaborate strategic plans or forecasts; indeed they did. However, those plans and forecasts pertained primarily (if not exclusively) to *products* and only secondarily to *processes* for making their products.[12] With the possible exception of the aluminum company case, products, product technologies, and product needs were designated as the *drivers* of process technology and of manufacturing more generally. Although not unusual in assembled goods industries—especially in the United States (see Hayes, Wheelwright, and Clark 1988; Clark and Fujimoto 1991; Dertouzos, Lester, and Solow 1989)—the hegemony of the product has critical implications for the process of technological choice that, to date at least, have been largely ignored in the strategic choice literature.

Most important, the subordination of process to product and of manufacturing to product design left managers and engineers in manufacturing without a strategy to guide their choices other than what they could infer from careful scrutiny of new product developments. In this regard the case studies offer a measure of support to critics of the strategic choice perspective (e.g., Rose and Jones 1987; Barley 1986) who contend that broad statements of strategic intent offer little insight as to the outcomes of technological change. However, the absence of an explicit strategy did not prevent managers and engineers from constructing strategies to guide their choices; instead, it meant that the strategies they constructed were likely to be implicit, rather than explicit, and therefore invisible except through detailed observation of the process of technological choice.

The case studies are especially useful for what they reveal about the managers' and engineers' behavior in the absence of an explicit strategy to guide their choice of technology. Most directly, they suggest that the subordination of manufacturing to design reduced the incentive—or raised the perceived risks—of engaging in technological innovation. Departures from precedent were rare, and opportunities to innovate with major new technologies were both coveted and feared—as we saw in virtually every case. When departures were contemplated, considerable care was taken to create fallback positions, to align powerful allies,

12. In every company I requested and received access to information about market conditions, strategic plans, and forecasts. In some cases this information took the form of planning documents and analyses; in others I was briefed by representatives from corporate or divisional strategic planning offices. I had signed nondisclosure agreements with all four companies and was given no reason to believe that strategic objectives were withheld or obscured for fear that I might leak them. By no means did these companies lack for research and planning. However, what's at issue is the extent to which those studies and plans *actually* informed decision making around new technology; my contention is that their effect was indirect at best.

and to shield development activities from the view of "outsiders," including other departments as well as lower-level managers and workers. Even when the opportunity to innovate was actively sought out, history and power relations played an important role in shaping the choice and configuration of new process technology. In the computer company case, for example, it took an unconventional effort—a virtual social movement among manufacturing engineers—to garner the knowledge, resources, and visibility necessary to make a case for surface mount technology. Still, once the technology proved feasible, the insurgency was rapidly co-opted by higher-level management and the design labs, leaving the status of manufacturing engineers and the structure of the organization largely unchanged.

Moreover, the subordination of process to product helps explain why manufacturing managers and engineers would adhere to traditional return-on-investment metrics. In most cases those metrics provided a functional substitute for an explicit manufacturing strategy. That is, the problem was *not* that other metrics were unavailable or that suitable ones could not be devised with some imagination; rather, in the absence of a manufacturing strategy, those other metrics *lacked meaning and therefore influence*.[13] Thus, when manufacturing managers and engineers were faced with product design organizations hostile to changes in manufacturing processes that did not meet with their prior approval and, more generally, when they were faced with higher-level decision makers for whom alternative measures made no sense, the default option was also the safest: to restrict the search for both problems and solutions that fit with traditional measures—even when doing so might produce deleterious consequences (e.g., increases in the volume of indirect labor). On those few occasions when managers and engineers chose to go out on a limb, they ardently resisted arguing for alternative measures because "having the numbers"—even numbers they may have ridiculed in private—enabled them to argue that their choices were legitimate. The numbers were legitimate because they had been screened through a *procedure* that was deemed to be legitimate and defensible.

In sum, the strategic choice perspective remains useful for the attention it draws to the *capacity* of people in organizations to choose technology and, through technology, to affect organizational structures

---

13. I return to the general issue of manufacturing strategy—and an interpretive framework supportive of manufacturing innovation—later in this chapter and at greater length in the final section of chapter 7.

and practices in ways that are consistent with particular interpretations of the organization and its environment. However, the case studies suggest that the strategic choice perspective has limited applicability because (1) it presumes that choices made at the top of the organization are strategic by definition, when in fact they may only be ratifications of decisions made elsewhere; (2) it characterizes the substrategies of the groups that occupy the intervening layers between the top and the bottom as unidimensional when they are instead multidimensional and, more important, proactive as well as reactive; and (3) it presents organizational strategy as an explicit and comprehensive guide to all an organization's major activities when, by contrast, strategy may pertain only to activities that are deemed strategic: that is, others may be left to operate within constraints over which they can exercise little direct control and within which, if they are to innovate at all, they must do so by nonsanctioned means.

The case study findings thus lead to an ironic conclusion: although the concept of strategic choice was formulated as a response to the failure of functionalist theories (e.g., technological determinism) "to give due attention to the agency of choice by whoever have the power to direct the organization" (Child 1972, 2), the strategic choice perspective restricts our attention to the behavior of top-level managers and to the implementation of their decisions. Like the functionalist theories it critiques, it leads us to conclude that history—as embedded in prior decisions about technology and structure—is largely irrelevant to understanding the range of new technologies or new social systems an organization is capable of or willing to adopt. And, finally, it leaves us to wonder how the very strategic choices that result in major technological changes *actually come about*.

CLASS ACTION?

Labor process theory—the other and in many ways more emphatic variant on social choice—also deserves scrutiny on the basis of the case study findings. Although Marx's admonition to enter the "hidden abode" of production spurred prodigious efforts to analyze the labor process under capitalism, the principal advocates of labor process theory in the United States largely ignored organizational processes and relations that did not seem to have a direct influence on the structuring of skills or the distribution of control over work. Braverman (1974), for example, argued that capitalists, aided by the managers and engineers they hired, used physical technology as a tool with which to divide, deskill, and ultimately dominate workers. Yet he gave only passing mention to the organizational forms and processes in and through which those technologies were designed and deployed. In other cases (e.g., Edwards 1979; Gordon, Edwards, and Reich 1982) differences in organizational size, scale, and market power were used to distinguish between "monopoly" and "competitive" or "core" and "peripheral" enterprises; but again, organizational and intraorganizational levels of analysis were treated as virtually transparent. Even some of the most insightful field studies, such as Burawoy's (1979) study of a machine shop, resort to con-jecture and theoretical assertion instead of empirical observation when trying to bridge the gap between the social organization of the shop floor and the macrodynamics of capitalist enterprises and economies.

Whether the researchers were content to assume that organizational processes and relations were inconsequential, were hampered by the difficulties of trying to assimilate organizations into a theoretical framework that only had room for classes, or were unable to gain access to data beyond the shop floor, the result was the same: researchers analyzed work processes in virtual isolation from the rest of the organizations in which they were located. Moreover, in treating technology as a tool in the hands of capitalists and managers, they gave it the appearance of being infinitely elastic and mutable, governed almost exclusively by a logic of class domination. Technological choice, in other words, would be little more than an extension of managerial objectives.

From the perspective of the case studies, labor process theory comes up short in three distinct areas. First, labor process theory assumes not only that capitalists and their agents share a common consciousness but also that they work in concert to enact common objectives through the design of both the technical and the social systems of production. Although *control* was frequently referred to in the cases as a concern or an objective associated with the introduction of new technology, the object of control was as likely to be *other* managers or departments as it was to be workers. Proponents of the aircraft company FMS declared the entire machining factory "out of control"; shop managers in that factory wanted an automated storage and retrieval system to get control over their parts flow. Shop managers in the CNC case wanted control over parts ordering and programming in order to serve their customers. Manufacturing engineers in the computer company wanted control over prototyping, board assembly, and even board design. Top-level auto company executives saw the design of the FMS cell as part of a strategy for enhancing control over the plants, and so on. At one level, each change proponent attached a different meaning to the term *control*; however, the breadth of concern and contention over control suggests that no group or objective could be identified as the *singular* focus of these many meanings of control.

If anything, what emerges from the case studies is a singular concern with creating spheres of activity within which *any group* (be it executives, managers, engineers, production supervisors, or workers) could enact their particular view of *the way things should work*. Indeed, as I argue in the next section, that concern represents one of the most important themes to come out of the case studies. It is also one of the most important underpinnings for a power-process analysis of technological choice and change in organizations.

Second, labor process theory substantially overlooks the role of engineers in the design of new technology. Theorists have been content to assume not only that engineers are an undifferentiated group but that they unconditionally and unreflectively obey the commands of their organizational superiors. Even Noble (1984) portrays engineers as largely devoid of aspirations or worldviews apart from a kind of presocial or antisocial consciousness in which machines are more trustworthy than human beings. Yet the case studies present a picture that differs in important ways. In some instances the engineers who design physical processes share their superiors' suspicion and disdain for workers *and* for lower-level managers.[14] But far more often they harbor conceptions of work systems that could just as easily upgrade as downgrade worker skills. What they tend to lack is the capacity, the language, and, most important, the power with which to make those visions real. They are, as I pointed out in the last section, no less constrained by history and power relations in these organizations than are the managers for whom they work or the plant supervisors and workers who are ultimately "impacted" by the technologies they design.

This point is most evident when, under admittedly unusual circumstances, opportunities arise that allow (or force) engineers to pursue conceptions of the labor process that depart from precedent. For example, in the auto and aluminum company cases, engineers were engaged in a way that changed the parameters of their assignments and enabled

14. This clearly seemed to be the case in the aircraft company, as depicted in chapter 2. However, it bears recalling that, as one engineer told me, "you repeat what you hear in order to get what you want." That is, mimicking the buzzwords and even the demeanor of one's superiors may be necessary in order to get the opportunity to do "real engineering."

them to work collaboratively with managers, supervisors, and workers to solve problems of *common* interest rather than narrowly defined problems of departmental, professional, or hierarchical interest.

Third, labor process theory has a great deal of difficulty explaining situations in which workers themselves play a central and collaborative role in the design and introduction of new technology. The only real allowance made for this occurrence is a variant on "false consciousness": workers are enticed into a form of self-exploitation by what only appear to be opportunities to gain greater control over the labor process. Certainly this has been at the core of labor process theorists' critiques of worker participation (cf. Parker 1985; Thomas 1988; Kelly 1987; Grenier 1988), Japanese management techniques (Parker and Slaughter 1985; Burawoy 1985; Yamamoto 1981), and new approaches to work organization such as lean production and flexible specialization (Hyman 1989; Bergren, Bjorkman, and Hollander 1991). Yet, although there is empirical evidence to support many of these criticisms, the case studies suggest that at least some of the success of new technologies like the rod caster and the effort to jointly design the auto company FMS must be attributed to the efforts of workers to realize in practice their desires to use new technology in ways that gave them a stake in both the process and the products of manufacturing. In other words, the ardent efforts of those workers to realize their own worldviews about the way things should work may reflect a false consciousness, but those same efforts also represented a source of enormous pride, too.

To draw attention to the limits of labor process theory is, once again, not to deny it completely as a source of insight on the social context within which technologies are chosen and used. There is no reason to quibble with the historical significance of class conflict as a "driver" of managerial efforts to enhance their control over production. However, it is to argue that class conflict is not the only axis of contention in the design and deployment of new technology. Other lines of cleavage are not inconsequential, and, more important, they are not simple derivations of a primordial struggle between labor and capital. Only in the absence of detailed study of the *process* of technological change is it possible to arrive at the conclusion that class conflict alone is the driver of technological choice.

In sum, the case studies do not call for a complete disregard for the insights to be drawn from the social choice perspective—any more than they warrant the total rejection of technological determinism. The value of a social choice perspective resides in its insistence on the inclusion of social and organizational context as mainstays in the analysis of technological change. Yet as I've tried to show, research based on the social choice perspective has not been attentive *enough* to the multiple, the complex, and the historically situated objectives called into play in the process of change.

THE POWER-PROCESS PERSPECTIVE: AN ELABORATION

The power-process perspective is distinguished by its intense concern with technological change as a *process*. It begins from the assertion that analyses of discrete episodes of change—especially analyses that are limited empirically to the observation of outcomes—implicitly deny the idea that history and organizational process have any effect on either the choice or the outcomes of technological change. From a power-process perspective, *before technological change is possible, before any impacts occur, many choices have to be made.* These choices are not limited to the features of a given technology or to the formal decision to adopt a given technology. In fact, the choices of greatest interest are *the choices about how choices will or can be made*; these are manifestations of history (prior choices) that take the form of a structure, a set of procedures, and a set of norms, precedents, and institutionalized understandings about the range of possible technologies and social systems an organization is willing and able to consider, much less to implement. The way an organization structures and conducts its search for alternatives offers valuable insights as to the effect of history not only on its current form and functioning but on its *possible* futures as well.

Rather than squander the opportunity to gain insight into what an organization is or could be by ignoring the things it chooses *not to be*, the power-process perspective pays close attention to selection among alternative choices. As I've tried to demonstrate in the case studies, the options an organization chooses *not* to consider seriously and the ones it rules out of bounds (the unorthodox propositions) can be as enlightening as the ones it chooses to pursue. Including the "paths not taken" forces any analysis, even the analysis of a discrete change, to attend to the effect of history on the framing of choice alternatives *throughout* the change process—not simply to the way past investments can lever choices about alternative futures during the initial stages of change but also to the way history influences different actors' conceptions of what is proper or possible at each moment in the process of change.

In these respects the power-process perspective has a dialectical quality: *it simultaneously diverges from and bridges the technological determinist and social choice perspectives.* It diverges from the technological determinist perspective by asserting that even in those instances in which a new technology (as an exogenous or an endogenous development) appears and carries with it demonstrable advantages over an existing technique, it must be recognized before it can have an impact. The technological determinist perspective, given its emphasis on technologies that have already had their "impact," is in the seemingly enviable position of being able to dispense with a concern about choice. Yet as I noted earlier, unless an organization is able or willing to recognize the existence of an alternative technology, it will not be able to implement it. Thus, the power-process perspective reintroduces a vital part of the analysis of technological change: how an organization's capacity for "seeing" (i.e., recognizing and evaluating) alternatives affects what it is likely to see.

The power-process perspective diverges from the social choice perspective by asserting that even in those instances where a change in technology is heralded as strategic, it is essential to investigate the activities that go into the framing of choice alternatives. The power-process perspective does not deny that technological choice can be an extension of organizational strategy—any more than it denies that choices between and within technologies establish a design space that limits the degrees of freedom available for modifying the technology in its use. However, by extending the investigation back in time—to the prehistory of a strategic choice—the power-process perspective forces us to confront the possibility that strategic intent may be mediated or attenuated in two directions, not one: *before* a formal decision is made (i.e., in the interpretation of strategic objectives that lead to proposals for change) and *after* a formal decision is made (i.e., in the interpretation of the intents embedded in the change).

The power-process perspective bridges technological determinism and social choice by arguing that the relationship between technology and organization is dynamic and interactive. At any given moment technological change may "cause" organizational adaptation; or organizational objectives may "cause" a change in technology. By extending the temporal and the organizational context for analysis, however, the power-process perspective forces us to recognize that technology and organization *structure one another* over time. That is, technological changes in one time period may not only cause organizational adaptation but may also impose constraints on the range of possible technologies an organization will be able (or willing) to consider at a future time. Likewise, social or strategic choices in one time period may not only cause technological change but may also impose constraints on the range of possible strategies (or structures) an organization will be able (or willing) to consider at a future time. In other words, the power-process perspective does not deny that the *proximate* cause or stimulus to change can come from either technology or organization; it does, however, suggest that neither can be analyzed independent of the other and, even more important, that neither can be completely subsumed by the logic of the other.

PURPOSIVE STRUCTURING

The power-process perspective recaptures the motion or interaction between technology and organization that is lost when history is segmented into discrete episodes of change. It does not deny that history (whether individual or organizational) may be recalled or even experienced episodically, for example, as a string of stirring images or critical events. But it does suggest that the connecting time between vivid episodes is much more important than either the technological determinist or the social choice perspectives let on. The intervening periods can be a time when changes already completed are routinized, when routines long in place are institutionalized, when the constraints associated with institutionalization are translated into pressures for change, and when the ideas, strategies, and technologies that will be put on the next agenda for choice are framed. In other words, it is the time when choices about how choice will be made are themselves made.

In this respect the power-process perspective parallels and extends structuration theory (cf. Giddens 1976; 1979), particularly as it has been applied to organizations (cf. Barley 1986; Barley 1990; Ranson, Hinings, and Greenwood 1980; Orlikowski 1992). Like structuration theory, the power-process perspective has at its core a dualistic conception of organizational structure. On the one hand, structure is a *constraint* on social action. Structure takes the form of historically derived rules, understandings, and patterns of interaction that shape the way organizational members perceive, respond to, and make sense of everyday life. On the other hand, structure is a *product* of social action. The same rules, understandings, and patterns of interaction constitute or create structure through their repetition. Unlike more traditional conceptions of structure as a static set of offices or rules, structure is portrayed as the object of constructive activity, particularly since the people who occupy the offices and who create, interpret, and obey the rules are active, creative subjects. Thus, institutionalized rules and norms may lend a measure of stability to organizational life, but rules and norms can neither anticipate every contingency nor provide an all-inclusive guide as to how organizational members interpret or respond to unanticipated events. Slippages between the "institutional template and the exigencies of daily life" (Barley 1986, 80) can appear, and like the proverbial grain of sand that may become the pearl, they may reconfigure the structure of social and organizational settings. Technological change can be a source of such a slippage.[15]

The power-process perspective and structuration theory contribute to our understanding of technological change in organizations in two key ways. First, and most directly, they force us to pay close attention to the interaction between external developments and the interpretive acts of people in specific social and historical contexts. More specifically, they suggest that we treat technological change as a *process of translation*. In order to be incorporated as part of routine organizational life, technology must be translated from a physical object into a social one. Organizational actors must recognize that technology exists and negotiate a set of understandings about what it is (and what it is capable of) and what it means: how it defines and redefines tasks, responsibilities, and relationships and how susceptible it is to social influence. In this sense both approaches give theoretical grounding to what others have described as the inevitable modification or reinvention of technologies as they are adopted by organizations (Rice and Rogers 1979; Leonard-Barton 1987; Nord and Tucker 1987).

---

15. The utility of these ideas is demonstrated in Barley's (1986) longitudinal study of the introduction of new imaging equipment in the radiology departments of a matched pair of hospitals. Although the same equipment was introduced in both cases, authority and control over its operation was centralized in one setting and decentralized in the other. Whereas a finding of this sort would have been lost in a cross-sectional study of the "impacts" of the new technology, Barley's close examination reveals that the differences in structural outcome (specifically, in the degree of centralization) were very much influenced by the social context and the meanings that end users attached to the technology and to their relationships with one another as mediated by the technology. In other words, the technical attributes of the new equipment may have challenged the extant structure of each radiology department, but the observed outcomes could be understood only as a joint product of technology and social interaction.

Second, both approaches force us to recognize just how contingent and variable outcomes can be. By attending directly to the context within which change takes place, to the alterations that must be negotiated in order for technology to be used, and to the reproduction of those alterations as durable changes in both meaning and practice, they suggest that efforts to predict (or explain) structural outcomes solely from the attributes of the technology itself are likely to be at best partial and incomplete. Moreover, they suggest that cross-sectional snapshots of structural change are likely to underestimate or miss entirely the stage or direction of structuring activity in organizations that are assumed to have been "impacted" by the same technology.

However, the power-process perspective extends beyond structuration theory in two important respects. First, structuration theory begs the question of *why* a given technology should appear on the scene such that it becomes an occasion for structuring. Even in Barley's studies (1986; 1990) the arrival of the technology is not questioned; new technology, in other words, is treated as largely an exogenous and unexplained event. Second, structuration theory offers only limited insight as to the conditions under which technological change (or any other slippage between institutionalized norms and everyday life) reinforces or modifies organizational structure.

The critical piece missing from structuration theory, in other words, is an explicit treatment of *purpose*. By attending primarily to the meaning that end users attach to a change in technology and by neglecting the process through which the technology is designed and configured, structuration theory makes technology appear fixed. Even more ironically, technology comes to be treated as the motive force behind change. The meaning of a new technology may, as Barley (1986, 106) has argued, be derived from the social context of its use; however, the *purpose* of a new technology can be understood only in terms of the objectives or ends that its proponents (or creators) seek to achieve by means of its use.

From a power-process perspective, purpose must be at the very heart of the analysis of technological change precisely because change is portrayed as a series of choices. In order to understand how and why exogenous developments come to be recognized or how and why strategic choices come to be made, *it is essential to understand who or what segments of an organization have the power with which to define the parameters of search for problems and solutions, the criteria with which alternatives are evaluated, and the manner in which a choice once made is implemented.* Of necessity, the power-process perspective accords a central role to power relations in organizations—those that are rooted in formal structure as well as those that arise out of the control of organizational resources (Pfeffer and Salancik 1978; Pfeffer 1978). As I argue in the next section, power relations are especially important and especially complex because technology is often represented (as well as perceived) as *apolitical*, that is, as governed by a logic that sets it apart from human or social interests.

THE POLITICAL HAND

A central issue in the debate over the relationship between technology and structure is the *location* of the stimuli to change. From the technological determinist perspective, change occurs as a result of exogenous events and forces that upset the equilibrium and cause organizational adaptation. From the social choice perspective, exogenous developments certainly play a role, but they are mediated either by top-level strategic choice or by an overarching managerial imperative. The power-process perspective can accommodate both those alternatives; more important, however, it offers a third alternative: in addition to the "invisible hand" of exogenous forces or the "visible hand" of strategic choice, change may occur as a result of a "political hand," that is, *change that is initiated in response to existing structure by means of technology.*

A review of the cases supports the emphasis on power relations—but it also calls into question whether resource dependence or strategic contingencies theories of power and politics (cf. Hickson et al. 1971) are themselves adequate to the task of analyzing what is, from a power-process perspective, a relationship of *mutual determination.* That is, when the cases are analyzed on their own, it is reasonably clear that the organizational units that controlled resources, that were relatively nonsubstitutable, and that managed what were deemed to be critical sources of uncertainty for the organization were far better positioned to choose the problems they deemed important and to impose technological solutions they felt appropriate. On a broader scale the manufacturing organizations in most of the companies studied were deemed less critical than product development organizations, were granted far less control over organizational resources, and were (to a varying degree) considered substitutable (e.g., the auto parts plant was told that unless it operated more efficiently, it would be closed altogether).

Yet the case studies also suggest that it may be as misleading to argue from a model of resource dependence or strategic contingencies alone as it is to argue from technology or strategic choice. As often as not, the choices of technology were influenced not simply by the extant power structure but by *efforts to alter that power structure by means of technology.* For example, a significant subset of the manufacturing engineers in the computer company envisioned SMT as a lever to make organizational change, that is, to mobilize disaffected peers to argue for the creation of a more centralized approach to circuit board assembly, one that would grant them an unprecedented level of control over manufacturing processes and, by extension, over product designers. Likewise, lower-level managers in the CNC and FMS cases sought to use technology to alter power relations in their organizations. In the aluminum and auto company cases, subordinate units sought to gain a measure of standing with more powerful R&D organizations in order to gain greater autonomy over their own affairs. In other words, *choices of technology could be influenced as much by efforts to alter structure and power relations as they could by efforts to reinforce or reproduce existing relations.* Resource dependency theory may emphasize the centrality of power and control, but it is far better equipped to explain *extant* power relations than it is to account for the dynamics of internally induced change.

Viewed from the power-process perspective, *technological choice represents a vehicle for the expression and enactment of the worldviews of its advocates and designers.* Physical technology—the aspect of organization that appears most objective, universal, and apolitical in and of itself—has the potential to be among the most effective tools in political struggle inside organizations. The use of technology either to alter or to reinforce internal power relations would, however, be all but invisible to the other perspectives. Technological determinists leave no room for the analysis of motives, other than those that can be attributed to an entire organization. Social choice theorists might attend to the strategic intentions of top managers or to the motives of capitalists/managers as a class, but they would very likely ignore the motives and activities of those who engaged in the choice and design of new technology. Even resource dependency and strategic contingencies theories would be hard-pressed to detect, much less to explain, efforts to alter structure through technology until *after* they had succeeded in doing so.

TECHNOLOGY POLITICS

Tempting though it might be to dismiss the politics of technological choice as "just politics" (i.e., the pursuit of self-interest), to write it off as an irritating but innocuous sort of friction, or even to view it as a sign of deviant or maladaptive organizational behavior, the power-process perspective suggests another and in many ways much more provocative interpretation: *political action might be a vital—though not necessarily a comfortable—part of technological change.* Rather than restrict the analysis of politics to its role as an impediment to, or a by-product of, technological change (cf. Kotter and Schlesinger 1979; Coch and French 1948; Lawrence 1954), it may make sense to consider political conflict as a precondition or even a stimulus to change. Politics could then be viewed as a generative or creative influence in organizational life.

By allowing for the possibility that politics can be a creative activity, the power-process perspective does not limit us to viewing politics as an expression of narrow self-interest—a Hobbesian "war of all against all"—and it gives us an alternative to the reductionist assumptions about human motivation that often characterize economic analysis. Instead, we can allow for the possibility that the worldviews of different organizational actors (as individuals, groups, or even entire categories) may contain both a large component of self-interest and a genuine commitment to notions of collective interest. Group worldviews are certain to be influenced by extant structure, rules, assignments, and the like, but the content of those worldviews and their potency (i.e., their potential to serve as the basis for action) cannot be directly inferred from structure.[16] Thus, when contention arises, it need not immediately be interpreted as one or another group's effort simply to gain power, as if power alone were the ultimate objective of every political struggle; instead, contention may represent an attempt to gain *through power* the means by which to put in place a set of relations and practices that more nearly approximate a group's view of the way things should work for themselves and for the organization as a whole.

In testimony to the vitality of different worldviews even in the face of historical, economic, technical, as well as ideological constraints, it is

16. Zald and Berger (1978) provide an extensive set of propositions about how internally induced change might come about based on characteristics of organizational structure. Structure is, however, used largely as a predictor of the availability of resources for mobilizing change efforts. Little attention is paid to explaining *why* people would engage in political action.

worthwhile to recall that the computer company manufacturing engineers undertook considerable risk in their dogged efforts to prove the value of SMT. Likewise, managers, technicians, and workers in the aluminum and auto companies went out on a limb in their efforts to influence not only the implementation of technology but also the parameters of its design. Once again, those efforts reflected both factional interests and what they genuinely believed to be collective interests. They were efforts formulated as much in response to historical structures, power relations, and dominant interpretive frames as they were unique manifestations of particularistic interests.

Obviously, not all the cases were characterized by overt challenges to the status quo. We might conclude, therefore, that the case studies from which these ideas are built are really quite unusual or special. This may be so. However, the case studies also suggest that the *absence* of such a challenge may indicate that other behaviors are substituted for the ones that lead to ferment, contention, innovation and change. For example, in the face of what are perceived to be immutable constraints, subordinate groups may *focus inward*, trying to cut out domains in which they can enact what their worldviews inspire; *resign* themselves to living within the rules, manifested in what can be described only as a bureaucratic mind-set; or *retreat* into a purely instrumental relationship with the organization, doing nothing more than what is necessary to get the job done. The senior engineers in the aircraft company who warned the RAC project team against excessive enthusiasm are a case in point. The manufacturing engineers in the computer company with their self-described "heroic efforts" to "thanklessly produce ugly boards" are another example. The R&D engineers in the aircraft and auto companies jealously guarded their opportunities to do what they believed to be "real engineering" because such opportunities were so infrequent and because they were so easily undermined by "others"—other engineers, other managers and supervisors, and workers.

In other words, frustration, resignation, and boundary warfare redirect energy that might be expended in experimentation or in innovative redesign of extant processes and relations into efforts either to channel changes along preexisting paths (e.g., incremental improvements at best) or to resist change altogether. In each case, the result is the same: the inertial relationship between technology and structure remains in effect, and with it comes a further institutionalization of assumptions and practices. Advances *within* a known technical system might occur, but they will proceed largely without deviation from a given trajectory.

CROSSING THE BRIDGE BETWEEN
DETERMINISM AND CHOICE

The power-process perspective offers a bridge between two opposed and in many respects contradictory perspectives on technology and organization. The power-process perspective incorporates, rather than denies, the idea that the logic that governs physical technology is distinct from the logic of social organization; thus, it leaves open the possibility that changes in technology can force the social system of an organization to adapt in patterned ways. So long as we can accept the idea that organizations operate in the same physical reality and are therefore subject to the same constraints, we can reasonably expect that identical physical technologies will leave identical imprints or "impacts" on those organizations.[17] Accepting that condition does not deny that people, groups, organizations, or even entire societies might discover or formulate new ways to think about or act on physical reality and thus set in motion new patterns of organizational structuring. Neither does it deny that the patterns we observe in the way people, organizations, and so on interact with or use physical technology may not also be the product of simple emulation or unreflective mimicry of the behavior of others.[18]

However, the power-process perspective identifies two critical limits inherent in this conceptualization. First, the physical technologies must actually be identical. Similarity in name only, as I argued earlier, is not sufficient; in fact, it can obscure significant differences in the design space available to end users (whether organizations or individuals) in *how* they use the technology in question and therefore in what impacts the technology can have. Second, the social conceptions of physical reality and physical technology must also be identical. That is, differences in culture and ideology can dramatically influence understandings of what physical technology is and how it should be used (cf. Benedict 1934; Geertz 1973; Tausky 1978). To give an extreme example: to an adult, a Rolex watch may be a precision instrument for measuring the passage of time, but to an eighteen-month-old child it may be an effective device for pounding pegs. More serious examples can be drawn

---

17. Indeed, unless we are willing to ascribe agency to technology, we have no choice but to accept that condition.

18. In other words, the patterns of technological impact could very well be influenced by what institutional theory refers to as "mimetic" pressures (cf. DiMaggio and Powell 1983) rather than efficiency considerations or the discovery of the "one best way" to use technology, organize production, compete, and so forth.

from the small but important comparative and cross-cultural literature on work organization.[19] There we find, for example, that some Japanese firms may employ equipment identical to their U.S. counterparts but operate it in dramatically different ways—for example, investing substantial sums in worker training as an extension *both* of a different conception of how technology ought to be used and, more broadly, of a different philosophy of human abilities and human potential. In other words, technological determinist arguments do hold, but they hold under very restrictive conditions. To understand what occurs when those conditions vary (or are not met), we need a perspective that draws explicit attention to *how and why* those conditions vary.

By characterizing technological change as a process of translation, the power-process perspective highlights the importance of culture and ideology in the perception of physical reality and physical technology. It incorporates human agency in the choice of technology in much the same way that the social choice perspective does. In that respect the power-process perspective does not deny that conceptions of what is physically possible or necessary may be guided by the strategic objectives of an organization or the interests of a class of similarly situated organizational actors. Nor does it reject the idea that when those objectives or interests vary, the choice and use of physical technology will vary, too.

However, the power-process perspective questions whether it is possible or even useful to conceive of organizations as characterized by a *single* set of objectives or interests—or, for that matter, to assume that organizations can be characterized as containing only one conception of physical reality. One worldview or interpretive frame may be dominant in an organization (or in a collection of organizations), but the dominance of that worldview cannot be taken for granted, it cannot be assumed to be permanent, and it cannot be assumed to be immune from challenges—from either *internal* or external sources. Thus, conceptions of technological choice drawn from strategic choice and labor process theories may hold, but they hold under very restrictive conditions: that is, that top managers or capitalists as a class must be able to articulate and consistently enforce a single, coherent, and comprehensive worldview that is capable of directing (and constraining) the thoughts and behaviors of all organizational participants, including themselves. Such a situation may arise, but its existence would presume unlikely

19. See, for example, Piore and Sabel (1984), Cole (1979; 1989), Locke (1991), Whittaker (1988), Kern and Schumann (1989), and Westney (1987).

levels of knowledge and power. Alternatively, such a situation could occur only in organizations that are remarkably stable, even inertial. Only under conditions of great stability and near unanimity in the worldviews of organizational participants could such all-inclusive preferences hold with so much force.

The key difference introduced by the power-process perspective is the possibility for technological change to be triggered by *internal* political action. Rather than limit the repertoire of explanations to exogenous developments, top-level strategic choices, or class-based interests, the power-process perspective points to internal organizational dynamics as a stimulus to change through technology. In that respect the power-process perspective need not resort to using events outside the analytical frame to explain action inside the frame.

The idea, once again, is that organizations are composed of multiple worldviews. These worldviews will overlap in significant ways; no organized activity could continue for long without shared understandings, experiences, and norms. Yet when sufficient desire, opportunity, and resources are available, organizational actors—especially groups of actors—may take actions in areas that fall outside the overlap or intersection of worldviews and in ways that may or may not be consistent with formal organizational objectives. Desires for status, recognition, redress of inequities, and spheres of autonomous action can all compel groups to go outside institutionalized rules in the effort to enact their views of the way things should work. Opportunities can arise in areas that are not covered by formal rules and objectives or in areas where it is not clear who has responsibility or power. Thus, opportunities need not be formally endowed or sanctioned to be used for the enactment of worldviews.[20] Finally, resources can be mobilized from many quarters when desires are strong and opportunities are available, as occurred in the efforts of manufacturing engineers in the computer company.

By drawing attention to the possibility for political action to influence the choice of technology, the power-process perspective does not suggest that it is the only influence. Political action is, however, an

---

20. Indeed, as I argue in the next section, the partitioning of opportunities to engage in innovation *inside* organizations is likely to stifle innovation generally or force non-sanctioned innovation. The distinction is important. Peters and Waterman (1982) wax lyrical in their praise of skunkworks approaches to innovation, and Kidder's (1981) story of the development of a new computer at Data General equally glorifies the behind-the-scenes efforts of product development engineers; but it should be recognized that in virtually every case these innovations take place in parts of the organization where they are considered legitimate even when they are not always considered conventional. However, the same activities undertaken in a part of the organization that is expected to be stable

influence on the process of technological change that is least likely to be recognized by static, unidirectional models of technology and organization and the least likely to be visible in snapshot studies of the outcomes of technological change. It can be detected only by extending the temporal and organizational context for analysis and thus by reanimating what is, in fact, a dynamic and interactive relationship.

THE POLITICS OF INNOVATION AND INNOVATIVE POLITICS

If political action can be viewed as a stimulus as well as a response to technological change, then it is appropriate to ask whether we can extend the idea further. That is, what role do politics play in the broader process of organizational innovation and change?

The topic of organizational innovation is both critical and elusive.[21] Innovation is critical to organizational survival in competitive environments. It is, however, elusive both theoretically and practically because at its core innovation is made up of contradictory activities that are joined in an ambiguous process. That is, innovation in general, but in organizations particularly, is simultaneously *a subversive and a constitutive activity*. It is subversive in the sense that it undermines or dissolves established practices or concepts. It is constitutive in the sense that it constitutes or creates new practices and concepts to take the place of the ones it subverts. In slightly different terms, to innovate, organizations must have the capacity to carry out two contradictory activities: promoting stability and consistency in performance along the lines of what Nelson and Winter (1982) characterize as routines while at the same time devising and engaging in activities intended to promote the *dissolution* of routines. The ambiguous process that connects these contradictory activities is a *social process of imagination*, that is, a process that

---

and quite conventional—for example, manufacturing—are usually treated with far less tolerance. To use another example, both fighter pilots and test pilots in the U.S. Air Force, as Wolfe (1979) showed, were formally prohibited from engaging in rule-breaking behavior (e.g., pushing the outside of the envelope), but informally they were encouraged to do so for reasons both of product development and organizational esprit de corps. However, one can easily imagine what would be the formal response to equally innovative or risk-taking behavior on the part of mechanics, supply logicians, or security guards.

21. Perhaps not surprisingly, it has spawned an enormous literature, not all of which can be reviewed or referenced here. For very effective overviews, see Van de Ven (1986), Marquis (1982), Kanter (1988), Burgelman (1984), Maidique (1980), Abernathy and Clark (1985), Kimberly (1980), Kimberly and Evanisko (1981), and Roberts (1968; 1988).

involves collaboration among people to generate a new concept or practice and then to articulate it in such a way that it can be understood and enacted.

Framed in those terms, innovation shares many of the features of combustion in an automobile engine. It is, as Schumpeter (1950) argued, simultaneously a creative and a destructive act. It can be a source of great power and motion, but it can also cause great damage. It must be contained and directed to prevent it from being dissipated or from destroying the very setting in which it takes place. Simply put, the problem of innovation for organizations is one of conducting a controlled explosion.

As useful as the engine analogy may be, it breaks down when we compare the physics of combustion with the sociology of innovation. We may not completely understand combustion, but we have a relatively high level of confidence about several aspects of the phenomenon: for example, that molecules of fuel, air, and so on, are not conscious or self-aware; that we need not worry about whether they are willing to participate in the explosion or whether they have alternative views about what they should be doing; and that the stimulus to the explosion is the one we have introduced. Not so, unfortunately, with either the elements or the interactions involved in organizational innovation: we may assemble the ingredients, contain and direct them, and introduce various stimuli, but we cannot say with great confidence that we understand the elements or their interactions. At one level we suffer from an inability to control the context adequately; and even if we could, the exercise of that much control could prevent the occurrence of the very thing we want to happen (or to study), or the thing we observe could turn out to be an artifact of the experimental context. At another and more important level, however, we suffer from the fact that the elements involved *are* conscious and self-aware. We are confronted with the existence of *many* individuals and therefore many motives, interests, and worldviews. Organizational managers (and organizational theorists) thus face an interesting challenge: they want the explosion to happen, and they want it to be contained and directed; but they don't know precisely how to make it happen, much less how to contain and direct it when it does.

Given the importance of innovation and the breadth of social science attention it has garnered, it is ironic that researchers tend to tread lightly when it comes to the role of politics and political action in the process of organizational innovation. Theories of innovation and the conditions that seem to facilitate or retard it have their roots in economics, psychology, organizational behavior, and sociology, but political conflict and resistance are almost always treated as outcomes of, or obstacles to, innovation. Researchers may readily agree that power or authority is an important ingredient in understanding how change occurs, but few seriously consider the possibility that political conflict may be a driver of innovation (including technological innovation) or that innovation may be pursued in ways that are difficult to square with formally stated organizational goals.

There appear to be three main reasons why power and political conflict are treated so gingerly. First, innovation is considered, almost by definition, to be in accord with a broader set of organizational objectives. For example, Kanter's (1988) life-cycle model of organizational innovation gives considerable emphasis to interest mediation and conflict; but little attention is given either to the innovation itself or to the motives that may be driving change proponents. Both are *presumed* to be consistent with organizational objectives in large measure because the analysis is restricted to those individuals and groups who are *sanctioned* to engage in innovation (most commonly, product development groups). Similarly, Walton (1987) explains conflict and failed implementation as the product of inadequate integration of organizational stakeholders in the implementation process but takes for granted the positive attributes of information technology. Politics and conflict are thus reduced to a regrettable (even preventable) mismatch between established routines and relationships and those called forth by a new product or process. In neither case, however, are the purposes attached to the technology scrutinized critically, and because of the limited focus of investigation, no allowance is made for nonsanctioned innovation. Innovation may thus be "colored by politics" without being seen as political by nature (Burns 1961, 259).

Second, most theories assume that goal consensus is the essential ingredient of organization. By definition, then, conflict is considered dysfunctional and indicative of organizational ineffectiveness. Competition may be tolerated or even encouraged, but only so long as it occurs within, and therefore reproduces, the established order. Although this is certainly a defensible assumption, it is also an extremely restrictive one because behavior that cannot be explicitly justified by reference to formal goals is considered deviant and therefore deleterious. Yet under these conditions it is difficult to imagine how innovation or change can occur—except from the top down (since the legitimate authority with which to set and interpret formal objectives is hierarchically arrayed) or from the outside in (in response to unavoidable external pressures). Left aside is the possibility that the object of action may be a change in the goals themselves.

Third, politics and conflict are tender topics precisely because they call into question the rationality of managerial action. Despite penetrating criticism and a paucity of empirical support, researchers still find it difficult to relinquish "rational actor" models of organizations and organizational decision making.[22] This reluctance can be explained, in part, by the demands for parsimony that encourage researchers to build into their theoretical models reductionist assumptions about human behavior and motivation.[23] More subtly—and perhaps more commonly—researchers may find it difficult to escape the bind imposed by what Burns (1961) called the dual linguistic code of organizational politics: politics and political action are undeniably real and meaningful aspects of organizational life, but both are essentially private, backstage behaviors. They are not openly discussed, especially with outsiders. To do so would contradict the preferred image of managerial and organizational action as rational and consensual (see also Pfeffer 1981, 9–15; Dalton 1959, 19). Thus, organizational analysts, like participants in the settings they study, may acknowledge the fallibility of rational actor models but refrain from making political conflict a central feature in their explanations of organizational behavior.[24]

However, from a power-process perspective, innovation and change in both technology and organization may be as much *products* of internal political action—of insurgency or even of movement politics—as they are products of exogenous forces, conscious design on the part of

22. For critiques, see Pfeffer (1981), March (1962; 1978), Cyert and March (1963), Allison (1971), and Feldman and March (1981).

23. Assumptions about rational and utility- or profit-maximizing behavior are deeply entrenched in economic models of organization. Modifications to these assumptions have slowly emerged with the growth of principal-agent and transaction cost models (see Jensen and Meckling 1976; Williamson 1975). However, substantial ground remains to be covered between sociological and economic theories of firm behavior and human behavior in organizations. For constructive treatments of this situation, see Arrow (1974), March (1981), Granovetter (1985), and Williamson and Ouchi (1981). For a critique, see Perrow (1981; 1986, chap. 7).

24. Other dangers are associated with "publicly" discussing or analyzing political behavior: researchers may alienate their organizational (managerial) sponsors and thus preclude further opportunities for investigation. See, for example, Dalton's (1959) methodological appendix and his later essay on the dilemmas of telling "insider stories" (Dalton 1964). For a modern version of this situation and the epistemological and ideological issues associated with "interviewing important people in big companies," see appendix 1 and Thomas (1993).

top organizational leaders, or the efforts of units formally sanctioned to engage in innovation. That is, by leaving the content of innovation largely unexamined and by limiting both the definition and the analysis of innovation to formally sanctioned activities, the literature on innovation overlooks the possibility that a new technology or a new approach to organization might come about as a result of efforts to enact the worldviews of groups who are *not* sanctioned to innovate and who are yet convinced of the necessity of change in the form they envision it. Political action of this sort would differ from the politics of self-interest by a strongly held conviction that change is essential not simply to a single group's interest but to the interests, objectives, and well-being of the organization as a whole. More than just a power play, such an insurgency would have to carry with it an idea, an interpretive framework, and a set of practices that depart from precedent but that are at the same time sufficiently robust to accommodate and attract adherents from many quarters.[25]

Unlike the concepts of "champion" or "intrapreneur" quite familiar in the literature on organizational innovation (cf. Burgelman 1984; Maidique 1980), insurgency is not likely to rest with a single individual. Charismatic movements are possible; but it is worthwhile to remember that, at least in Weber's (1978) analysis, charismatic individuals do not make change, movements do. Moreover, insurgent movements, especially charismatic ones, are inherently opposed to the status quo. Even when couched in the language of collective interest, they cannot usually be justified by the measures and criteria commonly used to evaluate competing options precisely because those metrics reflect ends and means *as they are defined by dominant groups*. And since the ideas and claims made by insurgent groups tend also to be untested on a scale large enough to allow generalization with any assurance, they are, for all intents and purposes, *unprovable*. In other words, they are taken as an article of faith by believers while commonly decried as unfounded, unscientific, and even mystical by members of the dominant group and adherents to the status quo.

Internal political movements are not likely to emerge full-blown from a single discovery or idea, and even if their objectives are ultimately realized in practice, they may be absorbed by the existing organizational

25. In this respect, such a movement would have to be "counter-hegemonic," to borrow a concept from Gramsci (1971): that is, it would have to be capable of establishing an interpretive frame that causes people to see the world in a way that is not only different from but superior to the dominant or hegemonic frame currently in place.

power structure (cf. Zald and Berger 1978; Pettigrew 1973). The most obvious case in point was the movement behind surface mount technology in the computer company. However, the aluminum and auto company cases are also enlightening in this regard: in the face of enormous constraints—including a historical prohibition against manufacturing organizations engaging in changes that did not meet with the prior approval of product designers—managers, engineers, and workers combined to engage in a substantial redefinition of traditional processes and relationships. For example, in the aluminum company case, the failure to bring out hard alloy products might have been resolved through traditional means; for example, the R&D center "doctors" could have been called in to save the day. Instead, plant managers and engineers organized an unprecedented effort to change the way they dealt with the R&D center. The collaborative approach they created helped forge an effective solution *and* a new way of thinking about the relationship between people and technology, too. In the auto company, the prospect of plant closure might have led local union leaders and workers to make concessions, as many locals did during that era, and to accept the new technology without question or reservation (cf. H. Katz 1985; Parker and Slaughter 1988). Instead, local managers and union leaders turned what had been promised as a technological marvel designed and deployed in a traditional fashion into an opportunity to redefine the technology and to restructure the process of change. In other words, essential to the achievement of a break with the past and with institutionalized expectations were deliberate efforts to change the rules that seemed to govern their organizations' approach not only to the introduction of new technology but to its design as well.

Political movements in organizations, much like their counterparts in society at large, are likely to gain momentum and members in periods of crisis—when rules and relationships that were once believed to be eternal verities begin to lose their ability to explain, much less to predict, anomalous events (cf. Gurr 1970; Tilly 1978; Gamson 1975). Crisis does not, however, guarantee that political movements will arise or that those that do appear will succeed. Rather, crisis can provide an opening for reconsideration of traditional practices or institutionalized conceptions and for experiments that might otherwise have been ruled out of bounds. In this respect the breakdown of the aluminum rod caster and the threat to the auto plant's future provided openings for political action *without* determining the exact nature of that action. Crisis brought into stark relief the manner in which historical precedents, institutionalized norms, and structural rigidities actually obstructed the path to survival. It not only highlighted the way boundaries between functional groups and levels inhibited the ability of individual groups to perform effectively but also forced into the open the stakes each group had with regard to the existing division of labor and to the creation of a new one. The maneuvers on the part of the auto plant manager to reveal the assumptions and prejudices of the different groups involved and to dispel myths each held about the others provided a marvelous example of just how difficult, and yet innovative, the process could be. Out of that experience came a confirmation for some participants that change in traditional relationships and practices was not only necessary but possible, too.

In sum, the power-process perspective argues that internal political action represents a real but largely overlooked stimulus to organizational, as well as technological, innovation and change. Because it focuses on internal activities of interpretation and action and because it views structuring as an active process, the power-process perspective is far more likely than other perspectives to detect and to explain those movements—whether or not they succeed in accomplishing their objectives. However, it is sufficiently robust as a perspective that it actually subsumes conventional definitions and explanations for innovation as a process (i.e., a controlled explosion) because it does not restrict innovation *only* to sanctioned groups and activities. In other words, the power-process perspective allows politics to be treated as a potentially integral and *creative* dimension of organizational innovation and change, rather than being dismissed as ephemeral, inefficient, nonrational, or embarrassing.

IMPLICATIONS FOR RESEARCH AND THEORY

In this book I've tried to take a fresh look at an old problem. Guided by an initial review of the most prominent theoretical perspectives, I set up a research design and a methodology for studying the process of technological change in organizations. Unlike many researchers in this field, I intended to make possible explicitly comparative case studies by dramatically expanding the temporal and the organizational analysis of technological choice.

Opening up the choice process encouraged me to propose what I believe to be a distinctive and, in many ways, provocative cut on technological change—the power-process perspective. At one level the power-process perspective brings to the study of organizations and organizational decision making a political sensitivity that has been out of the mainstream of technology studies for far too long. In this respect the power-process perspective and the book more generally answer pleas like those made by Perrow (1983) for greater attention to be paid to the social process of new technology design. At another level, however, the power-process perspective provides a framework, concepts, and even a language to researchers who have long been aware that power relations and political conflict can (and often do) play a decisive role in the process of technological change—but who have been unable to integrate either into their analyses. By not reducing politics to self-interest, the power-process perspective should encourage researchers to "talk politics," to borrow a phrase from Burns (1961), without feeling as if they should do so in hushed tones or that when they use the term they will be accused of unduly emphasizing the seamy side of organizational life. Indeed, as I suggested in the preceding section (and argue more vigorously in the next chapter), by emphasizing the *similarity* between insurgency and innovation, the power-process perspective opens the door to broader and more creative analyses of organizational innovation and change.

Bringing politics and power back in to the analysis of technological and organizational innovation has its costs, however. This approach requires researchers to seek out and then to weigh carefully the multiple and competing worldviews and rationalities that make up organizations. Cursory investigations, especially ones limited to brief peeks at organizational life through the eyes of official spokespersons and authorized accounts, need to be examined closely—not necessarily skeptically— because even the most forthright and frank spokesperson or account can present only so many realities at once.[26]

More specifically, the analysis of the case studies raises serious questions about (and for) research and theory about technology's impacts on organization and about the future of the industrial enterprise:

First, the case studies suggest that arguments about the trend toward upskilling as a result of the introduction of new technology made by

---

26. It helps, in this regard, to recognize that many organizational participants are amateur ethnographers; some are even quite accomplished. And contrary to those who have argued that the best observers are usually "marginal" actors (i.e., those who are familiar with but not fully incorporated into the social setting or scene they observe), my experience has been that subordinates in organizations (especially workers and lower-level staff) as well as boundary crossers are often quite attuned to the informal and formal pathways of power and the stakes that different groups hold in political contests.

Adler (1990), Hirschhorn (1984), Walton (1987), Zuboff (1988), and others need to be far more carefully investigated and substantiated. If the case studies are any guide, "post-industrial possibilities" (cf. Block 1990) will remain precisely that as long as extant worldviews, evaluative criteria, and organizational structures remain unchallenged and un-changed. As long as work designers are encouraged to pursue visions of "real engineering" that "cut costs and lose heads," that are undertaken in isolation from end users, and that are fueled by suspicion of and disdain for workers and lower-level supervisors, it is hard to imagine that upskilling will occur *as a result* of the technologies they devise. As the case studies have shown, work designers (i.e., process or manufac-turing engineers, equipment and software developers, and so on) are anything but ciphers; they may not be as visible as the people who manage them or the people who chart organizational strategy, but that does not mean that they are unimportant or without influence in the framing of technological alternatives.

Second, the case studies suggest that arguments about broader impacts of technology on organization—specifically arguments about the emer-gence of new manufacturing paradigms such as "flexible-specialization" (Piore and Sabel 1984) or "lean production" (Womack, Jones, and Roos 1990)—need to be carefully reexamined. New technologies may appear (and be perceived) as exogenous drivers of organizational change, but there is nothing automatic about the effects of technology on organiza-tion. Far more than the absorption of new technology must take place if organizations are to achieve the daring new forms and functions implied by flexible specialization and lean production. More important, re-searchers need to be much clearer and much more thorough in their investigations to demonstrate what has changed and what must change in the internal structure, operation, and, perhaps most critically, the worldviews of all levels of organizational participants if organizations are to use new technology to achieve new paradigms of production. Moreover, researchers themselves need to be far more incisive in their analyses of technological developments, especially in exploring the as-sumptions that get built into new hardware, software, and integrated systems by technology developers and vendors. If the auto case is any guide, many of the "new age" ideas about participatory work structures, flexible specialization, and the like have yet to reach those who are supposed to be designing "new age" technology.

Third, the case studies suggest that, although claims about the "trans-formation of industrial relations" (Kochan, Katz, and McKersie 1986) and the advent of strategic human resource management (Beer et al. 1985; Walton 1987) certainly have some empirical grounding, transformations may be far more difficult—and therefore far more superficial—than researchers have implied. An important case in point is the conception of a greatly expanded role for unions in the strategic decision-making process of the industrial enterprise, a conception found in both Kochan, Katz, and McKersie (1986) and Sorge and Streeck (1988). With the case studies providing a backdrop, the involvement of unions in strategic choices about new technology will require far greater energy, resources, and expertise than even the most "transformed" unions have mustered thus far. Yet anything less than intimate involvement in the setting of priorities, the definition of evaluative criteria, the establishment of goals and methods for work designers, and profound changes in the process of implementation would make unions' strategic participation of limited value—to unions, their members, and their contract partners. Involvement of this sort would require unions to find a way to make participation important *to their members*—something that does not appear to have happened in the aerospace, steel, and auto industries, where Kochan, Katz, and McKersie have found much of the evidence they offer in support of their transformation arguments.

Fourth, the case studies set an agenda of issues and questions about the process of technological change that are limited to industrial enterprises in the United States. To date, these issues and questions have not been researched extensively in other countries or economies, and we would therefore benefit greatly from explicitly comparative research. Not only would such comparisons allow for testing of the cultural and historical specificity of the concepts I've put forward (including the power-process perspective), but they could also help provide greater substance and detail about differences in process and outcome in, for example, Japanese, German, Korean, and Swedish manufacturing organizations. For example, works by Cole (1979; 1989), Westney (1987), Cusumano (1985), Dore (1986), and Clark and Fujimoto (1991) have provided tremendous insight as to differences in the structure of Japanese enterprises. These studies offer a solid foundation for comparative research; what we lack, however, is an equally solid foundation in *process*. For example, how are choices of technology made in Japanese firms? Are the worldviews of organizational participants so clearly aligned that the kinds of conflicts depicted in this book are specific to U.S. firms? If, as Clark and Fujimoto and Cusumano suggest, manufacturing processes are considered far more strategic in Japanese firms, how do those firms escape the traps of linear thinking that lead product to dominate process?

Fifth, and finally, the case studies suggest that the effort to revitalize manufacturing in the United States may itself represent a political movement worthy of further investigation by sociologists and political scientists. The absence of a serious effort to establish a national industrial policy has pushed manufacturing revitalization to the sidelines (even in an election year), but that should not distract attention from the fact that tremendous energy is being expended outside as well as inside industrial enterprises to elevate the status and power of manufacturing as a function and manufacturing managers as a group. Indeed, most fascinating about the growing financial and intellectual involvement of manufacturing organizations in academic institutions (including my own) has been their efforts to affect not only how manufacturing is viewed inside the academy but, in some ways more important, how academic institutions can be enlisted to support claims for greater status, resources, and power for manufacturing *inside* industrial enterprises.

These issues and questions have significant implications for future social science research. But more immediately, they have practical implications for the future of the industrial enterprise. In the final chapter I argue that future industrial enterprises will likely be built from ideas and practices that, from a historical perspective, don't make sense. Authoring the future is, of course, one of the things machines can't do.

SEVEN

The Politics and Aesthetics
of Manufacturing

"Should we change for the machines?"
Pat Cadigan, *Synners*

After hearing me present one of my case studies, a colleague from an engineering school asked pointedly why we couldn't just "fix" things so technological change wouldn't be so political. I hemmed and hawed. It seemed enough that I had demonstrated that technological change *was* a political process—that people had very different views about how they and their organizations should work and that technological choice provided them an opportunity to enact those views. So I mumbled something about his question missing the point and let it go. Still, the question lingered, irritating me like the words to a half-remembered song.

The more I thought about it, the more I came to recognize the significance of the unspoken assumption in my colleague's question. Politics and technology, he was telling me, just didn't mix. Politics was all about differences in interests and worldviews, whereas technology was all about indisputable facts and observable, objective relationships. Politics threw things into disarray; technology brought them under control.

My colleague intended his question to be a challenge to me. In fact, he identified one of the biggest challenges facing U.S. industry. If executives look to technology alone as the answer to the current era of turmoil, they may very well bring things under control—but they will do so at a very high cost.

In this chapter I offer two answers in response to the question posed by my colleague. First, I argue that the future industrial enterprise may be better served by *incorporating* the political aspirations of managers, engineers, and workers than by trying to subdue or eliminate them by

246

technical means. Success in this effort will require more than just structural change, however. In addition, it will require a serious reconsideration of the *status of manufacturing* in the industrial enterprise. Second, I
argue that until we develop an *aesthetic of process* comparable in influence
to the one that guides and invigorates product design, manufacturing will
continue to be treated as a secondary organizational activity—one that
lacks the potential to be a source of either innovation or competitive
advantage.

POLITICS AND CHANGE

The human and social systems that make up organizations and that give
rise to political action and political conflict *can* be eliminated. That is,
work *can* be automated. Organizational policies *can* be tightened and
more closely monitored. People *can* be made to go away. But the social
costs of unemployed and underemployed people and skills will be quite
high. And if the research I've described in this book is any guide, the
organizational costs of making politics go away will be higher still. In
fact, the organizational costs will take the form of a *diminished ability
to innovate*—a risky strategy to pursue in a global economy that demands innovation and change.

Rather than try to eliminate politics, industry must embrace politics.
This is not by any means to argue that the industrial enterprise ought to
revert to a Hobbesian "war of all against all." It is instead to argue that
political action and innovation bear more than a passing resemblance.
Both build from the creative impulses of individuals and groups: from
their aspirations to achieve something unique and uniquely satisfying, to
realize in practice a vision of the way things *should* work. In that sense,
both political action and innovation are intensely personal in nature. But
neither can survive in a vacuum; they must ultimately find some connection to broader notions of a *collective* good. Indeed, as I argued in the
preceding chapter, it is only in the extreme—when politics is reduced by
definition to the pursuit of individual self-interest—that political action
and innovation truly part company.

Embracing politics means enlarging the domain in which innovation
is considered to be a legitimate activity. Instead of partitioning organizations into spheres of innovation and "no innovation"—where some are
licensed to pursue their creative impulses and aspirations and others
who do the same are labeled malcontents or deviants—the challenge for
the industrial enterprise is one of simultaneously encouraging innova-

tion in all functions and at all levels and directing it toward collective goals. Instead of defining innovation as a *zero-sum proposition*—in which one group or function's opportunity to innovate comes only at the expense of some other's—innovation must be defined as an *integrative proposition*, a collective opportunity and a collective responsibility that enhances an organization's capabilities rather than balkanizes and diminishes them.

A brief look back at the case studies might help ground these ideas. In virtually every case engineers, workers, and managers aspired to achieve something more than their circumstances seemed to allow. For example, manufacturing engineers aspired to do "real engineering": they preferred problems and solutions that contained a technical challenge, especially one that allowed them to apply their skills in the creation of something that was visible, significant, and enduring. Workers aspired to do "real work": to make something of which they could be proud, to make it in a creative way, and to feel some sense of ownership in the process. Manufacturing managers, no less than engineers or workers, wanted to feel that they, too, did real work: the sense that they *and* their organizations were producing high-quality goods, goods they could be proud of, through processes that were themselves forms of creative expression.

However, when it came to undertaking technological innovation, two decidedly different approaches were evident. On the one hand, when responsibility for undertaking change was delegated to or claimed by one group exclusively, innovation rapidly became a zero-sum proposition. Design and implementation were carried out in isolation, often at some distance removed from the place and the people it would affect. Quite often, substantial conflict accompanied implementation of the change: in some cases the conflict could be resolved only through the exercise of formal power: in others implementation devolved into negotiations over suboptimal uses of the innovation itself.

On the other hand, when the number of parties authorized to participate in the process of change was expanded, innovation came to be defined as an integrative proposition. Changes carried out in an environment of openness and collaboration were no less contentious in their initial stages, and in the end they appeared no less effective than the others. But in many respects their solutions seemed far more robust. By engaging rather than ignoring the aspirations of the different groups involved, the integrative approach expanded the range of possible solutions; perhaps more important to the long run, it opened the door to a far more extensive rethinking of the process of production.

Accounting for the differences in process and outcome is by no means simple, certainly when dealing with complex technologies, complicated organizations, and widely varying industrial settings. However, there were subtle—but in many ways quite powerful—variations in the context within which change occurred. Those variations had much less to do with the attributes of the physical technologies or the products involved than with the *status of manufacturing* inside the industrial enterprise.

THE STATUS OF MANUFACTURING

Perhaps the most profound paradox of the modern industrial enterprise is the low status accorded to manufacturing. Although corporate executives frequently issue pronouncements to the contrary, manufacturing continues to be looked on as a secondary organizational activity—one that is largely expected to respond to orders, initiatives, and strategies issued from above, to execute the designs of the product development organizations, and to devote its energies to diminishing variation rather than creating it. Salary levels, career paths, prestige, and opportunities for (as well as expectations of) innovation were all clearly different for manufacturing managers and engineers in the companies I studied.[1]

Taken together, those factors provide an important source of explanation for why innovation and change—in technology and other domains—should be viewed as a zero-sum proposition. In the face of a limited ability to influence (often, even to anticipate) the nature and timing of products from the design organization, manufacturing managers were encouraged to look inward, to their organizations, as the thing that had to be controlled. Few saw any real alternative to conceiving of change as a zero-sum proposition. Limited resources, restricted opportunities to do real engineering, and control-oriented line managers encouraged manufacturing engineers to take a segmented, isolated, and guarded approach to the design and implementation of new work systems. Given what appeared to many as arbitrary and capricious behavior on the part of both higher-level managers and engineers,

1. Recent reports (e.g., Society for Manufacturing Engineering 1988) suggest that the organizations I studied are by no means unusual in this regard.

workers and supervisors constructed social systems in the shops that gave meaning to work life, if not to the work itself, and that provided a measure of insulation from "external" agents.

Breaking out of that vicious cycle is not a simple undertaking. In the auto and aluminum cases, the pursuit of an integrative approach was stimulated by crisis, by the formation of unlikely alliances, and by remarkably astute maneuvering. Each in a different way challenged the subordinate status of manufacturing and helped create an opening for innovation. In the process they revealed alternatives to traditional assumptions about the role that technology ought to play in the structuring of work and work relations. However, each opening was also temporary in nature. Very quickly, traditional assumptions and relations were reasserted by the larger organizations, leaving the participants to wonder whether their experiences were indeed reproducible or whether they were conjunctural after all.[2]

Therein, I suggest, resides the broader challenge for the industrial enterprise. In the face of resource constraints and a lack of influence in product design, manufacturing managers will continue to combat uncertainty by investing in machines—especially in what they hope are flexible machines—instead of investing in people or processes that could integrate the two. In the face of status inequality with their peers in design and in an effort to serve manufacturing management, manufacturing engineers will continue to invent opportunities and technologies that enable them to be real engineers. And in the face of managers and engineers who ignore and devalue their knowledge, shop-floor workers and supervisors will either choose technologies that give them some opportunity to do real work or throw up barriers in order to extract a price for change.

For these reasons it is essential to turn to a much more direct consideration of the relationship between design and manufacturing in the future industrial enterprise.

---

2. In this sense it is quite remarkable that most organizations, including the ones that participated in this project, do not make a practice of reviewing either their successes or their failures except in the most cursory form. Successes are more likely to be recognized, as they were in the aluminum company; but even then the focus is on outcomes, *not on the processes through which those outcomes were achieved*. Failures are painful, of course, but they can also lead to the most illuminating reviews. Unfortunately, as I found in this project, the people involved in failed or stalled efforts usually see (and often experience) such reviews as degrading and humiliating; they are thus encouraged to spend more energy generating creative and imaginative post hoc rationalizations than they spent in dealing with the problems they encountered in the process of failure.

DESIGN ↔ MANUFACTURING?

There is a growing recognition that traditional functional boundaries between design and manufacturing have significant and undesirable effects on the cost, quality, and serviceability of new products, as well as on the ability of manufacturing to be a source of competitive advantage (see, e.g., Hayes, Wheelwright, and Clark 1988; Clark and Fujimoto 1991; Liker and Fleischer 1992). Simply put, when product developers don't understand manufacturing, they design products that are hard to make. When manufacturing managers and engineers don't have the knowledge, the authority, or the incentive to participate in product development, they either make do (e.g., do what they can to build the product), drag their heels in hopes of negotiating a more producible design, or adopt a conservative attitude (e.g., claiming that the product can't be made).

In light of these findings, analysts have begun to prescribe changes in structure to strengthen the linkage between design and manufacturing and new strategies (e.g., design for manufacturability) to bridge the gulf between organizational functions.[3] For example, they propose the creation of matrix structures to compel managers and engineers in each domain to share information and ideas or "heavyweight" program managers who control vital resources and bring different types of expertise to bear on common objectives. Many turn to Japanese firms—particularly in the auto and electronics industries—as a source of alternatives.[4]

Though pointed in the right direction, most of those prescriptions do not go far enough. In the broadest sense, what they miss is a recognition of the opportunity for dramatic change not only in the way we structure the relationship between design and manufacturing but in the way we *think* about the relationship as well.

KNOWLEDGE AND POWER

Two issues have yet to be addressed completely. The first has to do with the nature of the knowledge flowing back into the design activity. The second has to do with the power or the influence of manufacturing as an

---

3. See especially Hayes, Wheelwright, and Clark (1988), Schonberger (1982), Adler (1990), and Womack, Jones, and Roos (1990).

4. There is, of course, an extensive literature on Japanese management practices. For some of the most insightful recent work, see Cusumano (1985), Womack, Jones, and Roos (1990), Cole (1989), Dore (1986), Cole and Yakushiji (1984), and Westney (1987).

organization and of manufacturing knowledge as a resource in the conduct of design.

Proposals to codify and incorporate manufacturing knowledge into design rules for product development (i.e., core features of DFM) are quite appropriate and necessary. They suggest that knowledge resident in the manufacturing organization ought to "flow back" and help developers design manufacturable products.[5] Missing, however, is a consideration of what *kind* of knowledge is being transferred. If, for example, the manufacturing knowledge flowing back into the design activity is historical knowledge—knowledge derived solely from past practice—then it will constrain the range of possible products the design organization can develop. Even if top executives order product and process design to be carried on simultaneously, as long as the manufacturing knowledge being communicated is bound by past investments in plant and equipment, by established procedures and routines, and by institutionalized assumptions about the capabilities of the social system of production, the benefits of structural reorganization will be limited at best. Newer and more manufacturable designs will come about, but the range of possible products will still be constrained by manufacturing capabilities.[6]

Equally problematic is the issue of whether (or how) product designers will use the knowledge communicated from manufacturing. At one level this issue is addressed by prescriptions such as DFM, simultaneous engineering, heavyweight program managers, and the like. That is, someone or some procedure (e.g., design reviews) will see to it that manufacturing has "bought off" on a proposed design. However, this approach is not likely to be adequate. The computer company case study, for example, suggests that even when manufacturing (or, to be more accurate, manufacturing engineering) uncovers a new process, the design organization may be unwilling or unable to recognize the potential contributions of the process.[7] Or, as was the case in the auto

5. Although it could be argued that this kind of interchange *did* take place prior to the "discovery" of DFM, the flow back usually lagged. That is, designers usually did not learn about problems of manufacturability until well after their designs had been finalized and the costs of changes were extraordinarily high. Adjustments or revisions could be accommodated economically only later in the life cycle of a product (cf. Abernathy 1978).

6. An esteemed professor of aeronautical engineering once commented to me that he had warned an aircraft manufacturer *not* to incorporate its historical records about manufacturing into its new CAD-CAM system for airplane design. His fear was that those records would *prevent* the generation of new designs, the use of new materials, and the development of new processes for manufacturing.

7. Alternatively, as I have seen and had reported to me by students doing internships

company, the temporal and organizational distance between the designers and the plants may be so great that even when a process engineering group is established to serve as a conduit, it may be unable to adequately translate manufacturing knowledge into the design activity.[8]

If organizations are to escape the gravitational pull of history, they will have to be propelled as much by innovation in *process* as by innovation in product. Thus far, analysts have stressed the competitive advantages to be achieved through greater attention to manufacturing *as a function*, that is, what it can contribute as an independent activity in terms of cost reduction, quality improvement, and accelerated new product introduction (or "time-to-market"). And as I noted earlier, efforts such as DFM emphasize the competitive advantages to be achieved through a closer relationship between manufacturing and design. However, I suggest that we need to push the bounds of conventional thinking even further: to look on manufacturing as an activity and an organization that can *not only respond to the demands placed on it by new products but might also stimulate product innovation and change.* In this respect assembled goods industries could benefit by emulating continuous process industries. In continuous process industries such as petrochemicals, the product and the process are so closely intertwined as to be virtually indistinguishable; investments in understanding and improving the process routinely unlock new product possibilities. If organizations in assembled goods industries were to dedicate themselves to achieving an equally intimate understanding of their own processes, there is reason to believe that they, too, could unlock new product possibilities.[9]

---

in "leading-edge" manufacturing companies, people from various functions and disciplines can be brought together in groups (e.g., in design-build teams) to exchange knowledge, but the simple fact of their aggregation does not by itself guarantee that anything will be said *or* heard.

8. Of course, as in that case, process designers may not share the perspective of the plants either. In that situation they may feel closer to the product design organization—and thus be guided by the latter's lead—or they may have a distinctive view of "how things should work" that is not congruent with either the design organization or the plants.

9. In this regard I am *not* suggesting that we should expect assembled goods industries to achieve the levels of automation achieved in continuous process industries or that there is an implicit evolutionary scheme underlying change in manufacturing organizations. The "logic of technical rationality" emphasized by theorists such as Thompson (1967) and Woodward (1965) does imply a trend toward the increasing automation of production, culminating in automated industries such as petrochemicals. What I am arguing is more on the order of what Piore and Sabel (1984) refer to as the "equifinality" of production systems: that is, that there are multiple paths to the same objective. However, I suggest that strategies for dealing with market differentiation, such as flexible specialization, are not likely to emerge, much less to succeed, *without* an integrative approach to the choice, design, and implementation of new technology.

This consideration brings me to the second issue: the power or influence of manufacturing as an organization and manufacturing knowledge as a resource in the conduct of design. A manufacturing organization may contain tremendously valuable knowledge, but if it cannot affect the design activity, the value of that knowledge is greatly diminished. In order for knowledge to "add value," its value has to be recognized and used. In order to be recognized and used, that knowledge must be backed by power—something that manufacturing lacks in most industrial enterprises.

Conventional thinking in organization theory would explain the relative powerlessness of manufacturing as a result of its lack of a claim to coping with critical organizational contingencies or sources of uncertainty, that is, its mundane, programmed, and insulated nature by contrast to the highly volatile (and high-velocity) world of product market competition faced by the design organization. According to this line of thinking, to make manufacturing strategic and manufacturing knowledge influential, it would be necessary to strip away the insulating layers of rules and buffering devices and expose manufacturing to an uncertain and volatile environment. In some respects this is actually happening (albeit in a segmented fashion) with the removal of inventory as a buffer through just-in-time inventory controls and the conversion of manufacturing organizations into profit centers. Efforts such as these draw greater attention to the *costs* of design errors in the form of scrap, rework, and delayed shipments (cf. Krafcik 1988). At minimum they make much more visible the *interdependence* of design and manufacturing.

However, although changes of that sort may increase manufacturing's influence over current or near-term products and processes, they do little to exploit the potential contribution of manufacturing knowledge for *future* products and processes. In other words, empowering manufacturing is not simply a matter of restructuring (i.e., moving boxes around) or writing new policies. Instead, *the empowerment of manufacturing requires a serious consideration of whether the temporal ordering of activities demands a hierarchical ordering of authority*. The idea that design must precede manufacture is not "wrong" by any means, and it certainly does fit with prevailing (Western) notions of time as a linear and directional flow, but it can also be an extremely restrictive idea. It blinds us, as I suggested earlier, to the possibility that investments in manufacturing capabilities may expand the array of future products. Moreover, it limits manufacturing to short-term and reactive adjustments in existing processes—thus reducing the likelihood that manufacturing will recognize, much less generate, innovations that provide real competitive advantage. In this sense, it can channel even the most dedicated efforts at continuous improvement into refinements of existing processes, not into the discovery of new ones. *If manufacturing is to influence the future, it must be viewed as a resource for the future, and it must have the power to help shape that future.*

PRODUCT AND PROCESS RECONSIDERED

If questions concerning the form and influence of manufacturing knowledge are to be addressed adequately, we need to think about the relationship between design and manufacturing in fundamentally different ways. Most important, we have to confront head-on the differences between products and processes.

A product is an object and a process is an activity. A product is discrete, physically bounded, and, in many ways, appropriable. A process, by contrast, is continuous, physically unbounded, and nonappropriable. A product may be the object of human labor and creativity, but a process is human labor and creativity *in action*. A product can be used or consumed without its creator or creators being present. A process *is* the activity of creation, and it therefore requires the presence of the creator or creators.

Stylized as it may be, let me offer an illustration of the difference. Consider a sculpture as both an object and a process. In object form a sculpture is a discrete, physically bounded entity that can be uniquely associated with its creator. Once installed in a garden or a museum, the sculpture is there to be consumed (e.g., viewed, climbed on, used as a teaching device, or simply employed as a resting place for pigeons). The sculptor need not be present for the sculpture to be consumed; the sculpture exists as a message from the sculptor to a public she is likely never to meet.[10]

When considered as a process, however, sculpture takes on a different aspect. In process, the sculpture may be thought of as linear and sequential stages of *becoming*—a drawing, a scale model, and then a completed piece—but even that conception disguises what is often a much more

10. Indeed, for many sculptors and other artists, it is tedious, even irritating, to create something that others feel has to be explained or that they themselves have to explain. An artist friend routinely confounds me by deflecting even my most careful questions about what he "means to say" with his paintings.

contingent and iterative activity.[11] The physical activity of sculpting has its own dynamic and its own aesthetic, and both are often only remotely visible in a finished product; in the process of sculpting, the sculptor is intimately involved in selecting materials, in translating ideas into physical action, in using the knowledge, experience, and craft that enable certain effects to be achieved, and in exploring the subjective state that accompanies the process itself. Finally, the process of sculpting is extremely difficult, if not impossible, to appropriate. A sculptor's style can be emulated, but the process through which it is made concrete usually cannot. Indeed, few artists can fully explain what it is they are doing while (or even after) they do it.[12] Process cannot be adequately described in words alone. Yet to the sculptor and to the community of sculptors, it is virtually indistinguishable from the finished product.

This amateur excursus on sculpture connects to the earlier discussion about design and manufacturing in much the same way that the sculpture product relates to the sculpture process: most design organizations are object-oriented, and most manufacturing organizations are process-oriented. The difference in orientation may be explained as the outcome of a division of labor, but the subordination of one to the other bespeaks a separation of far greater consequence than results from distance in time or space. It suggests that manufacturing is *not* an essential part of the creative process. To make matters worse, most industrial enterprises are managed as if the process were itself a product. The focus is on objects and, most important, on outcomes. The idea that a new product might emerge from a deeper understanding of and appreciation for process is therefore quite foreign to many managers and executives, if only because *products are supposed to determine processes.* Equally important, as I showed in the case studies, most industrial enterprises contain an aesthetic of products—a language, a set of concepts, and a framework for judging the beauty of products—but few contain an equally well developed *aesthetic of process.*[13]

11. This description also overlooks the myriad false starts, failures, repairs, uncompleted ideas, and so on that are not visible in a finished product.

12. Cf. Becker (1982) and Schon (1983).

13. A visit to the design studio of any major automobile manufacturer is like a trip to an art museum. Oil and watercolor paintings adorn the walls. Car "concepts" may be the principal product, but it is very clear that the language of design is a language of the fine arts. Even more directly, the industrial design gallery in the Museum of Modern Art in New York provides compelling testimony to the importance of artistic concepts and artistic expression in the design of helicopters, teapots, toasters, and even gearboxes. With the possible exception of "living museums" such as Greenfield Village (near Detroit) or the resurrected nineteenth-century textile mills of Lowell, Massachusetts, it's hard to find

The dominance of the aesthetics of product has significant effects on the design of manufacturing processes. For example, when manufacturing engineers describe real engineering in object form, they tend to talk in terms that bear a remarkable resemblance to the terms used by product engineers. In many respects this resemblance should hardly be surprising: whether they have assimilated the aesthetics of products/art objects or seek to achieve recognition from higher-status product designers/artists, they tend to employ the language, concepts, and objectives of the latter in the objects they produce, that is, the process-products. Thus, the aircraft company FMS *was* a sculpture to its designers: it was discrete, physically bounded, and uniquely identifiable with its creators.[14] And like sculptors, the project team did not want to have it be interpreted: in the best of all worlds, the FMS, like the sculpture, would "speak for itself": it would run by itself.[15]

In the absence of an aesthetic of process, there is little reason to believe that manufacturing engineers, their managers, or top-level executives will come to see manufacturing as anything more than a means to execute the artistic conceptions of product development organizations. In the absence of a language, concepts, and a framework for articulating what process is—as distinct from the product-object—it is unlikely that manufacturing will come to be seen as a domain in which creativity and innovation ought to be encouraged. In the absence of that encouragement and legitimation, it is unlikely that manufacturing will come to be a stimulus to future product possibilities or to be a source of current, as well as future, competitive advantage.

THE SEARCH FOR AN AESTHETIC OF PROCESS

The principal difficulty in fostering an aesthetic of process derives from its incompatibility with established ideas about products. Two important differences deserve attention: first, an aesthetic of process would need to have at its core an appreciation for the *performance* of the activity, not some end state or outcome of the activity; second, it would have to take into account the *collaboration among many performers* and

---

equivalent—or equally accessible—monuments to process design.

14. In fact, several of the engineers involved wanted to have a brass plaque with their names on it attached to one of the machines.

15. The sculpture metaphor may also help explain why many factories *look* like sculpture gardens, particularly those gardens in which the only apparent coherence to the collection of sculptures comes from the pathways that connect the pieces.

their tools (including, but not limited to, machines). An aesthetic of process would, in other words, be much more likely to be one that applies to a *performing art* than to an object art.

In this respect theater would be a more apt analogy for manufacturing than even the process of sculpting. Theater is not an object: it is an event, an ensemble of acts. Individual actors or scenes may be especially memorable, but it is the totality of the performance that is experienced and judged. There may be an end product, if one considers a particular state of mind a commodity,[16] but even the most powerful final act can have little meaning if it is taken out of context. And the most dramatic or sophisticated mechanical sets or props will not substitute for poor acting.

Repertory theater—even more so than the long-run Broadway production—can offer some useful insights for how an aesthetic of process can be applied to an organized human activity. Repertory theater companies stage several plays over the course of a season. The company seeks to perform each play at the highest level of quality; but it also seeks to perform a wide variety of plays in a relatively short period of time. Given finite resources, limited members, and a wide variety of roles and activities that have to be performed on a given night, in a given play, and across a given set of plays, repertory theater companies must quickly reach a high level of quality, sustain it, and simultaneously prepare to shift to another play. To achieve these objectives, the company deploys its members across roles and activities for the duration of a particular play but redeploys its members in different configurations for subsequent plays.[17] In this fashion the company and all its members must be able to think and act in accord with *different time horizons*: learning from the last play, performing the current one, and preparing for the next. To *be* a company, however, members must understand the roles— onstage and off—and their relationship. Without that breadth of knowledge about the process of performance, the company can neither achieve its objectives nor respond to the unforeseen events that could threaten its performance (e.g., an illness in the cast, a mechanical failure in the midst of a performance, etc.). Without a dedication to the performance *as* a

16. Certainly there are industries built up around selling a state of mind. Amusement parks, and Disneyland and Disneyworld in particular, are excellent examples. See Van Maanen and Kunda (1989).

17. For example, there are only so many roles in a given play. Thus, members who are not performers may be stage hands. In a subsequent play, someone who moved sets may take an onstage role.

process and a sense of fulfillment *through* the process, neither the company nor its customers would ascribe value to the product.

The performance of a season of plays and the manufacture of a line of automobiles are not as dissimilar as they may seem. The quality of performance or production in each case critically influences the quality of the outcome. Flexibility is no less important in the process of auto manufacturing than it is in repertory theater. Creativity and innovation are essential to effective performance in both. Yet the theater has a language, concepts, and a framework that enable the process *as a process* to be evaluated, critiqued, and, most important, improved. To this point, manufacturing does not.

Philosophies of total quality and the like may be precursors to an aesthetic of process. But to succeed, they must create means through which the qualities of process can be identified, enacted, and then enhanced—in much the same sense that the qualities of sculpting and performance have been identified, enacted, and enhanced over time. The aesthetic must enable all participants to engage in three distinctly different domains, each with its own time horizon, and to do so simultaneously: achieving mastery over *current* processes, promoting *continuous improvement* in those processes, and preparing for *transformational change*. An aesthetic of process in industry should share with theater traditional notions of craft and professionalism, but rather than preserve those traditions for their own sake, the point will be to use them as a foundation for expanding the skills of *all* participants—be they managers, engineers, or workers.

Thus, to the science of production we must add the art of manufacturing. That is, in the end, another thing machines can't do.

Talking Technology

Case studies in organizations are not simple undertakings. You can't just walk in unannounced and expect to strike up a conversation with whomever happens to be around. Neither can you simply hang out in order to observe the scene. Most organizations, no matter how small, have gatekeepers, people who keep an eye on the comings and goings of strangers. Business organizations, especially large ones with trade secrets to hide, usually have gates, guards, and security devices. Even welcome visitors encounter inner lines of defense: public relations departments, "official spokespersons," and whole levels of management who have been trained in how to represent the company to the outside world. Thus, gaining access—or as we usually put it, "getting in"—can be a tough business, even when the point of getting in is innocuous, well intentioned, or attractive to key people in the organization itself.[1]

The case studies I planned required not only that I gain access but that I have a virtual passkey to each organization. As I noted in chapter 1, my goal was to study the process of technological change in a way that most researchers had not.

First, I wanted to extend the *temporal context* of analysis. I was not interested in limiting my attention to the "impacts" of change in technology. Instead, I wanted to understand how and why a particular technology

---

1. See, for example, Buchanan, Boddy, and McCalman (1988) and Van Maanen (1978).

was chosen and what options were foregone as a result. This meant that I needed access to the complete paper trail associated with a given project—from concept to and through implementation—and, equally important, I needed to know about the competitor projects that failed or were eliminated from contention.

Second, I wanted to extend the *organizational context*. This meant, at minimum, a request for access to all the relevant participants in the change process. It meant I needed to cross-cut functional boundaries and hierarchical levels in search of people and data. Though I began with a simple list of the types of people I might need to see and interview, I also needed to follow leads as they developed in the course of the research.

Third, I wanted to include the broader *historical, economic, and industrial relations context* in order to ensure both that I understood the circumstances surrounding change and that I would be in a position to judge whether (and how) the data I was collecting—and the story I would construct—could be compared to similar instances of technological change in a given company or industry. Thus, it was essential for me to have a detailed history of each organization, its competitive position, the product markets in which it operated, and the structure and operation of its human resources or labor-management relations system.

GETTING ACCESS

As might be imagined, these three criteria were not easy to fulfill. Although many of the organizations I approached had had experience with case study research—especially with business school staff who develop cases for teaching purposes—few were prepared to fulfill my requests. Offers of meetings with a small and select group of company personnel were not a problem. Offers of factory tours abounded when it was learned that I was interested in the use of new technology. These were courtesies commonly extended to business school faculty and to the researchers responsible for the cases that are a staple of business school teaching. Most people froze, however, when I explained that I wanted the opportunity to interview everyone from executives to machine operators, that the research could not be confined to a few days of carefully orchestrated visits (or showcase presentations) but would instead stretch over weeks if not months, that the written materials I needed were not the ones offered by the public relations department, and that I would be directly involved throughout the project and not supervising a research assistant from a distance. In other words, "workplace tourism," as Berggren, Bjorkman, and Hollander (1991, 9) so aptly put it, was something most organizations could understand; detailed data collection of the sort I requested was not.

No stranger to the demands of fieldwork, I was still surprised by the amount of time, the size of the professional network, and the travel budget it took to get access to four different manufacturing companies. Over the course of the first year of the project I approached fifteen firms before the first one agreed to the project. Several companies invited me to make presentations ("pitches") to different groups of executives; in one instance I flew cross-country twice before it was confirmed that no one was interested. I began the first case study without concrete assurances that there would be any subsequent cases. Fortunately, as time passed, three companies that had initially balked at participating opened their doors. By the time I was three-quarters of the way through the project, two of the companies that had originally rejected me suddenly embraced the idea of the research. At that point, however, I was nearly two years into the effort and eager to bring it to a close.

My eventual success in "getting in" was aided enormously by my affiliation with MIT, the Sloan School of Management, and the MIT Leaders for Manufacturing program (LFM).[2] My association with MIT led many people to believe that I was an engineer and that I could therefore understand and appreciate technology.[3] Although I am not an engineer (despite my fascination with taking things apart) and made no pretense of being an engineer, the MIT imprimatur of "Mens et Manus" was sufficient to create the impression that I was not the average business school type. Being from the Sloan School meant that I was sensitive to—or at least interested in—the dynamics of business competition and the problems that managers and engineers face in a competitive environment. Even when I mentioned that I taught organizational studies, I was received far more warmly than if I had claimed expertise in either finance or sociology. In fact, on several occasions when I mentioned getting my doctorate in sociology or when I asked about financial and accounting practices, I was quietly but firmly advised to emphasize my role as a faculty member in organizational studies and

2. Leaders for Manufacturing is a program of education and research organized as a joint venture of the Schools of Engineering and Management at MIT and a consortium of thirteen major U.S.-based manufacturing firms.

3. Even those who noticed that I wasn't wearing a "brass rat"—a nickname for the insignia ring that MIT graduates wear—assumed that I must have obtained my degree from another engineering program.

industrial relations.[4] Being associated with the LFM program cemented the impression (accurate in my case) that I was interested in the revitalization of manufacturing in the United States. Even when people were unfamiliar with LFM, the connotation that I was a "leader" or involved with a "leading" program helped persuade people to talk with me.

Funding from the National Science Foundation and the LFM program was critical to my ability to maintain my status as an independent observer. Without that standing I would have had to choose between soliciting corporate support or conducting a superficial study. As it was, the direct costs of doing the research in the fashion I planned were remarkably high: the case study sites were spread all over the United States, and it was essential for me to have the ability to travel quickly, to stay near the sites themselves, and to have secure lodging for my computer and files. Moreover, it was invaluable to have my interview tapes completely transcribed in a timely manner. The methodological importance of complete and timely transcription is a topic I will return to later; here, however, I would note only that transcription expenses exceeded $27,000—a figure that may not seem like a great deal, but one that is staggering to most qualitative or ethnographic researchers.

Negotiations over access brought to the surface two aspects of the research process that were, in many ways, critical even though they are rarely discussed in the literature on research methods: the nature of the exchange between the researcher and those who are the "researched"; and questions as to confidentiality. Sociologists, among many other academics, frequently promise to exchange things such as final reports for the right to collect data. Almost as frequently, they fail to make good on their promises.[5] Or if they do deliver, what they present may not have a great deal of use-value to those who provided data, time, and even money. This situation was sufficiently familiar to the managers I interviewed that when I referred to it as the "smash and grab" approach I was greeted with knowing nods and smiles.[6] In return for access I promised to deliver presentations on my research findings or, if that wasn't considered useful, to provide free consultation on a problem that

4. Sociologists can take heart in the fact that financial experts are held in equally low esteem.

5. To my knowledge, no one has ever looked at this issue in depth. However, given the number of incidents that people in these organizations recalled, I suspect the phenomenon is not limited.

6. I borrow this colorful phrase from Maurice Punch (1986).

people deemed important. In two of the four companies, I was taken up on the latter offer. In the other two, I delivered drafts of the relevant chapters and used them as opportunities to check the accuracy of my reporting as well as to provide feedback to the companies and unions involved.

Questions of confidentiality posed important constraints on me and on the organizations I studied. I signed similar confidentiality agreements with all four companies. In effect, I agreed to guard trade secrets and to refrain from divulging what I had learned about corporate strategy. I signed these agreements without reservation; it was never my intent to report more than was necessary about the financial or technical operations of a given organization. Equally important, I refused any form of research support or remuneration for the advice or analysis I provided in exchange for data.

However, protecting the confidentiality and, by extension, the welfare of the people I interviewed was a central concern for me throughout the research. It was especially important to make clear at the outset that the people with whom I spoke had to remain anonymous and had to be assured that I alone would have access to the interview tapes and transcripts and that quotations from the interviews would be attributed in such a way as to conceal their origin. In no case was I pressured (formally or informally) to divulge the sources of my data by anyone inside the organizations. The only time the issue arose was when I prepared summary presentations to company and union audiences— particularly when I made arguments that ran counter to someone's opinion or interpretation. Having clearly established the principle of confidentiality and nonattribution, however, I felt free to refuse to disclose my sources.

GETTING TO "YES"

I suspect that for many readers the critical question as yet unanswered is why anyone would let me in in the first place. After all, I requested a level of access and a breadth of data unprecedented in most companies, and I did not promise a "program" or a solution at the end. From my perspective, there were four main reasons why I was able to gain entrance.

First, I was interested in learning about a set of processes that all the companies considered problems. In every case company representatives quickly latched onto one or another facet of the project I described. In some cases, the problem was interpreted as one of manufacturing strategy (or the lack thereof): that is, people saw in my research an opportunity to draw attention to the fact that their companies lacked a manufacturing strategy, or they sought to "test" whether it was possible to have a distinctive strategy for manufacturing. Not surprisingly, the people interested in manufacturing strategy were mostly to be found *in* manufacturing. In other cases, however, people were interested in solving problems they associated with technology transfer, for example, the diffusion of new manufacturing processes from a central R&D facility to actual factories. In at least two cases engineering managers were concerned because, although they and their companies had had some major successes in technology transfer, they could not be consistently successful, no matter how hard they tried. Thus, they saw my study as an opportunity not only to get an outsider's view but to catch a glimpse of how other companies solved similar problems. Finally, the unions that agreed to participate did so largely out of frustration that they knew little about how the companies made decisions about new technologies and even less about how those decisions might affect jobs and skills. In one case, the union pushed quite hard to encourage the company to allow me access; they saw it as part of their effort to promote collaborative labor-management relations. In the other two cases, the unions expressed cautious interest; most important, they did not refuse me the opportunity to speak with their members. They could see little of immediate use-value to my inquiry; but they were interested enough to want to have a claim on access to my findings.

Second, in at least two of the four companies, representatives of manufacturing announced their conviction that manufacturing had been ignored for far too long in favor of financial, marketing, or product development objectives. They explained their interest in my project as an extension of their efforts to raise manufacturing's profile—efforts that included speeches to civic and professional associations, lectures in business schools, and contributions in support of the rapidly growing manufacturing programs in major colleges of engineering. Without saying so directly, they sought both to achieve influence over the content of public and academic perceptions of manufacturing and to use external associations to gain greater say in the development of business strategy *inside* their own organizations. Thus, giving access to an MIT professor not only helped increase the chances that MIT would take manufacturing seriously but also added the imprimatur of MIT to their cause of manufacturing inside their companies.

Third, in addition to the internal purposes my research might advance, many people saw my project as an opportunity to learn more about a process that few could afford to study on their own. Beyond those few who simply wanted to have successes immortalized, there was a broader and genuine concern to get a more complete picture of how these organizations actually choose and implement new technology. Apropos of comments in chapters 6 and 7 about the weight of history and structure, many had difficulty gaining perspective on things they took for granted. My research promised to take apart the taken for granted, and, without embellishment, many managers and union representatives saw that as a very valuable approach—no matter how vehemently they may have disagreed with my interpretation.

Finally, data collection did not rely solely on the consent of high-ranking officials. It also depended very much on the willingness of people in the middle and lower levels to speak to me. Their motivations were equally mixed, but a pair of issues predominated. Some agreed to be interviewed because I was a curiosity: they had received a letter of introduction from their boss (or from the union) explaining my purposes and objectives; the letter stated clearly that participation was purely voluntary. Others, I suspect, perceived me to be a medium, a means for getting a message across to higher-level management, to the company as a whole, or to the union. The majority of people, however, seemed genuinely interested in talking about their work and their worldviews. Even though I made it clear that no one was obliged to be interviewed,[7] in only 2 cases out of 296 did anyone ask me to shut off the tape recorder (before or during the interview).

SITE AND CASE SELECTION

As I explained in chapter 1, my initial goal was to select a small array of technologies to allow for comparison across a range of firms. The firms would be chosen to represent different segments of the manufacturing economy. For reasons I've already discussed, this sampling scheme proved impossible. Instead, I focused on a set of technologies that met the following criteria: (1) all the cases were to represent instances of technological change considered to be substantial departures from prior processes employed by these organizations; (2) all the cases were to be

---

7. To be more specific: no one was required to answer my questions; the interview could be stopped at any time (without prejudice of any sort); and anyone could refuse to be tape-recorded.

instances of change in process technology, that is, in the physical and social organization of the production process;[8] and (3) all the sites within which the cases were located would be large, U.S.-based companies whose principal lines of business were the design and manufacture of industrial goods. In most companies I was offered several different cases from which to choose. In the first company, the aircraft manufacturer, I chose to do three separate case studies before I realized just how much time and energy each case would require. In subsequent sites I elected to limit my research to one case.

TYPES OF DATA AND THEIR USES

WRITTEN RECORDS

In negotiating access, I requested both written records and interview data. After the particular case was finalized, I sought out all the documentation, memos, reports, and letters that had been written or received in connection with the specific undertaking. These documents provided background that I could then use to guide the library research I did before commencing the interviews. In this respect the written records proved invaluable in helping me do three things: (1) gain familiarity with not only the technical system but also the structure of the organization and its accounting, budgeting, proposal development, and review practices; (2) formulate a list of *specific* people to interview; and (3) build a preliminary chronology of events for each case. In other words, rather than launching directly into interviews, I used the written records as both a platform and an excuse for preparing myself for the interviews and observation that would follow.

In retrospect, the documents and other materials played an even more important role in enabling me to anchor the interviews. Although relatively little time had passed since the completion of each project, people's memories were fallible—in some cases, perhaps purposely so. Thus, the chronology enabled me to focus questions as to timing and sequence of activities. In some instances this approach led to minor disputes as to the accuracy of my chronology; but in each case I requested and usually received additional documentation (from the inter-

---

8. Although several cases include significant changes in less visible elements of production technology—most notably in software and control systems—all are principally concerned with alterations in manufacturing techniques.

viewees) to settle the disputes. The chronology also served as a vehicle for comparing the details of sequence and timing between the case I was studying directly and ones that came before and after. This comparison was extremely helpful in my efforts to determine whether the case I studied deviated in significant ways from what participants considered routine practice. In this respect the chronologies also served as a refresher to the interviewees' memories and as a device for asking about change processes in the organization more generally.

INTERVIEW DATA

Once I had established an initial list of people to be interviewed, I made arrangements to meet these people in their offices or near where they worked. I introduced the project and explained the conditions of the interview as clearly as possible. The format of each interview was roughly the same. Opening questions were focused on the person's job or role in the organization. I started with questions about the individual's job for two reasons: (1) to avoid assuming that a job title was an accurate depiction of what someone actually did; and (2) to help the interviewees disengage from what they were doing immediately before the interview and focus on the topic I had introduced. From prior research (e.g., Thomas 1985; 1988), I'd found this approach especially helpful—in large measure because people needed the transition time before they could get fully engaged in what I was pursuing. The next set of questions targeted that person's specific role in the change process. I probed extensively for descriptions of activities but also for the interviewee's reflections on the major issues or problems they felt they had had to address during their involvement. I concluded this phase by asking people to compare their experience with this particular project or change with others that had come before or after (e.g., how typical or atypical was it? what, if anything, had they learned as a result?). The final set of questions was designed to elicit their perspectives on the case and on the change process in general. Specifically, I posed a hypothetical situation and asked them to respond: "If you had the opportunity I have—to study the process in detail, to move up and down in the company in search of insights, and to cross departmental boundaries—what sorts of questions would you ask? Who would you want to have answer those questions?" These questions were driven by my hypothesis (correct in most cases) that people viewed the interview as an opportunity to tell *their* stories. If that were the case, then it made sense to allow people to tell me who else they thought should be allowed to tell their stories, too, and to identify those people whose stories they would like to hear (and why they would like to hear them).

In addition to using the interviews as an occasion for soliciting participants' recollections, perspectives, and opinions, I also treated them as opportunities to gather more documents and observations. Specifically, I asked for any descriptive or documentary evidence the interviewees could provide to help me understand the project and their roles in it. Occasionally this request yielded surprising results: in three different instances engineers allowed me to read their personal notebooks. These notebooks, like the lab notebooks that scientists use to keep a running record of their activities and results, included meticulously annotated notes on meetings and telephone conversations as well as the output from various development efforts—all of which were laid out in chronological order.

Besides the added documentation, I also asked respondents to *show* me what they were talking about. As a result, I received multiple tours of the same facility or process, each time gaining a different perspective on the object of study.[9] For many people, especially those who had worked on a visible dimension of the project, this was a welcomed opportunity to "go beyond words," as one maintenance worker explained. It closed the loop in a way that words couldn't. Equally important, it gave me the chance to visualize what people had described, to add direct observation to my data collection, and to listen to the interchanges between people that took place during the tours. For example, engineers and the operators at work illuminated dimensions of the process or aspects of its history that my interview questions had not even begun to unearth. Usually, it also extended the interview well beyond the time originally agreed on—*without* any complaint from the interviewees.

The interviews averaged one and one-half hours in length. All but 12 of the 296 interviews were tape-recorded and transcribed verbatim.[10] This yielded nearly five thousand typed pages of transcripts, to which were added more than a thousand pages of field notes. Together with the

---

9. Howard S. Becker taught me this lesson many years ago when he chided me for refusing a tour: "Never," he said, "but never refuse a tour!"

10. In addition to the two cases where people asked me to not record, in ten additional cases circumstances (e.g., factory noise, faulty recording equipment, or lack of planning) precluded a verbatim transcript.

documentation and other research materials, they formed the basis for the analysis presented in the book.

The process of data collection (and data analysis, as I note below) was extremely time- and labor-intensive. The time it took to do library research, review written records, and conduct interviews averaged three months per site. However, this figure represented less than half the time I actually devoted to each case. I spent another year simply trying to collate and analyze what I'd learned from the combined cases. (Figure 11 provides a time line for the research.) Part of the large time budget I consumed I attribute to my decision to conduct all but a handful of the interviews myself. My earlier fieldwork experiences—in combination with extraordinary demands I made on would-be research assistants—led me to conclude that I needed *first-hand* involvement in order to arrive at a complete understanding of the phenomena. Obviously, this is not a strategy I would recommend for everyone; it was, however, essential for me to have confidence in what I wrote.

An additional contributor to the intensity of the research derived from my desire to maintain an ongoing dialogue with people in the organizations I studied. As I point out in the next section, this was an essential part of what I refer to as a "holographic" approach to data analysis. But it was also rooted in my desire to develop something closer to a research "praxis"—an interchange between theory and practice, as well as between theorist and practitioner, that would allow me and those with whom I interacted to test ideas as I and they generated them. Although not as intensive a process as is called for in Argyris and Schon's (1974) model of action research or Whyte, Greenwood, and Lazes's (1991) model of participatory action research, the approach I took resulted in an ongoing interchange with contacts I made in the various companies and unions. In some cases the dialogue has gone on for over three years now.

DATA ANALYSIS

Given my concern to extend both the organizational and the temporal context for studying the process of technological change, I deliberately set for myself a complex task of data analysis. On the one hand, I began the research with some fairly detailed ideas about what aspects of the change process had been neglected in prior research and what I needed to do (e.g., by means of the written records and interviews) to fill in the empirical and conceptual gaps. Thus, I did not begin with a blank slate.

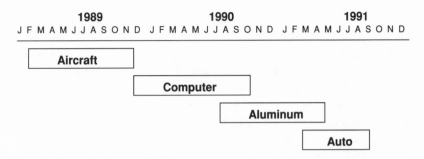

Figure 11. Timetable of research

Instead, I sought to get everything I suspected or hypothesized onto the surface as completely as possible. I did this precisely so I could be aware of my assumptions, biases, and predispositions and, by being aware of them, be better equipped to distinguish between what people were telling me and what I inferred from their remarks.

On the other hand, I wanted to create as many opportunities as possible to "discover" things I had not anticipated. That is, I wanted to allow for my hypotheses to be disconfirmed and, more important, to have my hypotheses shown to be *irrelevant*. I did this several ways. For example, I treated every interview as a separate piece of evidence—a document that had to be understood for itself and by itself. Indeed, I spent the better part of each case study attempting to extrapolate from each interview or encounter a story of the process *as a whole* from that interview. The process is one that I can best describe as a "holographic" approach to data analysis. In other words, I asked, What kind of story of the process would I see or create if this fragment (i.e., this individual interview) were the only fragment I could find? Unlike the physical characteristics of holography, of course, I was dealing with "multiple realities" (Silverman 1970): no individual fragment could be employed to re-create the whole of the image or process. Yet by engaging in holographic analysis, I was forced to confront many interpretations that did not coincide with each other and, more important, with my initial expectations.

This general approach is, I would argue, conducive to both testing of propositions *and* discovery of new forms of explanation. That it requires greater effort than either the artifice of a neutral stance or that of the "true believer"—what Davis (1973) refers to as the "Martian" and "Convert" approaches—may help explain why it is largely underplayed in the literature on qualitative methods.[11] As I describe it to my students, it requires the researcher to keep two sets of "mental books" simultaneously: one that is filled with the ideas, hunches, and hypotheses that are being tested, and another that is *being filled* with an analysis based on what one sees or hears. For example, in the computer company it was extremely tempting to evaluate the "official story" as presented to me by corporate staff as if it were the only data I needed. That is, I could simply take that very plausible and well-reasoned internal study, run it by my mental model, and then stop there. Doing so would not have violated any existing norms about depth or breadth of data collection; indeed, I have talked with enough researchers to know that, for many, an investigation of that sort is quite common.

Yet I had serious reservations about stopping there. Most important, I wanted to hold out the possibility that that story could, at minimum, be deepened by further investigation. I was not, however, looking for contradictory or conflicting evidence. The case study results, as depicted in chapter 3, confirm the usefulness of the approach I took: the "official" and the "unofficial" stories that emerged from the research describe two different *and* intersecting realities. By refusing to stop with the official story, I was rewarded with insights that partially supported the reality portrayed by corporate staff and partially disconfirmed it, too. Taken together, they provide a more compelling and complex account than either might have made possible. Equally important, together they forced me to substantially rethink my original expectations, for example, in regard to the extent to which technology could be infused with purposes or objectives more complex in nature than one would expect from either a technological determinist or a social choice perspective.

However, simply labeling a data analysis strategy as "holographic" is not the same as explaining how I actually constructed the accounts I give in chapters 2 through 5. To explain the process, let me describe what I did in two different ways: beginning with the mechanics of data analysis and then (in the next section) describing how (and why) I chose to report them.

The mechanics of data analysis were fairly straightforward. Every interview was transcribed directly onto the computer by means of a very

---

11. Arguably even Strauss (1987), who has developed one of the most systematic approaches to the analysis of qualitative data, skirts this issue when he encourages fieldworkers to use their prior experiences and ideas as a guide to collecting and analyzing data *but* then insists that "grounded theory" emerges solely from the data.

flexible word-processing program. I hired enough transcriptionists so that I could have completed texts back in my hands within three days from the time when I submitted them. This rapid turnaround enabled me to have ready access to the interview transcripts—certainly much more quickly than most researchers do—and I could therefore carefully read and annotate copies of the texts at the same time that I was doing new interviews in the same site. My written notes and the computer files allowed me to keep the enormous volume of detail I was receiving easily at hand; for example, I could rapidly check factual conflicts or differences in interpretation while my project was relatively fresh in the minds of the people I had interviewed. I could also rapidly amend or extend the chronology that served as an anchor for the interviews. Finally, I was also able to begin constructing an account of the process while I was at the site, thus making it possible to "pretest" my ideas with the people I had already interviewed or to frame new questions for those I had yet to interview.

I also began to construct coding categories from the earliest days in the field. Waiting until "all the data are in" may be an appropriate (even an unavoidable) strategy for survey research, but it can be quite inappropriate when the goal of the research is to *generate* theory (cf. Glaser and Strauss 1967). My initial codes were largely descriptive: they were based initially on *stages or moments in the change process* (i.e., categories derived from what I had sketched as a power-process perspective); on *relationships* among major groups of organizational actors (e.g., product engineering, process engineering, manufacturing management, etc.); and on characterizations of the *dynamics* of the process (e.g., conflict, bargaining, problem resolution strategies, etc.). Appendix 2 illustrates the coding scheme I had developed halfway through the computer case; Appendix 3 illustrates the formal definition of each coding category that I developed to render the coding activity consistent.

The codes were intended to serve as place markers or locators of aspects of the process to which I wanted to have easy access. The software package I used enabled me to code, count, and index passages in each file and then to retrieve them through a relatively simple set of macro commands. More important, perhaps, it allowed me to recode (change, add, or delete codes) without having to laboriously renumber pages by hand, reprint files, or lose earlier renditions of coded files. Not surprisingly, such a process required a great deal of memory (eight megabytes of RAM) and hard-disk space. This approach enabled me to build an account as I went along without sacrificing earlier coding schemes. It also allowed me to keep close track of where the evidence for my assertions resided, which points were well substantiated and which were conjectural, and what (or, more commonly, who) was the source of the evidence.

Keeping track of sources was particularly important because I wanted to avoid overreliance on a limited number of individuals or perspectives. Qualitative researchers, perhaps because of the visible role they play as the synthesizers and translators of the different realities that make up social life, are easy prey to critics who claim that their reports are biased by articulate or devious informants. Although I believe there is something to this critique,[12] I am also quite sensitive to the incompleteness and the biases hidden in what are more commonly presented as "objective" forms of data collection and analysis, for example, analyses that rely solely on surveys, secondary data sources, and the like. The critical question is, I would argue, not which approach comes closer to reality or "the truth," but instead which approach can maximize the possibilities that (1) the ideas the researcher wants to test are indeed *being tested* and (2) the researcher will find his or her a priori conceptual framework ruled irrelevant by what he or she learns *while doing the research*. In this respect my goal was to subject myself to these stringent criteria in a way that sophisticated quantitative analysts are encouraged to do (see, e.g., Schuman and Presser 1981; Schuman 1982).

Meeting these criteria has by no means proven to be a simple task. It has forced me, for example, to spend a substantial amount of time rechecking and cross-checking the facts as well as the assertions that underlie my accounts. Part of this I have done by way of follow-up interviews, circulation of drafts to many interviewees, presentations to both companies and unions, and last but not least, rereading and redrafting the case analyses themselves. Not surprisingly, my retelling of the accounts to participants has been an invaluable aid. But even when there has been disagreement as to my interpretation of events, I have been exceedingly careful to make sure that I got the facts right.

Differences in interpretation are inevitable, and although some of them stem from concerns about how "other people" will judge the company or the union, the ones that have to do with the underlying dynamics of the process have been reconsidered many times before they appeared in print. In this sense, even though I am the one telling the story—and therefore the story cannot exist independent of my telling—I

---

12. I, too, am skeptical of analyses based on superficial investigations, especially since I know how adept many organizations are at "staging" interviews and the like.

have made it a practice to make clear *how* I arrived at my version of the story and to provide enough data to allow others to construct their own account, too.

The objective of this project was not, however, to present a set of discrete cases. Rather, it was my intent from the very outset to compare the cases as I did them and to compare them after I was done with them all. Thus, just as I envisioned the inductive analysis of each interview holographically, I also conceived of the entire project (from case to case) in the same way. In this respect I began the project anew with each case, even though broader questions and hypotheses emerged out of each case I completed. Again, I consciously sought to keep two sets of mental books. I did this by trying to "live" each case as I collected the data and then to use the hiatus between cases to switch between books.

This process was eased enormously by what I created as a "macro" coding scheme, that is, a conceptual framework that began to absorb the major codes and relationships that I generated for the individual cases. Though extraordinarily complex—along the order of a system dynamics model (see Sterman 1989; Forrester 1971)—this conceptual framework allowed me to capture the peculiarities of the individual cases while abstracting common elements to guide the comparative analysis (in chapter 6).

REPORTING THE FINDINGS

The issue of "voice" is an important one in the reporting of findings from qualitative research and one that I labored over. Van Maanen (1988) has provided an extremely useful typology of voices or narrative styles used by ethnographers in the way they "tell their tales." In this book I have placed myself squarely between types: at times I venture into a "realist" mode where I adopt a third-person voice and portray events and explanations as if that is the way they "really were." At other times I am present as a first-person voice telling what Van Maanen refers to as a "confessional tale." In the latter mode I tell what "I" did, what I thought, and what I experienced. Early readers were decidedly split in their reaction to so many *I*'s. Some applauded this approach and bemoaned the drift into the realist mode later in the book; others recoiled at the idea. This latter group advised me that if I insisted on indicating my presence, I should do so in less obvious ways, for example, in anecdotal footnotes, in references to my role as interviewer in this appendix, and so on. My choice to fall in-between is a product of these conflicting pulls as well as my own concern that I not alienate completely those who expected (even demanded) a realist tale.

However, voice is important in another respect: Whose voice or voices will the author present in the telling of the tale? Who will be allowed to speak (in quotes, for example), and who will be spoken for? In this respect researchers who work with numbers—survey responses, production figures, mortality rates, and so on—appear to have a decided advantage over the qualitative researcher: their numbers, regression coefficients, and the like "speak for themselves," or so we are told. Qualitative researchers can make no such claim—even if they feel it to be a legitimate one—precisely because they are routinely confronted by many voices and many interpretations of the same essential phenomena, including interpretations backed by numbers. Thus, those who do fieldwork the way I have are forced to develop strategies not only for coding and analyzing those interpretations but for choosing which ones they will report as well.[13]

I pursued a relatively simple strategy. The chronologies in each case were used not only as anchors but as the closest thing to a factual backbone I could find. That is, the arguments and interpretations that people made in the interviews were carefully cross-checked against the chronology in my effort to determine whether such things as influence over the actual decisions, framing of decision alternatives, or efforts to shape the various proposals for change could be shown to have occurred at the time people claimed. Whenever someone claimed that they or someone else "did" something, I pressed hard for evidence to that effect. If evidence (in the form of memos, reports, etc.) could not be found, then I placed the remark into an inventory of leads to pursue (e.g., in subsequent interviews). If no further evidence in support of the assertion appeared, I either omitted it from the analysis or reported it in a provisional fashion in the text.

Reporting of interpretations *as interpretations* is handled in a different way. One of the greatest strengths of qualitative research, one that I

13. However, even within the community of field researchers there are important differences in the way in which voices are reported. Someone studying an occupational group or community can attribute remarks or observations in a far more general fashion than I have or than I can: e.g., one can refer to a remark made by a plumber or a neighborhood resident simply as someone who is part of the context; in my case studies, however, context is critical to understanding (as well as evaluating) the comments of any given individual. Context includes such factors as rank, profession or occupation, and relationship to the change under study. For these reasons I have had to be far more careful to specify the context within which the people speak while taking every measure to protect the identity of those who are speaking.

try to use to advantage in this book, is its emphasis on capturing and describing the multiplicity of interpretations that can reside in the same social space, be it an organization, a neighborhood, or a family unit. Because I wanted readers to experience the differences in interpretation that resided in these organizations, I have made a conspicuous effort to allow multiple voices to speak. Of course, this approach detracts from the traditional notion in social science writing that there should be a single integrated account. However, I am convinced that a single integrated account would be not only difficult but illusory as well. In other words, "official stories" are official in large measure because they have the backing of officials, that is, people with power and influence. They may be comforting to read because they are told with authority, but their authority must always be questioned. I chose to question authority not because I distrust those who tell official stories but because I am convinced that their stories, *like everyone else's*, are interpretations.[14]

Thus, rather than insisting that anyone has a monopoly on the truth or reality, I work from the assumption that reality is a *social* construct. In other words, contrary to reductionist assumptions in other disciplines, I do not believe this to be a Robinson Crusoe world. And given that I am in the business of educating people to live and work in an organizational world replete with multiple interpretations and identities, I would be extremely remiss if I were to argue for the supremacy of one reality—technical, managerial, or financial—over the others.

---

14. Of course, as one interviewee warned me, "If you do it well, chances are you'll never get to do it again."

Preliminary Coding Categories

COMPUTER AND ELECTRONICS COMPANY: SURFACE MOUNT TECHNOLOGY CASE

00–09 PRODUCT–PROCESS LINKAGES

01. Product's influence on process change/process attributes

02. Process's influence on product design

03. Process's influence on product attributes

04. Process's influence on designers and/or design process

05. Relations between product/design organization/lab and process or manufacturing organization

10–19 RELATIONS BETWEEN ORGANIZATIONAL UNITS

10. General

11. Relations of groups to corporate

12. Relations of divisions to corporate

13. Relations between divisions

14. Relations between surface mount manufacturing facilities (SMMF)

15. Relations between SMMFs and product development organization (PDO)

16. Relations between divisions and PDO

20–29 ECONOMIC EVALUATION/JUSTIFICATION
OF PROCESS TECHNOLOGY

20. General

21. Description of division-level evaluation/justification methods

22. Description of group- or corporate-level evaluation/ justification methods

23. Accuracy or confidence in evaluation/justification methods

24. Postimplementation evaluation or audit of change in process technology

25. Labor cost as a factor in evaluation/justification of change in process technology

26. Quality as a factor in evaluation/justification of change in process technology

27. Other factors in evaluation/justification of change in process technology

30–39 ATTITUDES TOWARD NEW
MANUFACTURING/PROCESS TECHNOLOGY

30. General

31. Company attitudes (general)

32. Divisional attitudes (general)

33. Engineers' attitudes

34. Managers' attitudes

35. Workers' attitudes

40–49 INFORMATION SHARING

40. General

41. Information sharing between divisions

42. Information sharing between divisions and corporate (including SMMF and PDO)

43. Site-specific information

50–59 MANAGING TECHNOLOGICAL CHANGE

50. General
51. Managing workers through transition
52. Worker involvement in technological change
53. Impact of new technology on jobs and/or skills
54. Impact of new technology on numbers of workers and/or composition of labor force

60–69 WORK ORGANIZATION/WORK ENVIRONMENT

60. General
61. Description of work process before technological change
62. Description of work process after technological change
63. Comparisons of work process before/after technological change

70–79 QUALITY CONTROL PRACTICES

70. General
71. Total Quality Control (TQC)
72. Statistical Process Control (SPC)
73. Worker involvement in quality control

80–89 TRAINING

80. General
81. Training required of or provided to production workers in connection with technological change
82. Training required of or provided to managers or engineers in connection with technological change
83. Quality-related training

84. Availability/quality/adequacy of training

85. Cost of and/or justification of training

90–99 LABOR FORCE CHARACTERISTICS
       AND MANAGEMENT

90. General

91. Temporary or contract workers (general)

92. Advantages/disadvantages of temporary or contract workers

93. Relations between regular employees and temporary or contract workers

94. Management issues associated with temporary or contract workers

95. Training issues associated with temporary or contract workers

96. Technology transfer issues associated with temporary or contract workers

97. Job performance issues associated with temporary or contract workers

Definition of
Coding Categories

COMPUTER AND ELECTRONICS COMPANY:
SURFACE MOUNT TECHNOLOGY CASE

00–09 PRODUCT–PROCESS LINKAGES

01. *Product's influence on process change/process attributes*

How the product being produced or being designed influences the choice of process. Includes the limits that the product or the design process places on what is deemed feasible in the organization of production.

02. *Process's influence on product design*

How the existing or anticipated production process influences the way products are designed. Includes the limits that the production process places on what is deemed feasible in the design lab.

03. *Process's influence on product attributes*

How the existing or anticipated production process influences the attributes of the product. Includes the limits and the opportunities for change in the product as a result of changes in the production process.

04. *Process's influence on designers and/or design process*

How the existing or anticipated production process influences what designers do or what they need to know in order to utilize new production technology.

05. *Relations between product/design/lab and process or manufacturing organization*

How relations between the product designers or labs and process engineers or manufacturing personnel are characterized.

10–19 RELATIONS BETWEEN
        ORGANIZATIONAL UNITS

10. *General*

Nonspecific references to the relationship between organizational units.

11. *Relations of groups to corporate*

References to past, present, and future relations between the groups and corporate. Includes issues of strategic planning, centralized versus decentralized decision making, group autonomy versus corporate control, resource sharing between groups and corporate.

12. *Relations of divisions to corporate*

References to past, present, and future relations between the divisions and corporate. Includes issues of strategic planning, centralized versus decentralized decision making, divisional autonomy versus corporate control, resource sharing between divisions and corporate.

13. *Relations between divisions*

References to past, present, and future relations between different divisions. Includes issues of resource sharing, competition, cooperation, and conflict.

14. *Relations between SMMFs*

References to past, present and future relations between different SMMFs. Includes issues of resource sharing, competition, cooperation, and conflict.

15. *Relations between SMMFs and PDO*

References to past, present, and future relations between SMMFs and the PDO. Includes issues of resource sharing, competition, cooperation, and conflict.

16. *Relations between divisions and PDO*

References to past, present, and future relations between division-based technology change efforts and corporate staff in PDO. *Excludes* surface mount technology and SMMFs, but includes issues of resource sharing, competition, cooperation, and conflict.

20–29 ECONOMIC EVALUATION/JUSTIFICATION OF PROCESS TECHNOLOGY

20. *General*

Nonspecific references to the economic evaluation/justification of process technology.

21. *Description of division-level evaluation/justification methods*

Description of how the division or site evaluates or justifies investments in new process technology. Includes references to budgeting practices, methodology, formal and informal measures, and benchmarks used in the evaluation/justification process.

22. *Description of group or corporate level evaluation/justification methods*

Description of how the group or the corporation evaluates or justifies investments in new process technology. Includes references to budgeting practices, methodology, formal and informal measures, and benchmarks used in the evaluation/justification process.

23. *Accuracy or confidence in evaluation/justification methods*

Assessments and/or opinions of the accuracy or degree of confidence that is placed in the data and the methodologies of evaluation/justification.

24. *Postimplementation evaluation or audit of change in process technology*

Reference to or description of evaluations, postmortems, or audits of investments made in new process technology. Includes assessments/opinions and indications that such evaluation or audit was never done.

25. *Labor cost/head count as a factor in evaluation/justification of change in process technology*

Reference to the cost of labor or increase/decrease in the amount of production labor needed as a result of a change in process technology. Reference to labor cost or head-count reduction as criteria in evaluation/justification of a change in process technology.

26. *Quality as a factor in evaluation/justification of change in process technology*

Reference to improvements/reduction in *either* product or process quality as a result of a change in process technology. Reference to quality improvement as criteria in evaluation/justification of a change in process technology.

27. *Other factors in evaluation/justification of a change in process technology*

Reference to factors other than product cost, labor cost, or quality as criteria in evaluation/justification of a change in process technology. For example, prototyping speed, worker safety, etc.

30–39   ATTITUDES TOWARD NEW MANUFACTURING/PROCESS TECHNOLOGY

30. *General*

Nonspecific comments or remarks regarding attitudes toward new process technology.

31. *Company attitudes (general)*

References to the attitude of the company to new process technology. Includes comments about the perceived importance (strategic and otherwise) of new process technology to the competitiveness of the company. Assessments of the company's status as a leader or follower of developments in new process technology.

32. Divisional attitudes (general)

References to the attitude of the division to new process technology. Includes comments about the perceived importance (strategic and otherwise) of new process technology to the competitiveness of the division. Assessments of the division's status as a leader or follower of developments in new process technology.

33. Engineers' attitudes

References by engineers to the importance (strategic and otherwise) of new process technology to the division or the company.

34. Managers' attitudes

References by managers to the importance (strategic and otherwise) of new process technology to the division or the company.

35. Workers' attitudes

References by workers to the importance (strategic and otherwise) of new process technology to the division or the company.

40–49 INFORMATION SHARING

40. General

Nonspecific references to information sharing in the site, division, group, or company.

41. Information sharing between divisions

References to and/or evaluations of information sharing between divisions. Includes references to the types of information that get shared or *do not* get shared.

42. *Information sharing between divisions and corporate (including SMMFs and PDO)*

References to and/or evaluations of information sharing between divisions and corporate organizations, including the SMFF and the PDO. Includes references to the types of information that get shared or *do not* get shared.

43. *Site-specific information*

References to information, techniques, or data generated by an individual site (including an SMFF) pertaining to the site's own operation. Includes references to information, techniques, or data *not* shared with other organizational units.

50–59 MANAGING TECHNOLOGICAL CHANGE

50. *General*

Nonspecific references to the problems, issues, and solutions associated with managing technological change.

51. *Managing workers through transition*

References to the specific issues or practices associated with workers during the transition from one process to another. Includes descriptions of how workers were (or will be) recruited, distributed, and/or deployed in the new process.

52. *Worker involvement in technological change*

References or assessments of the involvement of production workers (including technicians) in the selection, qualification, installation, or arrangement of new process technology.

53. *Impact of new technology on jobs and/or skills*

References to or descriptions of the real or anticipated effects of a change in process technology on job characteristics or skill requirements.

54. *Impact of new technology on numbers of workers and/or composition of labor force*

References to or descriptions of the real or anticipated effects of a change in process technology on the number of workers required, labor productivity, or the kinds of people employed in the production process.

60–69 WORK ORGANIZATION/WORK ENVIRONMENT

60. *General*

61. *Description of work process before technological change*

62. *Description of work process after technological change*

63. *Comparisons of work process before/after technological change*

70–79 QUALITY CONTROL PRACTICES

70. *General*

Nonspecific references to or descriptions of the role of quality control in the manufacturing end of the enterprise.

71. *TQC*

Specific references to the existing or planned efforts at TQC, including evaluations of their effectiveness.

72. *SPC*

Specific references to the existing or planned efforts at SPC, including evaluations of their effectiveness.

73. *Worker involvement in quality control*

References to or descriptions of the role that production workers (and/or technicians) play in quality control.

80–89 TRAINING

80. *General*

Nonspecific comments on training of all levels of employees.

81. *Training required or provided in connection with technological change*

References to or descriptions of training that were (or will be) required of or provided to production workers in connection with a change in process technology.

82. *Managerial and/or professional training required or provided in connection with technological change*

References to or descriptions of training that were (or will be) required of or provided to managers or engineers in connection with a change in process technology.

83. *Quality-related training*

84. *Availability/quality/adequacy of training*

References to who or what organization provides training. Assessments and/or opinions regarding the availability, quality, and/or adequacy of training as currently provided.

85. *Cost of and/or justification of training*

References to or descriptions of the cost of training and the justification (economic or otherwise) that must be made to pay for training.

90–99 LABOR FORCE CHARACTERISTICS AND MANAGEMENT

90. *General*

Nonspecific references to or description of the characteristics of the current or anticipated labor force.

91. *Temporary or contract workers (general)*

General references to or description of the temporary or contract employees. Includes description of the system for hiring, deploying, and/or retaining these employees.

92. *Advantages/disadvantages of temporary or contract workers*

Assessments of or opinions regarding the advantages/disadvantages of using temporary or contract workers.

93. *Relations between regular employees and temporary or contract workers*

References to or descriptions of relations between different types of production employee. Includes issues of competition, cooperation, and/or conflict.

94. *Management issues associated with temporary or contract workers*

References to or descriptions of specific management issues (e.g., management style or practice) associated with the employment of nonregular employees.

95. *Training issues associated with temporary or contract workers*

References to or descriptions of training issues associated with nonregular employees. Includes whether or not nonregular employees are provided with training.

96. *Technology transfer issues associated with temporary or contract workers*

References to skills and/or knowledge that is gained or lost through the use of nonregular employees.

97. *Job performance issues associated with temporary or contract workers*

References to or assessments of job performance of nonregular employees. Includes comparisons with regular employees in terms of productivity, commitment, quality, etc.

References

Abernathy, William. 1978. *The Productivity Dilemma*. Baltimore: Johns Hopkins University Press.

Abernathy, William, and Kim Clark. 1985. "Innovation: Mapping the Winds of Creative Destruction." *Research Policy* 14:3–22.

Abernathy, William, Kim Clark, and A. M. Kantrow. 1983. *Industrial Renaissance*. New York: Basic Books.

Abernathy, William, and James Utterback. 1978. "Patterns of Industrial Innovation." *Technology Review* 50 (7):40–47.

Abraham, Katherine. 1990. "Restructuring the Employment Relationship: The Growth of Market-Mediated Work Arrangements." In K. Abraham and R. McKersie, eds., *New Developments in the Labor Market*, 85–120. Cambridge: MIT Press.

Adler, Paul S. 1986. "New Technologies, New Skills." *California Management Review* 29 (1): 9–28.

——— 1987. "Automation and Skill: New Directions." *International Journal of Technology Management* 2 (5–6): 761–72.

——— 1990. "Managing High-Tech Processes: The Challenge of CAD/CAM." In M. A. Von Glinow and S. A. Mohrman, eds., *Managing Complexity in High Technology Organizations*, 98–125. New York: Oxford.

Allen, Thomas. 1981. *Managing the Flow of Technology*. Cambridge: MIT Press.

Allison, Graham. 1971. *The Essence of Decision*. Boston: Little, Brown.

Argyris, Chris, and Donald Schon. 1974. *Theory in Practice: Increasing Professional Effectiveness*. San Francisco: Jossey-Bass.

Arrow, Kenneth. 1974. *The Limits of Organization*. New York: Norton.

Bacharach, Samuel, and Edward J. Lawler. 1980. *Power and Politics in Organizations*. San Francisco: Jossey-Bass.

Bachrach, Peter, and Morton Baratz. 1962. "The Two Faces of Power." *American Political Science Review* 56:947–52.

Bailyn, Lotte. 1980. *Living with Technology: Issues at Mid-Career*. Cambridge: MIT Press.

Barley, Stephen. 1986. "Technology as an Occasion for Structuring." *Administrative Science Quarterly* 31:78–108.

——— 1990. "The Alignment of Technology and Structure Through Roles and Networks." *Administrative Science Quarterly* 35:61–103.

Becker, Howard S. 1982. *Art Worlds*. Berkeley and Los Angeles: University of California Press.

——— 1986. *Writing for Social Scientists*. Chicago: University of Chicago Press.

Bedeian, A. 1980. *Organizations: Theory and Analysis*. Homewood, Ill.: Dorsey.

Beer, Michael, Bert Spector, Paul Lawrence, D. Quinn Mills, and Richard E. Walton. 1985. *Human Resource Management*. New York: Free Press.

Benedict, Ruth. 1934. *Patterns of Culture*. Boston: Houghton Mifflin.

Benson, J. Kenneth. 1977. "Organizations: A Dialectical View." *Administrative Science Quarterly* 22:1–21.

Berggren, Christian, Torsten Bjorkman, and Ernst Hollander. 1991. "Are They Unbeatable?" Working paper, Royal Institute of Technology, Stockholm, Sweden.

Blau, Peter, Cecilia McHugh Falbe, William McKinley, and Phelps Tracey. 1976. "Technology and Organization in Manufacturing." *Administrative Science Quarterly* 21:20–40.

Blauner, Robert. 1964. *Alienation and Freedom*. Chicago: University of Chicago Press.

Block, Fred. 1990. *Post-Industrial Possibilities*. Berkeley and Los Angeles: University of California Press.

Bourdieu, Pierre. 1977. *Outline of a Theory of Practice*. Cambridge: Cambridge University Press.

Bower, Joseph. 1970. *Managing the Resource Allocation Process*. Boston: Harvard Business School Press.

Bowles, Samuel, and Herbert Gintis. 1976. *Schooling in Capitalist America*. New York: Basic Books.

Braverman, Harry. 1974. *Labor and Monopoly Capital*. New York: Monthly Review Press.

Bright, J. R. 1958. "Does Automation Raise Skill Requirements?" *Harvard Business Review* 36 (4): 85–98.

Buchanan, David, and David Boddy. 1983. *Organizations in the Computer Age*. Aldershot, Eng.: Gower.

Buchanan, David, David Boddy, and James McCalman. 1988. "Getting In, Getting On, Getting Out, and Getting Back." In A. Bryman, ed., *Doing Research in Organizations*, 53–62. London: Routledge.

Burawoy, Michael. 1979. *Manufacturing Consent*. Chicago: University of Chicago Press.

——— 1985. *The Politics of Production: Factory Regimes Under Capitalism and Socialism*. London: Verso.

Burgelman, Robert A. 1984. "Managing the Internal Corporate Venturing Process." *Sloan Management Review* 25 (2): 33–48.

Burns, Tom. 1961. "Micropolitics: Mechanisms of Institutional Change." *Administrative Science Quarterly* 7:257–81.

Burns, Tom, and George Stalker. 1961. *The Management of Innovation*. London: Tavistock.

Cadigan, Pat. 1991. *Synners*. New York: Bantam.

Carroll, John, and Eric Johnson. 1990. *Decision Research*. Newbury Park, Calif.: Sage.

Carter, E. E. 1971. "The Behavioral Theory of the Firm and Top-Level Corporate Decision." *Administrative Science Quarterly* 16:413–29.

Cebon, Peter. 1990. "Managing Secondary Objectives in Organizations: The Case of Energy Management in Universities." Master's thesis. Massachusetts Institute of Technology.

Chandler, Alfred D. 1962. *Strategy and Structure: Chapters in the History of the American Industrial Enterprise*. Cambridge: MIT Press.

———. 1977. *The Visible Hand: The Managerial Revolution in American Business*. Cambridge: Harvard University Press.

Child, John. 1972. "Organization Structure, Environment, and Performance: The Role of Strategic Choice." *Sociology* 6:1–22.

———. 1985. "Managerial Strategies, New Technology and the Labour Process." In D. Knights, H. Willmott, and D. Collinson, eds., *Job Redesign: Critical Perspectives on the Labour Process*, 107–41. London: Gower.

Chinoy, Eli. 1955. *Automobile Workers and the American Dream*. Boston: Beacon.

Clark, Jon, Ian McLoughlin, Howard Rose, and Robin King. 1988. *The Process of Technological Change*. Cambridge: Cambridge University Press.

Clark, Kim, and Takahiro Fujimoto. 1991. *Product Development Performance*. Boston: Harvard Business School Press.

Coch, Lester, and John French. 1948. "Overcoming Resistance to Change." *Human Relations* 1:520–32.

Cohen, M., James March, and J. Olsen. 1972. "A Garbage Can Model of Organizational Choice." *Administrative Science Quarterly* 17:1–25.

Cohen, Stephen, and John Zysman. 1987. *Manufacturing Matters*. New York: Basic Books.

Cole, Robert E. 1979. *Work, Participation, and Mobility*. Berkeley and Los Angeles: University of California Press.

———. 1989. *Strategies for Learning: Small Group Activities in American, Japanese, and Swedish Industry*. Berkeley and Los Angeles: University of California Press.

Cole, Robert E., and T. Yakushiji. 1984. *The U.S. and Japanese Automobile Industries in Transition*. Ann Arbor: University of Michigan Center for Japanese Studies.

Comstock, Donald, and W. Richard Scott. 1977. "Technology and the Structure of Subunits: Distinguishing Individual and Workgroup Effects." *Administrative Science Quarterly* 22:177–202.

Cornfield, Dan. 1987. "Labor-Management Cooperation or Management Control." In D. Cornfield, ed., *Workers, Managers and Technological Change*, 331–54. New York: Plenum.

Crozier, Michel. 1964. *The Bureaucratic Phenomenon*. Chicago: University of Chicago Press.

Cusumano, Michael. 1985. *The Japanese Automobile Industry*. Cambridge: Harvard University Press.

Cyert, Richard, and James March. 1963. *A Behavioral Theory of the Firm*. Englewood Cliffs, N.J.: Prentice-Hall.

Cyert, Richard, Herbert Simon, and Donald Trow. 1956. "Observation of a Business Decision." *Journal of Business* 29:237–48.

Dalton, Melville. 1959. *Men Who Manage*. New York: Wiley.

——— 1964. "Preconceptions and Methods in *Men Who Manage*." In P. Hammond, ed., *Sociologists at Work*, 58–110. New York: Basic Books.

Davis, Fred. 1973. "The Martian and the Convert." *Urban Life and Culture* 2:333–43.

Dean, James, Jr. 1987. "Building the Future: The Justification Process for New Technology." In J. Pennings and A. Buitendam, eds., *New Technology as Organizational Innovation*, 35–58. Cambridge, Mass.: Ballinger.

Denzin, Norman. 1978. *The Research Act*. 2d ed. New York: McGraw-Hill.

Dertouzos, Michael, Richard Lester, and Robert Solow. 1989. *Made in America*. Cambridge: MIT Press.

DiMaggio, Paul, and Walter Powell. 1983. "The Iron Cage Revisited: Institutional Isomorphism and Collective Rationality in Organizational Fields." *American Sociological Review* 48:147–60.

Dore, Ronald. 1986. *Flexible Rigidities*. Stanford: Stanford University Press.

Drucker, Peter. 1988. "The Coming of the New Organization." *Harvard Business Review* 66 (1): 45–53.

Eccles, Robert. 1981. "The Quasi-Firm in the Construction Industry." *Journal of Economic Behavior and Organization* 2:335–57.

Edwards, Richard. 1979. *Contested Terrain*. New York: Basic Books.

El-Hout, Jamal N. 1990. "Organization and Management at the Interface of Product and Process Engineering." Master's thesis. Sloan School of Management, Massachusetts Institute of Technology.

Emery, Fred, and Einar Thorsud. 1976. *Democracy at Work*. Leiden: Martinus Nijhoff.

Emery, Fred, and Eric Trist. 1960. "Socio-Technical Systems." In C. W. Churchman and M. Verhust, eds., *Management Science Models and Methods* 2:83–97. London: Pergamon.

Fantasia, Rick. 1988. *Cultures of Solidarity*. Berkeley and Los Angeles: University of California Press.

Feldman, Martha, and James March. 1981. "Information as Signal and Symbol." *Administrative Science Quarterly* 26:171–86.

Fleck, Ludwig. [1935] 1979. *The Genesis and Development of a Scientific Fact*. Chicago: University of Chicago Press.

Fligstein, Neil. 1985. "The Spread of the Multidivisional Form Among Large Organizations." *American Sociological Review* 50:377–91.

Forrester, Jay. 1971. "The Counterintuitive Behavior of Social Systems." *Technology Review* 43 (1): 52–68.

Francis, Arthur. 1986. *New Technology at Work.* London: Oxford University Press.

French, John, and Bertram Raven. 1968. "The Bases of Social Power." In D. Cartwright and A. Zander, eds., *Group Dynamics,* 259–69. New York: Harper and Row.

Gamson, William. 1975. *The Strategy of Social Protest.* Homewood, Ill.: Dorsey.

Garson, Barbara. 1975. *All the Livelong Day.* New York: Vintage, Random House.

Gartman, David. 1989. *Auto Slavery.* Cornell: ILR Press.

Geertz, Clifford. 1973. *The Interpretation of Cultures.* New York: Basic Books.

Giddens, Anthony. 1976. *The New Rules of the Sociological Method.* New York: Basic Books.

———— 1979. *Central Problems in Social Theory.* Berkeley and Los Angeles: University of California Press.

Glaser, Barney, and Anselm Strauss. 1967. *The Discovery of Grounded Theory.* Chicago: Aldine.

Gold, Bela. 1983. "Strengthening Managerial Approaches to Improving Technological Capabilities." *Strategic Management Journal* 4 (3): 209-20.

Goldman, Paul. 1983. "The Labor Process and the Sociology of Organizations." *Research in the Sociology of Organizations* 2:49–81.

Gordon, David, Richard Edwards, and Michael Reich. 1982. *Segmented Work, Divided Workers.* New York: Cambridge University Press.

Gouldner, Alvin. 1954. *Patterns of Industrial Bureaucracy.* New York: Free Press.

Graham, Margaret. 1990. *R&D for Industry.* New York: Cambridge University Press.

Gramsci, Antonio. 1971. *Selections from the Prison Notebooks.* New York: International Publishers.

Granovetter, Mark. 1985. "Economic Action and Social Structure: The Problem of Embeddedness." *American Journal of Sociology* 83:1420–43.

Grenier, Guillermo. 1988. *Inhuman Relations.* Philadelphia: Temple University Press.

Gurr, Ted R. 1970. *Why Men Rebel.* Princeton: Princeton University Press.

Hammer, Tove, and Robert Stern. 1986. "A Yo-Yo Model of Union-Management Cooperation." *Industrial and Labor Relations Review* 39:337–49.

Harbour Associates. 1989. *A Decade Later: Competitive Assessment of the North American Automobile Industry, 1979–1989.* Southfield, Mich.: Harbour Associates.

Hauser, John, and Don Clausing. 1988. "The House of Quality." *Harvard Business Review* 66 (3): 63–73.

Hayes, Robert, and Kim Clark. 1985. "Exploring the Sources of Productivity Difference at the Factory Level." In K. Clark, R. Hayes, and C. Lorenz, eds., *The Uneasy Alliance: Managing the Productivity-Technology Dilemma,* 151–88. Boston: Harvard Business School Press.

Hayes, Robert, Steven Wheelwright, and Kim Clark. 1988. *Dynamic Manufacturing*. New York: Free Press.

Henderson, Rebecca. 1988. "The Failure of Established Firms in the Face of Technical Change." Ph.D. diss. Harvard University.

Henderson, Rebecca, and Kim Clark. 1990. "Architectural Innovation: The Reconfiguration of Existing Product Technologies and the Failure of Established Firms." *Administrative Science Quarterly* 35:9–30.

Hershizer, Brian. 1987. "Union Officials Assess the Labor Movement and Labor-Management Relations." *Labor Studies Journal* 12 (1): 26–47.

Hickson, David, D. S. Pugh, and Diana Pheysey. 1969. "Operations Technology and Organization Structure: An Empirical Appraisal." *Administrative Science Quarterly* 14:378–97.

Hickson, D. J., C. R. Hinings, C. A. Lee, R. E. Schneck, and J. M. Pennings. 1971. "A Strategic Contingencies Theory of Intraorganizational Power." *Administrative Science Quarterly* 16:216–29.

Hirschhorn, Larry. 1984. *Beyond Mechanization*. Cambridge: MIT Press.

Hoerr, John. 1989. *And The Wolf Finally Came*. Pittsburgh: University of Pittsburgh Press.

Hrebiniak, Lawrence, and William Joyce. 1985. "Organizational Adaptation and Environmental Determinism." *Administrative Science Quarterly* 30:336–49.

Hunt, R. G. 1970. "Technology and Organization." *Academy of Management Journal* 13 (2): 235–52.

Hyman, Richard. 1989. "Flexible Specialization: Miracle or Myth?" In *New Technology and Industrial Relations*, edited by R. Hyman and W. Streeck, 48–60. London: Basil Blackwell.

Jaikumar, Ramchandran. 1986. "Postindustrial Manufacturing." *Harvard Business Review* 64 (6): 69–76.

Jenkins, Craig. 1984. *The Politics of Insurgency*. New York: Columbia University Press.

Jenkins, Craig, and Charles Perrow. 1977. "Insurgency of the Powerless: Farm Worker Movements, 1946–72." *American Sociological Review* 42:249–68.

Jensen, Michael C., and William H. Meckling. 1976. "Theory of the Firm: Managerial Behavior, Agency Costs, and Ownership Structure." *Journal of Financial Economics* 3:305–60.

Jick, Todd. 1983. "Mixing Qualitative and Quantitative Methods: Triangulation in Practice." In J. Van Maanen, ed., *Qualitative Methodology*, 135–48. Beverly Hills: Sage.

Johnson, H. Thomas, and Robert Kaplan. 1987. *Relevance Lost: The Rise and Fall of Managerial Accounting*. Cambridge: Harvard Business School Press.

Jones, Bryn. 1982. "Destruction or Redistribution of Skills? The Case of Numerical Control." In S. Wood, ed., *The Degradation of Work*, 179–200. London: Hutchinson.

Kanter, Rosabeth. 1988. "When a Thousand Flowers Bloom: Structural, Collective, and Social Conditions for Innovation in Organizations." *Research in Organizational Behavior* 10:169–211.

Kaplan, Robert. 1984. "Yesterday's Accounting Undermines Production." *Harvard Business Review* 62 (4): 95–101.

—— 1986. "Must CIM Be Justified by Faith Alone?" *Harvard Business Review* 64 (2): 87–95.

Katz, Fred. 1965. "Explaining Informal Work Groups in Complex Organizations." *Administrative Science Quarterly* 10:204–23.

Katz, Harry. 1985. *Shifting Gears: Changing Labor Relations in the U.S. Automobile Industry*. Cambridge: MIT Press.

Kelley, Maryellen. 1986. "Programmable Automation and the Skill Question." *Human Systems Management* 6:223–41.

—— 1990. "New Process Technology, Job Design, and Work Organization." *American Sociological Review* 55:191–208.

Kelly, John. 1987. "Management's Redesign of Work." In D. Knights, H. Willmott, and D. Collinson, eds., *Job Redesign*, 30–51. Aldershot, Eng.: Gower.

Kern, Horst, and Michael Schumann. 1989. "New Concepts in Production in Western German Plants." In P. Katzenstein, ed., *Industry and Politics in West Germany*, 87–110. Ithaca: Cornell University Press.

Khandwalla, Pradip. 1974. "Mass Output Orientation of Operations Technology and Organizational Structure." *Administrative Science Quarterly* 14:378–97.

Kidder, Tracy. 1981. *The Soul of a New Machine*. Boston: Little, Brown.

Kimberly, J. R. 1980. "Initiation, Innovation, and Institutionalization in the Creation Process." In J. R. Kimberley and B. Miles, eds., *The Organizational Life Cycle*, 18–43. San Francisco: Jossey-Bass.

Kimberly, J. R., and M. J. Evanisko. 1981. "Organizational Innovation: The Influence of Individual, Organizational, and Contextual Factors on Hospital Adoption of Technical and Administrative Innovations." *Academy of Management Journal* 24:689–713.

Kochan, Thomas, Harry Katz, and Robert McKersie. 1986. *The Transformation of American Industrial Relations*. New York: Basic Books.

Kofman, Fred. 1992. "Double-Loop Accounting: A Language for the Learning Organization." Working paper, Sloan School of Management, Massachusetts Institute of Technology.

Kotter, J. P., and L. Schlesinger. 1979. "Choosing Strategies for Change." *Harvard Business Review* 57 (2): 106–14.

Krafcik, John. 1988. "Triumph of the Lean Production System." *Sloan Management Review* 30 (1): 41–52.

Krafcik, John, and John Paul MacDuffie. 1989. "Explaining High Performance Manufacturing: The International Automotive Assembly Study." Working paper, International Motor Vehicle Program, Massachusetts Institute of Technology.

Kuhn, Thomas. 1967. *The Structure of Scientific Revolutions*. Chicago: University of Chicago Press.

Kunda, Gideon. 1992. *Engineering Culture*. Philadelphia: Temple University Press.

Latour, Bruno. 1987. *Science in Action*. Cambridge: Harvard University.

Lawrence, Paul R. 1954. "How to Deal with Resistance to Change." *Harvard Business Review* 32 (3): 49–57.

Lawrence, Paul R., and Jay W. Lorsch. 1967. *Organization and Environment*. Cambridge: Harvard University Press.

Leonard-Barton, Dorothy. 1988. "The Mutual Adaptation of Technology and Organization." *Research Policy* 17 (5): 251–68.

Liker, Jeffrey, and Mitchell Fleischer. 1992. "The Organizational Context for Design for Manufacturing." In G. Susman, ed., *Integrating Design and Manufacturing for Competitive Advantage*, 228–64. New York: Oxford University Press.

Lindblom, Charles E. 1959. "The Science of Muddling Through." *Public Administration Review* 19:79–88.

Lipsky, Michael. 1978. *Street-Level Bureaucrats*. Chicago: University of Chicago Press.

Locke, Richard. 1991. "Local Politics and Industrial Readjustment." Ph.D. diss. Massachusetts Institute of Technology.

MacDuffie, John Paul. 1990. *Beyond Mass Production: Flexible Production Systems and Manufacturing Performance in the World Auto Industry*. Ph.D. diss. Sloan School of Management, Massachusetts Institute of Technology.

Maidique, M. A. 1980. "Entrepreneurs, Champions, and Technological Innovation." *Sloan Management Review* 21:59–76.

Mangin, Charles-Henri. 1990. *Managing the SMT Challenge*. Bedford, Eng.: IFS Publications.

Mao Tse-Tung. 1976. *Selected Works of Chairman Mao*. Vol. 1. New York: International Publishers.

March, James. 1962. "The Business Firm as a Political Coalition." *Journal of Politics* 24:662–78.

———. 1978. "Bounded Rationality, Ambiguity, and the Engineering of Choice." *Bell Journal of Economics* 9:587–608.

———. 1981. "Decisions in Organizations and Theories of Choice." In A. Van de Ven and W. Joyce, eds., *Perspectives on Organizational Design and Behavior*, 205–44. New York: Wiley.

March, James, and Herbert Simon. 1958. *Organizations*. New York: Wiley.

Marglin, Steven. 1974. "What Do the Bosses Do? The Origins and Functions of Hierarchy in Capitalist Production." *Review of Radical Political Economics* 6:70–92.

Marquis, Donald. 1982. "The Anatomy of Successful Innovation." In M. Tushman and W. Moore, eds., *Readings in the Management of Innovation*, 42–50. Cambridge, Mass.: Ballinger.

Marx, Karl. 1967. *Capital*. Vol. 1. New York: International Publishers.

McGregor, Douglas. 1960. *The Human Side of Enterprise*. New York: McGraw-Hill.

Mechanic, David. 1960. "Sources of Power of Lower Participants in Complex Organizations." *Administrative Science Quarterly* 7:349–64.

Mintzberg, Henry. 1979. *The Structuring of Organizations*. Englewood Cliffs, N.J.: Prentice-Hall.

Mintzberg, Henry, D. Raisinghani, and A. Theoret. 1976. "The Structure of Unstructured Decision Processes." *Administrative Science Quarterly* 21:246–75.

Mohr, Lawrence. 1972. "Organizational Technology and Organizational Structure." *Administrative Science Quarterly* 16:444–59.

Montgomery, David. 1987. *The Fall of the House of Labor.* New York: Cambridge University Press.

Morris, Aldon. 1986. *The Origins of the Southern Civil Rights Movement.* New York: Free Press.

Nadler, David, and Michael Tushman. 1980. "A Congruence Model for Diagnosing Organizational Behavior." In I. Rubin and J. McIntyre, eds., *Organizational Psychology*, 48–62. Englewood Cliffs, N.J.: Prentice-Hall.

Nelson, R. R., and G. S. Winter. 1982. *An Evolutionary Theory of Economic Change.* Cambridge: Harvard University Press.

Noble, David. 1984. *Forces of Production: A Social History of Industrial Automation.* New York: Knopf.

Nord, Walter, and Sharon Tucker. 1987. *Implementing Routine and Radical Innovations.* Lexington, Mass.: Lexington Books.

Orlikowski, Wanda. 1992. "The Duality of Technology: Rethinking the Concept of Technology in Organizations." *Organization Science* 3 (3): 398–427.

Parker, Mike. 1985. *Inside the Circle: A Union Guide to QWL.* Boston: South End Press.

Parker, Mike, and Jane Slaughter. 1988. *Choosing Sides: Unions and the Team Concept.* Boston: South End Press.

Pavadore, Lori. 1990. "QWL Programs in Unionized Settings." M.S. thesis. Sloan School of Management, Massachusetts Institute of Technology.

Perrow, Charles. 1967. "A Framework for the Comparative Analysis of Organizations." *American Sociological Review* 32:194–208.

——— 1981. "Markets, Hierarchies and Hegemony." In A. Van de Ven and W. Joyce, eds., *Perspectives on Organizational Design and Performance*, 371–86. New York: Wiley.

——— 1983. "The Organizational Context of Human Factors Engineering." *Administrative Science Quarterly* 28:521–41.

——— 1984. *Normal Accidents: Living with High-Risk Technologies.* New York: Basic Books.

——— 1986. *Complex Organizations: A Critical Essay.* 3d ed. New York: Random House.

Peters, Thomas, and R. Waterman. 1982. *In Search of Excellence.* New York: Harper and Row.

Pettigrew, Andrew. 1972. "Information Control as a Power Resource." *Sociology* 6:188–204.

——— 1973. *The Politics of Organizational Decision-Making.* London: Tavistock.

——— 1983. "On Studying Organizational Cultures." In J. Van Maanen, ed., *Qualitative Methodology*, 87–104. Beverly Hills: Sage.

Pfeffer, Jeffrey. 1977. "Power and Resource Allocation in Organizations." In B. Staw and G. Salancik, eds., *New Directions in Organizational Behavior*, 235–65. New York: St. Clair.

———— 1978. "The Micropolitics of Organizations." In Marshall Meyer, ed., *Environments and Organizations*, 29–50. San Francisco: Jossey-Bass.

———— 1981. *Power in Organizations*. Marshfield, Mass.: Pitman.

Pfeffer, Jeffrey, and Gerald Salancik. 1978. *The External Control of Organizations*. New York: Harper and Row.

Piore, Michael, and Charles Sabel. 1984. *The Second Industrial Divide*. New York: Basic Books.

Punch, Maurice. 1986. *The Politics and Ethics of Fieldwork*. Newbury Park, Calif.: Sage.

Ranson, Stewart, Bob Hinings, and Royston Greenwood. 1980. "The Structuring of Organizational Structure." *Administrative Science Quarterly* 25:1–17.

Rice, Ronald, and Everett Rogers. 1979. "Reinvention in the Innovation Process." *Knowledge* 1 (4): 499–514.

Roberts, Edward B. 1968. "Entrepreneurship and Technology: A Basic Study of Innovators." *Research Management* 11:249–66.

———— 1988. "Managing Invention and Innovation." *Research-Technology Management* 31 (1): 11–29.

Rogers, Everett, and Judith Larsen. 1984. *Silicon Valley Fever: Growth of a High-Technology Culture*. New York: Basic Books.

Rose, M., and B. Jones. 1987. "Managerial Strategy and Trade Union Response in Work Reorganization Schemes at the Establishment Level." In D. Knights, H. Willmott, and D. Collinson, eds., *Job Redesign*, 81–106. Aldershot, Eng.: Gower.

Rothschild, Emma. 1973. *Paradise Lost: The End of the Auto-Industrial Age*. New York: Vintage, Random House.

Roy, Donald. 1952. "Quota Restriction and Goldbricking in a Machine Shop." *American Journal of Sociology* 57:427–42.

Sabel, Charles. 1982. *Work and Politics*. New York: Cambridge University Press.

Sahal, Devendra. 1981. *Patterns of Industrial Innovation*. Reading, Mass.: Addison-Wesley.

Salancik, Gerald, and Jeffrey Pfeffer. 1974. "The Bases and Uses of Power in Organizational Decision-Making." *Administrative Science Quarterly* 19:453–73.

Saltzman, Harold. 1992. "Technology Design and Productivity, Skill and Quality of Worklife." In T. Winnograd and P. Adler, eds., *The Usability Challenge: Technology, Learning, and Organization*, 98–119. New York: Oxford University Press.

Schein, Edgar. 1985. *Organizational Culture and Leadership*. San Francisco: Jossey-Bass.

Schon, Donald. 1983. *The Reflective Practitioner: How Professionals Think in Action*. New York: Basic Books.

Schonberger, Richard. 1982. *Japanese Manufacturing Techniques*. New York: Free Press.

Schuman, Howard. 1982. "Artifacts Are in the Eye of the Beholder." *American Sociologist* 17:21–28.

Schuman, Howard, and Stanley Presser. 1981. *Questions and Answers in Attitude Surveys.* New York: Academic.

Schumpeter, Joseph. 1950. *Capitalism, Socialism, and Democracy.* New York: Harper and Row.

Schurmann, Franz. 1970. *Ideology and Organization in Communist China.* Berkeley and Los Angeles: University of California Press.

Schwenk, Charles. 1985. "The Use of Participant Recollection in the Modelling of Organizational Decisions." *Academy of Management Journal* 10 (3): 496–503.

Seattle Times. 1985. "Making It Fly." 25–28 June.

Selznick, Phillip. 1949. *TVA and the Grass Roots.* New York: Harper.

Shaiken, Harley. 1985. *Work Transformed.* New York: Holt, Rinehart, Winston.

Silverman, David. 1970. *The Theory of Organizations: A Sociological Framework.* London: Heinemann.

Society for Manufacturing Engineering. 1988. *Countdown to the Future: The Manufacturing Engineer in the Twenty-First Century.* Dearborn, Mich.: Society for Manufacturing Engineering.

Solomon, Janet. 1987. "Union Responses to Technological Change: Protecting the Past or Looking to the Future?" *Labor Studies Journal* 11 (3): 51–64.

Sorge, Arndt, and Wolfgang Streeck. 1988. "Industrial Relations and Technological Change: The Case for an Extended Perspective." In R. Hyman and W. Streeck, eds., *New Technology and Industrial Relations,* 204–19. London: Blackwell.

Spenner, Kenneth. 1983. "Deciphering Prometheus: Temporal Change in the Skill Level of Work." *American Sociological Review* 48:824–37.

Stanfield, Gary. 1976. "Technology and Organization Structure as Theoretical Categories." *Administrative Science Quarterly* 21:489–93.

Sterman, John. 1989. "Modeling Managerial Behavior: Misperceptions of Feedback in a Dynamic Decisionmaking Experiment." *Management Science* 35 (3): 318–39.

Stinchcombe, Arthur. 1990. *Information and Organizations.* Berkeley and Los Angeles: University of California Press.

Strauss, Anselm. 1987. *Qualitative Analysis for Social Scientists.* New York: Cambridge University Press.

Tausky, Curt. 1978. *Work Organizations.* Itasca, Ill.: F. E. Peacock.

Thomas, Robert J. 1985. *Citizenship, Gender, and Work: The Social Organization of Industrial Agriculture.* Berkeley and Los Angeles: University of California Press.

——— 1988. "Participation and Control: A Shopfloor Perspective on Employee Participation." In S. Bachrach and R. Magjuka, eds., *Research in the Sociology of Organizations,* 1988. Greenwich, Conn.: JAI.

——— 1989. "Blue Collar Careers: Meaning and Choice in a World of Constraints." In M. Arthur, B. Lawrence, and T. Hall, eds., *The Handbook of Career Theory,* 354–79. New York: Cambridge University Press.

——— 1991. "Technological Choice and Union-Management Cooperation." *Industrial Relations* 30 (1): 162–92.

——— 1993. "Interviewing Important People in Big Companies." *Journal of Contemporary Ethnography* 22 (1): 80–96.

Thomas, Robert J., and Thomas A. Kochan. 1992. "New Technology, Industrial Relations, and the Problem of Organizational Transformation." In P. Adler, ed., *Technology and the Future of Work*, 210–31. New York: Oxford University Press.

Thompson, James D. 1967. *Organizations in Action*. New York: McGraw-Hill.

Tilly, Charles. 1978. *From Mobilization to Revolution*. Reading, Mass.: Addison-Wesley.

Trist, Eric. 1981. "The Sociotechnical Perspective." In A. van de Ven and W. Joyce, eds., *Perspectives on Organizational Design and Performance*, 19–75. New York: Wiley.

Turner, Ralph, and Lewis Killian. 1972. *Collective Behavior*. Englewood Cliffs, N.J.: Prentice Hall.

Tushman, Michael, and Philip Anderson. 1986. "Technological Discontinuities and Organizational Environments." *Administrative Science Quarterly* 31:439–65.

Tushman, Michael, and William Moore. 1988. *Readings in the Management of Innovation*. 2d ed. Cambridge, Mass.: Ballinger.

Tushman, Michael, and Elaine Romanelli. 1985. "Organizational Evolution: A Metamorphosis Model of Convergence and Reorientation." *Research in Organizational Behavior* 7:171–222.

Udy, Stan. 1959. *Organization of Work*. New Haven: Human Relations Area Files Press.

Utterback, J. 1971. "The Process of Technological Innovation Within the Firm." *Academy of Management Journal* 14:75–88.

Van de Ven, Andrew. 1986. "Central Problems in the Management of Innovation." *Management Science* 32 (5): 590–607.

Van Maanen, John. 1978. "On Watching the Watchers." In P. Manning and J. Van Maanen, eds., *Policing*, 309–49. New York: Random.

——— 1988. *Tales of the Field*. Chicago: University of Chicago Press.

Van Maanen, John, and Stephen Barley. 1984. "Occupational Communities: Culture and Control in Organizations." In B. Staw and L. Cummings, eds., *Research in Organizational Behavior* 6:287–365. Greenwich, Conn.: JAI.

Van Maanen, John, and Gideon Kunda. 1989. "'Real Feelings': Emotional Expression and Organizational Culture." In L. Cummings and B. Staw, eds., *Research in Organizational Behavior* 11:43–103. Greenwich, Conn.: JAI.

Van Maanen, John, and Edgar Schein. 1979. "Toward a Theory of Organizational Socialization." In B. Staw and L. Cummings, eds., *Research in Organizational Behavior* 1:209–69. Greenwich, Conn.: JAI.

Von Hippel, Eric. 1988. *The Locus of Innovation*. New York: Oxford University Press.

Vonnegut, Kurt. 1952. *Player Piano*. New York: Delacorte.

Walker, Charles R., and Robert H. Guest. 1952. *The Man on the Assembly Line*. Cambridge: Harvard University Press.

Walton, Richard. 1981. "Establishing and Maintaining High-Commitment Work Systems." In J. Kimberly et al., eds., *The Organizational Life Cycle*, 2–90. San Francisco: Jossey-Bass.

—— 1987. *Innovating to Compete*. San Francisco: Jossey-Bass.

Weber, Max. 1978. *Economy and Society*. Berkeley and Los Angeles: University of California Press.

Wells, Donald. 1986. *Empty Promises*. New York: Monthly Review Press.

Westney, Eleanor. 1987. *Imitation and Innovation: The Transfer of Western Organizational Patterns to Meiji Japan*. Cambridge: Harvard University Press.

Whalley, Peter. 1986. *The Social Production of Technical Work*. Albany: SUNY Press.

Whittaker, D. Hugh. 1988. "New Technology and Employment Relations." Ph.D. diss. Imperial College, University of London.

Whyte, William F. 1961. *Men at Work*. Homewood, Ill.: Dorsey.

Whyte, William F., Davydd Greenwood, and Peter Lazes. 1991. "Participatory Action Research and Action Science Compared." In W. Whyte, ed., *Participatory Action Research*, 19–55. Newbury Park, Calif.: Sage.

Wildavsky, Aaron. 1964. *The Politics of the Budgetary Process*. Boston: Little, Brown.

Wilkinson, Barry. 1983. *The Shopfloor Politics of New Technology*. London: Heinemann.

Williamson, Oliver. 1975. *Markets and Hierarchies*. New York: Free Press.

Williamson, Oliver, and William Ouchi. 1981. "The Markets and Hierarchies and Visible Hand Perspectives." In A. Van de Ven and W. Joyce, eds., *Perspectives on Organizational Design and Behavior*, 347–70. New York: Wiley.

Winner, Langdon. 1977. *Autonomous Technology*. Cambridge: MIT Press.

Wolfe, Tom. 1979. *The Right Stuff*. New York: Bantam.

Womack, James, Daniel Jones, and Daniel Roos. 1990. *The Machine That Changed the World*. New York: Rawson Associates and Macmillan.

Wood, Stephen, and John Kelly. 1982. "Taylorism, Responsible Autonomy, and Management Strategy." In S. Wood, ed., *The Degradation of Work?* 74–89. London: Hutchinson.

Woodward, Joan. 1965. *Industrial Organization: Theory and Practice*. London: Oxford University Press.

Workman, John. 1991. "Racing to Market: An Ethnography of New Product Development in the Computer Industry." Ph.D. diss. Sloan School of Management, Massachusetts Institute of Technology.

Wright, Erik Olin. 1978. *Class, Crisis, and the State*. London: New Left Review Books.

Yamamoto, Kyoshi. 1981. "Labor-Management Relations at Nissan Motor Co., LTD." *Annals of the Institute of Social Science* (University of Tokyo) 21:24–44.

Zald, Mayer. 1962. "Power Balance and Staff Conflict in Correctional Institutions." *Administrative Science Quarterly* 7:22–49.

Zald, Mayer, and Michael Berger. 1978. "Social Movements in Organizations: Coup d'Etat, Insurgency, and Mass Movements." *American Journal of Sociology* 83:823–61.

Zimbalist, Andrew. 1979. *Case Studies in the Labor Process.* New York: Monthly Review Press.

Zuboff, Shoshana. 1988. *In the Age of the Smart Machine: The Future of Work and Power.* New York: Basic Books.

Zucker, Lynne. 1983. "Organizations as Institutions." In S. Bacharach, ed., *Research in the Sociology of Organizations* 8:1–42. Greenwich, Conn.: JAI.

Zussman, Robert. 1985. *Mechanics of the Middle Class: Work and Politics among American Engineers.* Berkeley and Los Angeles: University of California Press.

Index

Abernathy, William, 8, 20n
Academic institutions: Leaders for Manufacturing (LFM), 263–64; and manufacturing, 245; MIT, 263. *See also* Research
Adler, Paul S., 242–43
Aesthetics: of manufacturing, 246–59; process, 7, 247, 250n, 256–59; product, 256–57
Aircraft company, 47–48, 268; CNC, 42, 76–82, 85–86, 205–6, 212, 216, 220; control in, 52–54, 57, 64, 82, 87, 133–34, 205, 220; design organization, 44–46, 47, 86–87; employment policies, 47, 60–61, 81n, 89; engineers, 42, 45, 46, 47, 55–75, 81–87, 231, 257; FMS, 42, 48–65, 83, 84, 85–86, 205, 211, 215, 216, 220, 257; industrial context, 42–46; managers, 42–43, 49–65, 70–87, 206, 215, 216, 229; manufacturing/operations organization, 44, 46, 47, 86–87; organization, 41, 42–46, 47, 86–87; politics, 55, 75, 81–82, 83–87, 205–6; RAC, 42, 65–75, 84, 85–86, 205, 231; workers, 47–64, 67, 79–81, 82, 85–86, 89. *See also* Choice of new aircraft technology
Air Force, U.S., 235n
Allen, Thomas, 206n, 207n
Alloys, hard/mechanical, 142
Aluminum company, 137–39, 229; collaboration, 149–65, 240; engineers/technicians, 138, 144–65, 240; industrial

context, 135–36; managers, 139, 144–65, 177, 231, 240; NIH syndrome, 206n; organization, 137–38, 150; politics, 145–46, 163; technology, 139–65; workers, 139, 148–65, 231, 240. *See also* Choice of new aluminum company technology
Anderson, Philip, 209
Argyris, Chris, 271
Authority: organizational, 5, 6, 18–20, 164, 177–78. *See also* Managers
Automation, 12–13, 207–8, 253n; automobile company, 171; computer company, 104, 107, 125–27, 131, 132; "fixed," 48. *See also* Flexible machining system (FMS)
Automobile company, 168–71, 229; collaboration, 185–201; control in, 167–79, 187, 191–92, 197–98, 220–21; employment policies, 169; engineers, 171–201, 206, 240; industrial context, 139, 166–68, 173; managers, 169–201, 231, 240; manufacturing organization, 177, 180–82; organization, 169–71, 174–76, 180–82; politics, 182, 186–88, 206; product design organization, 176, 256n; technology, 171–201, 210n, 211, 220–21; tours, 166–67, 172n, 198–99, 210n; workers, 169–79, 183–201, 216, 231, 240. *See also* Choice of new automobile company technology
Autonomy: in automobile company, 176–78; in computer company, 91–92

Compositor: Printed Page Productions
Text: 10/13 Sabon
Display: Sabon
Printer and Binder: BookCrafters, Inc.